Praise for

BATTLE FOR THE BIG TOP

"A blow-by-blow account of the rivalry among James Bailey, John Ring-ling, P. T. Barnum, and other players in the American circus world.... Fans of the circuses of old, as well as students of popular culture, will enjoy this look back." —*Kirkus Reviews*

"A zippy history of Ringling Bros. Barnum & Bailey Circus.... Standiford packs the account with colorful circus lore.... Readers will relish this entertaining portrait of a bygone American institution."
—*Publishers Weekly*

"Exercising his eye for exotic detail, Les Standiford gives us the charming and captivating saga of the outsized characters who dreamed, connived, and maneuvered to bring Gilded-Age America its most compelling source of entertainment—the circus. What a surprise to learn that behind all those bejeweled elephants and hair-raising acts lay a cutthroat battle to create the Greatest Show on Earth."
—Erik Larson, author of *The Splendid and the Vile*

"A mesmerizing, larger-than-life tale from brilliant storyteller Les Standiford—P. T. Barnum himself would tell you it's well worth the price of admission. With acrobatic grace and escalating suspense, Standiford documents the evolution of the American circus, in a masterful work of nonfiction as spell-binding as the monsters, mermaids, balletic elephants and charismatic ringleaders that fill its pages."
—Karen Russell, author of the *New York Times*
bestseller *Swamplandia!*

"*Battle for the Big Top* is as rollicking, infectious, and enthralling as the subject it covers. With verve and style to spare, Les Standiford spins an unforgettable and addictively readable yarn about the three great showmen of the wildest of all entertainments—the American Circus. What a blast."
—Dennis Lehane, author of *Mystic River* and *Shutter Island*

"An epic work of Americana that gives you a front row seat inside the big top. Les Standiford delves deeply into the history of one of America's favorite and oldest pastimes, examining the three dynamic men who revolutionized it."

—Brad Meltzer, bestselling author of *The Lincoln Conspiracy*

"Les Standiford understands that to know the American soul, one needs to understand the circus. Ambitious, insightful and chock full of exotic lore, *Battle for the Big Top* goes beyond the ballyhoo and delivers the strange and fascinating history of the Greatest Show on Earth."

—Stewart O'Nan, author of *The Circus Fire*

"Les Standiford takes us under the big top and behind the curtain in this richly researched and thoroughly engaging narrative that captures all of the entrepreneurial intrigue and spirit of the American circus. Fascinating and endlessly entertaining, you won't be able to put *Battle for the Big Top* down."

—Gilbert King, Pulitzer prize–winning author of *Devil in the Grove*

BATTLE
FOR THE
BIG TOP

LES STANDIFORD

BATTLE
FOR THE
BIG TOP

P. T. BARNUM, JAMES BAILEY, JOHN RINGLING, *AND THE* DEATH-DEFYING SAGA *OF THE* AMERICAN CIRCUS

PUBLICAFFAIRS

New York

PublicAffairs
Hachette Book Group
1290 Avenue of the Americas, New York, NY 10104
www.publicaffairsbooks.com
@Public_Affairs

Printed in the United States of America

Originally published in hardcover and ebook by PublicAffairs in June 2021
First Trade Paperback Edition: July 2022

Published by PublicAffairs, an imprint of Perseus Books, LLC, a subsidiary of Hachette Book Group, Inc. The PublicAffairs name and logo is a trademark of the Hachette Book Group.

The publisher is not responsible for websites (or their content) that are not owned by the publisher.

Print book interior design by Amy Quinn.

Library of Congress Cataloging-in-Publication Data

Names: Standiford, Les, author.
Title: Battle for the big top: P.T. Barnum, James Bailey, John Ringling and the death-defying saga of the American circus / Les Standiford.
Description: New York: PublicAffairs, [2021] | Includes bibliographical references and index.
Identifiers: LCCN 2020056749 | ISBN 9781541762282 (hardcover) | ISBN 9781541762268 (ebook)
Subjects: LCSH: Circus—United States—History. | Bailey, James Anthony, 1847–1906. | Barnum, P. T. (Phineas Taylor), 1810–1891. | Ringling, John, 1866–1936. | Ringling Brothers Barnum and Bailey Combined Shows.
Classification: LCC GV1801 .S73 2021 | DDC 791.3092—dc23

LC record available at https://lccn.loc.gov/2020056749

ISBNs: 9781541762282 (hardcover); 9781541762268 (ebook); 9781541762275 (trade paperback)

LSC-C

Printing 1, 2022

This book is for Kimberly, who, as is her wont,
opened another brand-new world for me. And for
Hannah, Jeremy, Ben, Brian & Stella,
for whom the wonders should never cease.

Two things only the people actually desire. Bread and circuses.

—Juvenal

When entertaining the public, it is best to have an elephant.

—P. T. Barnum

CONTENTS

Photo section A appears after page 80
Photo section B appears after page 166

INTRODUCTION

I WAS ONE AMONG THE MANY IN THE SELLOUT CROWD AT NASSAU COLISEUM on the evening of May 21, 2017, there to witness the final performance of the Ringling Bros. Barnum & Bailey "Greatest Show on Earth." I had not dressed up as a clown or in the manner of a favorite performer, though many in the stands had. In addition to the acolytes in costume, it seemed that a cross section of society had turned out: grandparents with every age child, from toddlers to teens, in tow, families, gen-Xers, millennials, boomers, all cultures present and accounted for. The background music pumping from the coliseum speakers was a reasonable facsimile of a wheezing calliope, and all the people there seemed to be genuinely united as one, drawn to a far-flung nook on Long Island by a common, palpable purpose.

Before the show began, Kenneth Feld, the CEO of Feld Entertainment, which had purchased the circus from Ringling heirs a half century before, led a contingent of fifty or so family members—children, grandchildren, and great-grandchildren—out to the ring beneath the coliseum's dome (the show hadn't been staged beneath an actual canvas big top since 1956) to bid America good-bye. The truth is that the Greatest Show on Earth had been a shadow of its former self since long before the Felds took over, but Feld still spoke of the joy that keeping the circus going all these years had brought him and the members of his family. It had always been a touch and go proposition, Feld said, but in 2015, the company had finally yielded to the pressure brought to bear by animal rights activists and had decided to retire their seventeen still-working elephants from the show. And following that decision, attendance fell off a cliff—the Greatest Show on Earth, featuring a hundred somewhat less impressive animals and requiring a crew of five hundred to move and stage, could no longer be supported.

There might have been a murmur of sadness concerning the elephants—outside the arena gloating picketers shook signs reading "Good Riddance," and the like—but inside the arena anger and outrage seemed on holiday. As one woman in attendance said, "The circus is all about being happy." In closing, Feld told his audience, "We must embrace change," and he and his family trooped out to wild applause.

Johnathan Lee Iverson, ringmaster for nearly twenty years, lamented that with the show's closing, the world was losing "a place of wonder," a concept echoed by audience member Autumn Luciano, a thirty-something photographer who had flown from Lansing, Michigan, to see the last show, a reminder for her that humans can do anything. "You go to the circus and see human beings doing insane things, but the truth is, we all have the ability to do crazy things."

During his performance, lion tamer Alexander Lacey turned his back on a dozen great cats, all of whom sat quietly at their places while he came to the edge of the big cage to address the audience. "People are not really concerned with lots of wildlife until they can feel it and see it, enjoy it and love it as much as I do, until they've seen it with their own eyes," Lacey said.

"Support good, well-run circuses," he said. "Support good, well-run zoos. Support good, well-run public parks that look after these animals." His passion so distracted him that he would finally turn to his patient cats to apologize. "I'm sorry, boys, I don't usually do that. I've confused you." The cats seemed willing to oblige him, and the show went seamlessly on.

As the lions and tigers (and a single leopard) went through their jaw-dropping paces, and while acrobats performed triple somersaults, and motorcyclists roared about in circular cages suspended high above the audience, and the clowns did their clowny things, my attention kept returning to a section of the floor, off to one side, where earlier in the show a half-dozen or so giant pigs had been brought out by a trainer to improbably hop over one another, perform handstands on platforms, nudge beach balls back and forth with their snouts, and, perhaps most notably, climb a set of sturdy steps and launch themselves—on their backs—down a ten-foot sliding board into a catch basin. The trainer had long since vanished, but the pigs were still at their acrobatics and were, one after another, still lining up for a turn down the slide.

At the end of the show, ringmaster Iverson called out to the crowd, "You mean the circus isn't antiquated?" They were already on their feet, but the noise grew. "You mean you love the circus?" A thunderous response, off the charts.

When it all died down, Iverson brought out some three hundred of the crew, including the animal wranglers, cooks, vets, stage technicians, schoolteachers, drivers, and others who composed what he called "a town without a zip code." Everyone in the arena joined in a rendition of "Auld Lang Syne," for the ages, and with that, a 146-year-old institution, older than Major League Baseball, one formed when there were still only thirty-seven states, was no more.

It would be the first time in a number of years that those many cast and crew members would not be scrambling to make connections for the next day's setup location and performance, I thought, as I made my way to the parking lot past the still enthusiastic program and souvenir vendors. And though many of the performers and staff had long ago made preparations for retirement or transition to other jobs, it occurred to me that precious little accommodation had been undertaken for those of us who might not be out of a job but who were certainly now out of a circus.

It had been quite some time since I'd seen the Greatest Show on Earth, but it had always been somehow reassuring to know that the show still went on, just as it somehow mattered to me that the Harlem Globetrotters were still tossing buckets of confetti into shrieking crowds and beating the bejesus out of the Washington Generals long after the team had relinquished its role— thankfully—in providing the only available gainful employment to a number of the nation's most talented Black basketball players.

At one time the circus had been an entertainment leviathan, and some of the nation's most accomplished entrepreneurs had been attracted to it, vastly enriched by it, and in turn, had enriched the lives of those who flocked to see it, moving the needle on the communal and cultural life of the country to virtually the same extent as did organized religion. Entrepreneurs like James Bailey, P. T. Barnum, and John Ringling were not only canny businesspeople but also secular prophets, each with a keen understanding of the human psyche and a way to provide for it some reassurance and some comfort, if only for a night. Bailey had fought Barnum, but once they teamed up, they had fought Ringling for control of the circus. Given the stakes, it was a bare-knuckle, no-holds-barred fight to the finish. And even though Ringling was the last man standing, even he was no match for Father Time or the talking Technicolor "pictures" or television.

"We must embrace change." Those wise words of Kenneth Feld echoed as I reached my car and glanced back at the glow of the coliseum. *Sure*, I thought. But I also thought about how hard Bailey and Barnum and Ringling and Feld had fought for the circus. Because the circus mattered to them, not simply for practical reasons, but because they believed the enterprise contributed significantly to the world about them. That was something worth looking into, I decided. Grown men, able and accomplished men, entranced by the circus, fighting to keep it alive. Who shouldn't want to know why?

ONE

WORLD ON FIRE

On July 6, 1944, about 170,000 people lived in Hartford, Connecticut, making it then the fifty-first-largest city in the United States. Just a month earlier, Allied forces had landed on the beaches of Normandy, and citizens of Hartford were hopeful that D-Day would mark a turning point in a war that had cost the lives of so many of the area's young men. Residents were regularly tending their victory gardens in an effort to ease food shortages, and able-bodied men who had stayed home to work were making about $50 a week, if the job was a decent one. Rent might take a week's pay, but a loaf of bread was only a dime, and gas, if it could be had, cost 14.9 cents a gallon—drivers could even put together a set of china if they saved enough coupons from filling up.

One person working in Hartford on that July day was county detective John F. Reardon, who had been called out to the four-acre site on the outskirts of town where the Ringling Bros. and Barnum & Bailey Circus had set up for the day. Hartford might have been a big, sophisticated city, but this was still "The Greatest Show on Earth," and about seven thousand paying customers—most of them women and children—were packed inside the sawdust-strewn big top, happy to be distracted from their daily concerns for a few hours. Ordinarily, security was not a problem with the Ringling show, but there was always the possibility of a pickpocket or a fistfight and a city simply didn't bring 5 percent of its population together without some kind of a police presence involved.

More than a few parents who sat on the bleachers with their spellbound children were old enough to remember when only three big days punctuated the course of the American year: the Fourth of July, Christmas, and the day the circus came to town. Everything stopped on those days. Businesses closed. Banks were shuttered. Schools went on holiday. And though movies had eaten into the public's fascination with the circus, and wartime made everything more difficult, this was still a special event. All those people jammed side by side in a sweltering tent, the air thick with the scent of animals and hay and wood shavings, and never mind the fact that it was in the nineties outside and thunderstorms threatened. The circus had come to town.

Opening the show was a spectacular parade about the three vast rings of elephants and other exotic animals and bespangled performers—gorgeous equestriennes atop broad-backed, high-stepping white horses, fez-sporting bears dancing along on their hind legs, lumbering hippos, caged panthers, lions, and tigers, Pomeranians trotting atop the iron-rimmed wheels of the wagons, the steam-driven calliope hooting and whistling above it all like no other music-making machine on earth. Then the troupe of woeful-faced clowns had followed, reducing adults and kids alike to tearful laughter.

Owing to the weather forecast, circus managers Fred Bradna and George Smith had quietly determined to shorten the program, and the famed Wallenda high-wire artists had already begun their act two slots ahead of the normal schedule. No net protected them from the circus floor, though cutting across the hippodrome track that circled the arena lay the runway cage through which Alfred Court's clawed menagerie—forty lions, thirty tigers, thirty leopards, and a score of bears for good measure—would soon travel from their steel cages outside the tent to the center ring.

The Wallendas had been headliners with the circus since John Ringling had spotted them performing in Havana in 1927. Ringling had been in the business for nearly a half century at the time, and though he was always on the lookout for something new, he was not a man easily impressed. But when he saw German-born Karl Wallenda mount a chair balanced on a bar spanning the shoulders of two men on bicycles riding across a thin wire fifty feet above the ground, only to have a lithe teenaged beauty spring onto his shoulders to complete a three-level, four-person gliding pyramid, Ringling had signed them on the spot. The group had been about to debut in Madison Square Garden the following year, but roustabouts reported that the safety net had somehow been lost in shipping and the act would have to be canceled. The Wallendas had instead gone on without the net, received a standing ovation said to have lasted for fifteen minutes, and had been performing without a safety net since.

Detective Reardon was no less fascinated than anyone else by the spectacle in front of him, and the twenty minutes that had passed since the opening fanfare were little more than the blink of an eye. Reardon was standing just inside the main entrance to the big top, behind the bleachers, or "blues," of Section A, so when the trouble started, it was behind his back. Later, Reardon speculated that someone had dropped a cigarette close to the canvas wall, and he lamented that if he had noticed the glowing embers of sawdust, or the initial wisps of smoke, or even the tiny fingers of flame that began to lick at the sidewall, all could have been averted with a simple pail of water.

But there were the dazzling Wallendas, forty feet above, in stunning white costumes, cavorting impossibly atop a slender wire, seemingly oblivious to the fact that no safety net was stretched beneath them, balancing, tumbling, and catching beautifully. Whose eyes could be torn away? Regretfully, the tent that had been hoisted up that day by a crew reduced from its normal number by wartime exigency was not the new fire-resistant model, which had proved to leak rain prodigiously upon its initial deployment. This was the old big top that had been pressed back into service, the one that had been coated with a mixture of eighteen hundred pounds of paraffin wax dissolved in twenty-three thousand gallons of gasoline. It did not leak. The hazard may seem unimaginable in our OSHA-conscious era, but at that time, in all its seventy-three-year history, John Ringling's circus had yet to experience the loss of a single patron's life.

Photographer Dick Miller had just finished snapping the last shots of the clowns disappearing down the chute from Clown Alley when he turned and saw the flames running from the sidewall up a guy rope toward the top of the tent. "Fire!" he cried, and Detective Reardon and scores of others were soon echoing the call, the Wallendas sliding down lines not yet burning toward the chaos on the ground.

Fanned by a breeze out of the storm-laden west, the flames advanced at a speed that astonished witnesses. Three ushers ran through the main entrance carrying buckets to fight the fire, but the instant they were inside, the intense heat set their hair and clothing smoldering. They were forced to retreat, using the water they carried to douse themselves.

One roustabout told a reporter, "It was like you'd opened hell's doors. You had all you could do to get your hands over your face and run the other way."

One policeman stationed outside saw what looked like the glowing end of a giant cigarette pressed from the inside against the roof of the tent, the spot widening at great speed before it ultimately erupted into flame. By this time, the caged animals had become aware of the fire and were screaming in a jungle cacophony.

Inside, great sheets of flaming canvas rained down upon audience members, who clambered—or tumbled—from the bleachers. The lucky ones scrambled through crevices in the bleachers toward safety. Others clawed helplessly as the heavy benzene-soaked fabric enveloped them, then vaporized into flame.

Other audience members dashed frenziedly away from the advancing flames but found themselves cut off by the animal runway that cut across the hippodrome track. Before they could turn back, they were trapped, then crushed and trampled by the thousands stampeding behind them.

One woman rolled out from under the tent's sidewall, her face blackened with soot, her clothes charred. She stood to gather herself, then ran back toward the main entrance of the flaming tent before a policeman tackled her. "My God," she cried, thrashing in his grasp. "My God. My kid's in there."

Through it all, the circus band, led by organist Pete Heaton and stationed at the east end of the big top, opposite Section A, blasted "Stars and Stripes Forever"—the traditional signal for disaster—right up to the moment when the towering main poles toppled and the last remnants of the flaming roof dropped down. And then, as suddenly as it had begun, it was over, the entire big top gone, the bleachers charred, the dead and the dying strewn everywhere.

Circus director Bradna—the man whom titan John Ringling himself had fought to install—his hair burned away as he pulled more than a dozen trapped children from the mass at the animal chute, stared in disbelief at the smoke and dust-palled ruin about him, bodies piled four and five deep, the animals still screeching and wailing hellishly. It seemed impossible. The worst circus fire in all history—far more Hartford lives lost than lost in the assault on Normandy—started and finished in less than fifteen minutes.

Conceivably, this could have meant the end. The end of the Ringling Brothers empire, if not of an era itself.

TWO

BEFORE THE BIG TOP

THE CIRCUS WOULD IN FACT SURVIVE THE AWFUL TRAGEDY, AND THE RINGLING show would not cease the use of the "big top" tent for another dozen years. But the Hartford disaster was a significant punctuation point in a process of reorganization and downsizing of the once-formidable circus industry, which had been ongoing since 1929, when John Ringling himself had struggled to keep his "greatest show on earth" afloat amid the economic wreckage brought by Black Tuesday of October 29.

Those struggles for Ringling, who was by the 1920s a highly diversified and successful businessman with far-flung holdings in railroading, banking, planned community development, and oil, might have seemed impossible scant years before the Depression, when the American circus reigned as far and away the most compelling form of popular entertainment in the nation, and indeed the world. At the turn of the century, when the big top was raised and the pachyderms paraded from the rail station to the circus grounds, an entire community turned its attention to the event that was about to unfold.

Nor were the financial implications of the industry insignificant. In the months leading up to the stock market crash, Ringling cleared about $1 million from $2.5 million in receipts. To gain some appreciation of those sums in terms of contemporary dollars, we could use the Bureau of Labor's somewhat conservative formula to adjust for inflation and peg Ringling's 1929 profits at about $15 million in today's money. But economists Michael Keppler and Robert Gunther, who compare the relative value of wealth against the gross national product of a given year, would suggest Ringling's 1929 circus generated the equivalent of at least $250 million in revenue, with profits equating to $100 million or more. That *the circus* once commanded such social and economic significance may be difficult to fathom today, when Super Bowls that draw less than a hundred million viewers are belittled, when television audiences can access four hundred or more channels, and when movie executives measure true success as film releases that gross in the hundreds of millions of dollars.

But, indeed, the circus did command the world of American entertainment during the greatest part of the nation's rise to world prominence and, in time, it became an inextricable part of the national identity. Just as the American frontier had been tamed by political leaders and adventurers, so had the most fearsome wild creatures been brought into détente with their human trainers. For a can-do nation that prided itself on the ability to overcome any technological obstacle to progress, what better metaphor might there be than a troupe of acrobats or gymnasts defying gravity? And if an audience member's attention might wander back to some cold reality outside the tent for a moment, the Joe-ordinary, never-catch-a-break clowns were there to remind them: we are all in this mess together.

Despite all the twentieth-century technological advancements in entertainment—movies, television, computers, and gaming consoles among them—it would be nearly a hundred years from when John Ringling had first grappled with a brave new world to the final performance of the Ringling Bros. and Barnum & Bailey Circus, testimony of how deeply ingrained in the American consciousness the institution of the circus had become.

As the final show in 2017 approached, Kenneth Feld, whose family had purchased the show from Ringling heirs in 1967, pointed out that the business model for the circus was in fact 146 years old, a form of mass entertainment that attempted to incorporate a bit of everything for audiences of all types and tastes. In this modern era, when technology allows for ever-narrowing "entertainment channels," the circus had suffered in the same way that big department stores and print newspapers have. Given the high costs of mounting such a diverse, labor-intensive show, the Felds' circus had long been an enterprise on life support, and with the 2015 decision to retire the pachyderms came the final blow, proof of P. T. Barnum's hoary observation: "When attempting to entertain the American public, it is best to have an elephant."

Yet even if the end had been in sight for some time, many in the crowd on May 17, 2017, were distraught. Shawn Goberdhan, a thirty-one-year-old pharmacy manager who had brought his two-year-old son to see the show, held out hope that the circus would somehow find a way to return, retrofitted in some way for a twenty-first-century audience. "If it doesn't," Goberdhan said, "I can't even think about it."

★ ★ ★

Part of the reason for Goberdhan's inability to comprehend the end of the circus likely has to do with the fact that the roots of the American circus date to colonial days, more than a hundred years before the arrival of Barnum and Bailey and the Ringlings and the Greatest Show on Earth. And actually, the roots of the circus itself go back two thousand years, to the Roman circus, a fixture of public entertainment dating from the fifth century BCE. During the hundred-day opening of the Colosseum in Rome, some nine thousand animals were killed, and it was commonplace for the Romans to sacrifice captured soldiers and army deserters to be trampled by elephants or brought down by lions and tigers in the arena. The emperor Commodus prided himself on having stalked and killed a hundred bears in a single day inside an artificial forest created in the Colosseum. Earlier even than the Roman circus was a Greek version called a hippodrome, primarily consisting of horse and chariot racing, which had been included in the Olympic Games as early as the seventh century BCE.

Though very little of what audiences viewed in those ancient venues, including gladiatorial contests and the slaughter of wild beasts, survived antiquity, it would be nearly thirteen hundred years after the collapse of the Roman Empire until a single dictionary or encyclopedia wavered from the common definition of the term:

> Circus: A wall-encircled arena, with its slanting tiers of seats, its gaping multitudes of spectators, its horse, foot, and chariot races, its naval shows, its athletic combats, and its groups of gladiators clashing arms, with mournful greeting, below great Caesar's throne.

To appreciate the evolution of the American circus, then, and its emergence as "one of the most important achievements of mankind," as one commentator has put it, requires a bit of backstory. And while Barnum and Bailey and Ringling might not have created "the greatest show" out of whole cloth, their accomplishments may seem even more remarkable given their ability to transcend what had been a staple of the world's entertainment for upward of two millennia. One measure of creativity, poet and scholar Brewster Ghiselin asserts, is "the combining of familiar elements into a form never before apprehended." Indeed, that was the watchword for many who experienced the full flowering of circus productions during the institution's golden age: "I've never seen anything like it."

Here is how it happened.

THREE

THE PERIODIC TABLE OF CIRCUS ELEMENTS

SLAUGHTER, NAVAL BATTLES, AND CAESAR'S THRONE THANKFULLY DISAP-peared from the circus with the passing of the Roman Empire, but when the world reemerged from the Dark Ages, what are generally regarded as the three essential elements of the modern circus were stirring: acts that can be presented in a ring, including riding, tumbling, juggling, and balancing; clowns; and the ring itself. Over time, three other elements added color and vitality: the menagerie, the sideshow, and the parade.

Historian Isaac J. Greenwood writes of a troupe of latter-day Eastern *desultores*, or horsemen, who caused a stir in the thirteenth century when they arrived by ship at Constantinople. "They stretched their ropes for dancing from one ship's mast to another, and in riding stood erect upon their horses, mounting, dismounting, and turning somersaults at full gallop. In sixteenth-century England, even Shakespeare made reference to the fabled silver-shod Marocco, a trained horse who could count coins and walk about on its hind legs: 'How easy it is . . . the dancing horse will tell you.'"

By 1652, one William Stokes was to publish his illustrated *Art of Vaulting*, which showed how he might mount one horse via a mighty leap over other stationary horses, sometimes choosing to land neatly in the saddle or at other times atop his chosen steed. And Greenwood shares an account of John Evelyn, dated 1682, describing the regular visits of the Moroccan ambassador and his retinue to Hyde Park, where crowds gathered "to watch their extraordinary activity in horsemanship, and in flinging and catching their lances; they rid [*sic*] very short, and could stand upright, managing their spears with incredible agility, and the ambassador himself charging his gun all at full speed."

More tightrope walking had been reported throughout the Middle Ages, including one account of a man who, in 1385, climbed from the top of a bridge in Paris to a church tower while holding a pair of lighted candles.

And at Saint Bartholomew's fair in London was introduced the curiosity or "monster," an attraction that would one day find its way to the circus sideshow. Among the earliest on display there was a "Miracula Natura," elsewhere billed as "O'Brien the Irish Giant the Tallest Man in the Known World Being Near Nine Feet Hight," who soon had company, including "a man with one head but two bodies, a hermaphrodite, a woman with three breasts, and a child with three legs, as well as a man without hands or legs who nonetheless managed to play the oboe and paint pictures that were offered for sale."

A number of royals and wealthy nobles of the Middle Ages were fond of keeping exotic beasts, including elephants, lions, tigers, leopards, bears, and giraffes, in private collections. By the fourteenth century, French rulers had established a public menagerie at the Louvre featuring lions, and soon the practice spread about Europe.

As to the antecedents of that most essential element of the circus, the clown—the figure who bridges the gap between the superhuman performer and the ordinary gawkers in the audience—it was in Italy during the Renaissance that the clown as a distinguishable modern performing figure began to take shape, in a genre known as the commedia dell'arte, loosely structured plays that tended to be bawdy and highly improvised and that were often dominated by a chief actor who could tell jokes, dance, sing, juggle, mime, and do acrobatics, all to keep a show from flagging. The most well-known clown, prior to American Emmett Kelly, was an early-nineteenth-century London performer: Joey Grimaldi. He never appeared in a circus ring, instead earning his reputation in vaudeville-styled performances at Sadler's Wells and other theaters, but his work set the bar for all the clowns to come. According to one commentator, all Grimaldi had to do to send his audiences into screaming laughter was don his outlandish makeup—his face described as a startling mask, his mouth "a blood-red wound, a mile-wide smear of jam"—then walk onstage and ask, "Well, how are you?"

Grimaldi was also a gifted singer, using musical performances to humanize his comedy. He would take his place, seated at the footlights, flanked on one side by a huge codfish's head and on the other by a giant oyster that opened and closed its mouth along with the music. Grimaldi sang "An Oyster Crossed in Love," which sent the adults in the audience into paroxysms. At the same time, he projected such pathos for the oyster's unrequited efforts that all the children were in tears.

So great was Grimaldi's impact upon the genre that the slang industry term for *clown* to this day is "Joey." He may never have set foot in a circus, but his outlandish makeup, his kaleidoscopic costumes, his wild array of wigs—Mohawks, purple plumes, thatches of orange and green thistle—and his shoes and gloves that left not an inch of skin showing created the archetypal look for all clowns.

Thus, with all the disparate elements of the modern circus alive in the popular imagination, there remained only the need for some individual to pull things together. In seventeenth-century England, public exhibitions of skilled horsemanship had become popular, with a man named Thomas Johnson among the first performers. As an October 1758 issue of *Grand Magazine* rhapsodized: "This Artist has, for some weeks past, entertained the town with his singular method of Riding. He first gallops round the field, standing upon one horse; he next mounts a pair, one foot on each horse, gallops then full speed round the course; and afterwards does the same with three horses. . . . He has even rode the single horse standing on his head."

The good Dr. Samuel Johnson himself was drawn to witness this equestrian at work and came away impressed: "Such a man, Sir, should be encouraged; for his performances show the extent of human powers in one instance, and thus tend to raise our opinion of the faculties of man . . . so that every man may hope, by giving as much application, although, perhaps, he may never ride three horses at a time, or dance upon a wire."

Thomas Johnson may have been adroit enough to capture the attention of Samuel Johnson, but the individual often recognized as the father of the modern circus was Londoner Philip Astley, a former cavalry rider and veteran of the Seven Years' War who set up a permanent performance arena in a field near Westminster Bridge. Astley staked out an open ring on his rented property and performed a series of stunts on his horses in full view of passersby. There were no viewing stands, but to help attract attention Astley erected a small platform in the middle of the rope-encircled ring where one or two pipers played, accompanied by Mrs. Patty Astley on bass drum. Handbills were posted about and thrust upon bewildered commuters, who must have wondered what on earth was causing the commotion in the middle of what had been so recently just a vacant, marshy lot.

As pipers piped and the drummer drummed, Astley mounted his horses and began to ride . . . and in such a fashion as most had never seen before. Standing on one foot, and then on two—though one per horse—standing on his head, standing on his hands, leaping from mount to mount, all the while at a gallop around the circular track. Astley soon had crowds stumbling down the pathway to stand transfixed about his crude ring, and just before the moment when he would dismount with a flourish, and while the cheers and the applause still sounded, wife Patty would leave off her drumming and slip smilingly through the crowd to collect, in the words of one commentator, "such gratuity as the crowd might be pleased to bestow."

Some say that the extraordinary skill that Astley exhibited resulted from a simple discovery that he had made: riding horses about a circular ring created a centrifugal force that aided him in keeping his balance. The harder the horses went, in fact, the easier it was for Astley to stand upright. Although some dispute the notion that Astley was the first trick rider to discover the benefits of ring riding, and others quibble about whether he or a colleague hit upon the ideal ring size of forty-two feet in diameter (still the standard size for today's circuses), it is indisputable that he was the equestrian to stamp the practice as a sine qua non for the trick rider and eventually for the grand institution of the circus that long outlived him.

Astley's modest endeavors at Halfpenny Hatch proved an enduring success, and by 1770, he moved his enterprise a few hundred yards away to a new site beside the southern end of Westminster Bridge (just south of today's London Eye and the Tate Modern), where he built a set of covered grandstands and charged a shilling for entry. Overhead galleries were set aside for the gentry, and stables for the horses, and the sides of the buildings that faced the roadways were painted into brightly colored billboards that advertised the attractions. Not only would audiences witness amazing feats of horsemanship, the posters promised, but many other delights as well.

One of Astley's most famed attractions was a pony named Billy that he had acquired for a nominal price at the Smithfield Market. Astley applied his fabled skills to the animal, and soon enough, Billy was featured on the program under the sobriquet "The Little Military Learned Horse." Among Billy's many feats were his abilities to jump through hoops, play dead, play hide-and-seek, add and subtract, set a table for tea, and pour the boiling water into the cups. His master was fond of introducing the act by coming upon the tiny animal lying motionless in the ring. Feigning dismay, Astley would turn to his audience and proclaim: "My horse lies dead apparent in your sight / But I'm the man to set the thing aright." Soon enough, Billy would be miraculously resuscitated, able to dance, paw out sums, and cavort beyond all logic, with Astley providing explanatory doggerel through their routine.

Eventually, Astley combined the features of the ring with those of the theater, building a stage at one end of a new amphitheater of his design. Equestrian acts were performed in the ring, while ropewalking, skits, and freak shows (also known as monstrosities), which had become quite popular, took place onstage. Some of the "monsters" might seem somewhat tame by later standards: one of the first to be featured in Astley's show is described in rather poetic terms by an early historian: "We are told of a certain fair one, from the south of France, who walked around the ring, gravely attended to by Mr. Astley bearing lighted candles, the better to display the wealth of golden tresses which trailed several feet upon the ground."

Astley also came up with the so-called hippodramatic spectacle, a kind of dramatic presentation performed on horseback and in pantomime. Performances might feature the exploits of some biblical-era character such as the chariot races of Ben-Hur or a reenactment of any fabled battle from the time of Hadrian through the Crusades. In the latter, men drove chariots and brandished swords and fired cannons and muskets while exotic animals stormed about the ring and up and down the entrance ramps. Military music blared, thunder shook the rafters, and lightning illuminated the frenzy in flashes. In time, no circus worthy of the name could fail to include such a "spectacle" on its program.

To all this Astley added acrobats arranged into human pyramids, tightrope walkers, tumblers, and a trainer with a troupe of dancing dogs. Truly, at the foot of Westminster Bridge, the modern circus had finally been born.

FOUR

ON AMERICAN SHORES

By way of prelude to his discussion of the early circus in America, pioneering historian Isaac Greenwood points out what a luxury was the horse in the New World, the species not being native to the colonies and quite expensive to bring across the Atlantic aboard ship. Given that there was no other practical way for people to travel to any inland destination, however, it was not long before many equines had been imported, and a healthy business in the breeding and training of horses was established throughout the colonies. By extension, Greenwood points out, any person whose livelihood depended upon the ability to travel—whether a physician, an attorney, a judge, a sheriff, a tinker, or a trader—became, to some degree, a horseman.

Thus the ability to "handle" a horse, or to train one, naturally was a skill of pertinence, potential distinction, and even a possible source of entertainment, just as centuries later in a highly automotive-centric nation the ability to handle a car, or race one, or jump one over some awe-inspiring impediment or another might distinguish an individual and lead to the creation of any number of eagerly attended contests and exhibitions: the demolition derbies, the tractor pulls, the drag and stock-car races, the jumps over the Grand Canyon, and the Indianapolis and Daytona 500s among them.

The first widely publicized organized exhibition of horsemanship in the colonies seems to be the one mentioned in the November 19, 1771, issue of the *Essex Journal* of Salem, Massachusetts, which informed readers that John Sharp, "High-Rider and Performer in Horsemanship, late from England, but last from Boston," would be riding that same afternoon for "the Entertainment of the people of Salem." The notice advised that, among other things, Sharp would be riding two mounts, with a foot upon each, "*in* full speed," and would also be mounting and dismounting many times, also pell-mell.

Other exhibitors followed in Sharp's lead, and soon Jacob Bates, who had preceded Philip Astley as an equine performer in London and upon the Continent, was advertising in the May 31, 1773, issue of the *New York Gazette* that he was beginning a series of outdoor performances featuring "Different Feats of Horsemanship" that would last through August 3. Though the announcement promised that seats would be made proper for both ladies and gentlemen, Bates also advised, "He will take it as a particular Favour, if Gentlemen will not suffer any Dogs to come with them." Tickets were priced at a dollar.

Bates intended to follow up his New York run with a set of performances in Boston, but the selectmen there, still feeling the effects of their Puritan heritage, were wary of unvetted "entertainments." Bates's application, even though he was careful to avoid any mention of theatricality or entertainment, was denied. If such an action seems an imponderable today, it should be understood that a number of the colonies had passed legislation forbidding theatrical performances, following the Puritan-dominated British Parliament of 1648, which had declared the theater immoral and likewise defamed the players in it:

> Whereas the Acts of Stage-Playes, Interludes, and common Playes, condemned by ancient Heathens, and much less to be tolerated amongst Professors of the Christian Religion is the occasion of many and sundry great vices and disorders, tending to the high provocation of Gods wrath and displeasure, which lies heavy upon this Kingdom, and to the disturbance of the peace thereof . . . all Stage-players and Players of Interludes and common Playes, are hereby declared to be . . . Rogues.

Article 8 among the Articles of Association of the First Continental Congress, agreed upon in October of 1774, in fact stated:

> We will, in our several stations, promote economy, frugality and industry, and promote agriculture, arts and the manufactures of this country,

especially that of wool; and we will discountenance and discourage every species of extravagance and dissipation, especially all horse-racing, all kinds of gaming, cock-fighting, exhibitions of shows, plays and other expensive diversions and entertainments.

"It was no more fun being President of the United States of America in 1793 than it has been during the hundred and thirty-eight years that have followed," observes a circus historian in introducing another figure important to the development of the institution on these shores. John Bill Ricketts—a Scotsman who had been a star pupil of Charles Hughes at the Royal Circus and who was a cousin of George Washington—had come to the States in 1792 to establish a riding academy in Philadelphia. He and Washington, himself an accomplished rider, often met on horseback for early morning tours of the nearby countryside. The impetus for the observation about Washington's state of mind derives from the fact that in 1793, France and Great Britain—which relied on American shipping for the transport of necessary goods—were at war, and both were angling for the new nation's favor, a matter that would have undoubtedly come up for discussion between the two men.

For his part, Ricketts's friendship with Washington had likely been cemented by their common interest. He told Washington's adopted son, G. W. P. Custis, "I delight to see the General ride, and make it a point to fall in with him when I hear he is abroad on horseback. His seat is so firm, his management so easy and graceful that I, who am a professor of horsemanship, would go to him and learn to ride." What he might have said to Washington about the political quandary he faced is not certain, but there is reason to suspect that at some point during their conversations, Ricketts suggested a way that Washington might get his mind off his troubles.

On the evening of April 22, 1793, Ricketts opened the doors to a new eight-hundred-seat building he had erected on the grounds of his riding academy, where he presented a program that is today generally described as the first true circus performance in the country. Ricketts performed as the star equestrian, along with his son Francis, and another boy named Strobel. Also on the bill was ropewalking by a Signor Spincuta, further riding displays by Mme. Spincuta, and comic riding and miscellaneous foolery by Mr. McDonald, the clown. Among other things, Ricketts is said to have "rode around the ring with a boy on his shoulder in the attitude of Mercury and danced a hornpipe on the saddle while his horse galloped at full speed."

In attendance at the show, the *Philadelphia Inquirer* pointed out, was none other than President Washington, who earlier on the same day had solved his dilemma with the British and the French by issuing his Proclamation of Neutrality, a bit of political ingenuity that left American merchants and ships able to carry on trade with either foreign power. Though it is nowhere recorded, subsequent historians may be forgiven for theorizing that Washington, once he had signed his proclamation, uttered something like the following, if only to himself: "There, that's taken care of. Now, I'm going to the *circus*."

Whether or not Washington's appearances mattered a great deal (he is said to have attended other performances, including the July closing), Ricketts's show proved a hit, and he went on to stints in New York, Boston, and Hartford in ensuing seasons. He returned to Philadelphia to open a new and expanded amphitheater, modeled after the designs of Hughes and Astley in London. There he pleased audiences with such additions to the program as the acrobatic "Polander Dwarf" and his taking two horses at full gallop toward a stretched ribbon twelve feet high over which he would vault, alighting upon his mounts again.

By 1797, Ricketts had added a second amphitheater on Greenwich Street in New York and was taking his troupe on occasional road excursions to settings as far away as Albany. But his luck would not hold forever. In 1799, his circus in New York burned down, and then, on the evening of December 6 of that year, while a version of *Don Juan* was being performed in pantomime on his arena stage in Philadelphia—just as the drama had reached the point where the hero was descending into Hell to be punished for his many sins—flames being produced by the prop crew got out of control. In moments, the entire building was engulfed, and although there were no deaths, the $20,000 loss sent Ricketts into bankruptcy.

The fire also claimed the hotel next door to the amphitheater, where Ricketts lived. Finding himself broke and homeless, Ricketts scrambled to survive. He leased the grounds of a ruined circus, where he advertised that his shows would go on in the open air, "after the manner of the old Amphitheaters of Rome," but he could not turn a profit. Next, thinking a circus might possibly prove a draw in the West Indies, he outfitted a ship to transport himself and his horses to the islands. But pirates ran the ship aground, seized the horses, and salvaged the lumber with which Ricketts had planned to build the ring. Ricketts did catch a piece of luck when a fellow merchant from Guadeloupe bought up the loot and hired Ricketts as a partner to produce a circus. According to reports, Ricketts earned back his losses in short order, but one of his riders fell ill and died, and his son was imprisoned under murky circumstances.

Dispirited, Ricketts booked passage on a ship for England, where he hoped to find better fortune, but luck once again deserted him. The ship that Ricketts was aboard went down in a storm, taking him and all who were on it to their doom.

FIVE

PACHYDERM ON THE HALF SHELL

THE DEMISE OF J. B. RICKETTS MARKED A MILESTONE IN THE DEVELOPMENT OF the American circus. After his passing, the institution's progress on these shores encountered something of a lull. Ricketts, despite his undeniable talents, was not himself an American, and the shows that he had staged, as artful as they were, reflected the tastes and practices of another culture and a different age. Furthermore, with Ricketts gone, no other individual seemed willing or able to rekindle the interest of such a wide spectrum of Americans with the sort of spectacle that he had mastered.

There were occasional performances of European shows: Robertson and Franklin in New York in 1802 and 1803, and Pepin and Breschard's Circus, which performed in Boston and elsewhere in Massachusetts from 1807 to 1810. But most historians agree that it was not until 1812, when a most unusual element—the pachyderm—was added to the proceedings, that a truly indigenous American circus emerged.

Decades later, after his entrance into the business, P. T. Barnum would proclaim, "Clowns and elephants are the pegs upon which the circus is hung." He is also credited with the apparently irrefutable observation regarding the power of the elephant over audiences. The benefits of clowns may indeed approach the profoundly existential, but perhaps the best explanation for the elephant comes from latter-day Ringling Brothers press agent F. Beverly Kelly, who quipped, "The Elephant is the largest animal you'll ever see this side of delirium tremens." All jokes aside, the elephant in essence and by dint of size alone is the one member of the animal kingdom that comes closest to equating with the impossible-ness of the circus's human performers. It is inconceivable to stand near an elephant and not feel a certain awe at its very existence.

There had never been an elephant in the United States until 1796, when Captain Jacob Crowninshield brought a three-year-old female specimen to New York aboard his ship. The New Englander had purchased the creature in Bengal for $450. "Crowninshield's elephant" toured the former colonies for a number of years, drawing crowds from upstate New York down to South Carolina. Adults paid twenty-five cents to view the beast, and children half that. "In size he [sic] surpasses all other terrestrial creatures," gushed one handbill, "and by his intelligence makes as near an approach to man, as matter can approach spirit." Flyers also made much of another of this particular elephant's human-oriented proclivities—it was apparently something of a lush, with a fondness for "all kinds of spirituous liquors; some days he has drank 30 bottles of porter, drawing the corks with his trunk." It was not until 1812, however, that the elephant and the circus were cojoined, when the Italian troupe of Cayetano, Codet, Menial & Redon presented Crowninshield's elephant at a performance in New York City.

As fabled as that first elephant has become in circus lore, the creature's place in the circus was cemented by the second pachyderm to cross the Atlantic in or about 1805. This was Old Bet, a female African elephant purchased by the sea captain brother of Hachaliah Bailey, a farm owner from Stephentown, in the far north of New York's Westchester County. Bailey's brother purchased Old Bet at auction in London for all of $20, but Hachaliah was happy to hand over $1,000 for the creature, which he quickly had ferried up the Hudson and put on display in local barns and tavern yards.

Old Bet was too big to be carted inside any conveyance of the time and had to be led along the roads from one venue to another. But Bailey was clever enough to travel at night with his charge so that no one could catch a free glimpse of what he would soon be exhibiting for a fee. According to contemporary showman W. C. Coup, who eventually joined forces with P. T. Barnum, Hachaliah Bailey's practice, and that of menagerie owners to follow, led enterprising locals to pile stacks of brush along the roadsides and set them ablaze when circus menageries approached, thus allowing the creatures to be viewed.

In turn, promoters sent scouts in advance of their processions. When the scouts spotted the makings of a bonfire, Coup said, "the showmen would blanket a horse and send him ahead, shouting 'Mile up! Mile up!,'" a command known to be used by elephant trainers. "On hearing this call," Coup said, "the farmers would light their bonfires only to discover, on the approach of the draped horse, that they had been fooled. And bitter would be their disappointment when, after the last flickering ember of their fire had died out, the huge object of their curiosity would pass unseen in the darkness."

In any case, Old Bet proved such a sensation that by 1808 Bailey was leasing the creature out to a pair of menagerie-owning neighbors, Andrew Brown and Benjamin Lent, who agreed to pay $2,400 for a year's exhibition rights. In 1816, Bailey partnered with a youngster named Nathan Howes, who made Old Bet part of a small traveling menagerie. When Howes failed to deliver the agreed-upon split in profits, Bailey tracked him down in New Bedford, Massachusetts, and demanded his money. Howes was resolute: there had been no profits. Bailey took a look at the crowds surging through the gates and told Howes that Old Bet's days with this outfit were at an end.

Howes shook his head. "I have a contract," he told Bailey, and walked off.

The next morning Howes went to the barn he had rented for the elephant, ready to move Old Bet to the next stop on the tour. Inside, he found Bailey with a loaded musket trained upon the elephant, ready to shoot the creature. Howes panicked. "Stop!" he cried. "Half that elephant is mine!"

"I'm only aiming at my half," was Bailey's Solomonic reply.

It was enough to convince Howes to pony up Bailey's share of the profits, so the story goes, and Old Bet's tour continued, though not for long. One Sunday in late July 1816, Howes's menagerie was passing from a run at Boston into the District of Maine (which would not become a state until 1820). Bet and her handler plodded down a narrow road near the hamlet of Alfred when there came a sudden rustling in the brush. A series of shots rang out, and suddenly Bet collapsed to her knees, then toppled over, blood pouring from wounds to her head that proved fatal.

Later, a local citizen named Daniel Davis was apprehended for the crime. Davis told authorities that his actions were precipitated for the good of his fellow citizens. He said it was the same as stealing to charge hard-working farmers a quarter of a dollar just to gaze at a giant, useless creature. And besides, the menagerie was traveling on the Sabbath Day, a sin in its own right. Davis spent three days in jail before he was released.

Hachaliah Bailey had Old Bet's remains—all seven thousand pounds of her—carried back to Somers, New York, and buried next to his Elephant Hotel, which he'd built with the proceeds from various exhibitions. The fine redbrick Georgian building still stands as the Somers Town Hall, and a tall granite pillar capped by a statue of Old Bet stands on the lawn.

Bailey's successes with Old Bet spurred something of a cottage industry in the area, to the point that nine competing entities, including one with Bailey as a principal, met in Somers on January 14, 1835, to execute a rather remarkable merger. All the property and animals owned by the various concerns, valued at some $330,000 and including such exotics as elephants, camels, bison, and antelope, would thenceforth be managed by a board of five directors who would lay out a network of noncompeting routes and carry out business in a way equally beneficial to all. The new entity was to be called the Zoological Institute, a name calculated to clarify to the world at large that a trip to the circus was not an exercise in heathen tomfoolery but rather a most proper endeavor in scientific education.

Shortly after the formation of the syndicate, a rival circus announced plans to stage an exhibition in the state of New York. A group from the Zoological Institute quickly sent word to the interlopers: "We put our foot down flat, and shall play New York," meaning that the territory was their exclusive domain. In short order, competitors formed a dismissive name for the Zoological Institute: ever after known as "The Flatfoots."

The formation of the Zoological Institute created such a concentrated center for circus-related activity that later commentators have labeled the area—comprising some twenty square miles and extending as far eastward as Fairfield, Connecticut—the "Cradle of the American Circus." The traveling menageries, spurred by Bailey's success with Old Bet, formed the initial focus of circus activity, but it was not long before the animal-centric traveling exhibitions incorporated jugglers, acrobats, and trick riders, folding the elements of the European-styled circus into the shows. Thus were the two enterprises of traveling menageries and fantastical performances, entirely distinct until that time, combined into a singularly American phenomenon, pointing the direction for the development of the industry ever after.

Furthermore, the traveling menagerie of the early nineteenth century was just that: a relatively modest enterprise that moved about from town to town, rarely extending its stay and, when the nature of the show called for it, performing outdoors. A plank floor would be laid in a field surrounded by a fence or canvas draping, and audiences would circle the exhibitions or sometimes watch from a hillside or hastily erected bleachers, which were scrapped once the show moved on.

In time, shows began to carry their own necessary paraphernalia, and as the productions became ever more complex, a support industry grew up in and around Flatfoot country. Animals were bred, trained, and housed in winter; wagons and rolling cages built; tents fabricated; portable bleachers designed; programs, bills, and posters printed—all of it supporting a thriving economy that benefited the entire region. Though Somers native Joshua Purdy Brown is said to have staged a performance under a "pavilion," or wood-sided tent, in Wilmington, Delaware, in November 1825, credit is given to one Aaron Turner, a former partner of Hachaliah Bailey, for adding another essential element to the American circus: the canvas tent.

To avoid the ever-present possibility of a show's being canceled owing to in-clement weather, and to create a far more pleasant space for audiences, animals, and performers alike, Turner designed a round tent, ninety feet in diameter, which could be hauled about by wagon and readied for an exhibition in a mat-ter of hours. When Turner took his show out for the season of 1826 and staged the proceedings in his marvelous new enclosure, the notion of the "big top" was born. The big top would free the circus to travel in all its glory to virtually any location. Quite likely, it is the practical innovation most responsible for the spread of the institution's popularity across the nation.

Shows such as Turner's eventually incorporated both animals and traditional circus acts, but considerable time would pass before the two elements were fully integrated into a seamless show. Generally, once a production arrived in town and the tent was readied, tickets were sold for an afternoon matinee so audi-ences could view the animals on display. A separate nighttime performance, with a separate admission fee, featured the riders and tumblers and acrobats. This system provided promoters an additional advantage: in a particularly con-servative area, it could be argued, though circus performances might lie outside the bounds of the permissible on a Sunday, the exhibition of exotic animals, whose pedigree could be traced all the way back to the Ark, was a godly, if not scientific, enterprise, and surely no protest could issue regarding an announce-ment of the same for an upcoming Sabbath.

A glance at W. C. Coup's invoice book gives some idea of the economics involved in the maintenance of a traveling menagerie in the nineteenth cen-tury. Although the cost of cages varied according to the size of what was being kept inside them, the average was about $350 apiece. A pair of lions cost Coup $2,000, as had two "royal" tigers. He acquired two leopards for $400, a yak for

$150, two camels for $300, and a brace of elephants for $3,000. Topping the list, a hippopotamus and a rhinoceros had cost him $5,000 each.

All in all, Coup reckoned, it cost about $86,000 to outfit the typical "million-dollar circus."

The Flatfoot era of the American circus prevailed from 1835 to 1870 or so. It was a time marked by the existence of a myriad of smaller shows that criss-crossed the nation, some more menagerie than circus, others the opposite. Some troupes were polished and impressive; others, flea-bitten. A number of them were backed by syndicate interests, others were fiercely independent, and a few had roots in England and the Continent. No small portion of the dubious business practices often associated with the circus can be attributed to the Flatfoot brain trust, which honed the art of competition to a fine and fierce point.

Unlike the Astleys and other circus pioneers, several of the syndicate insiders were not performers but businessmen with little personal connection to the shows they bankrolled. But these men were experts at scheduling shows at a moment's notice, sliding a troupe into a town a day ahead of a competitor, using the cover of night to plaster their own banners over those previously posted, planting scandalous rumors about a competitor, shamelessly demeaning the quality of a rival show, hiring toughs to disable another troupe's wagons or threaten its workmen, and even burning down bridges to keep another show from making its dates.

Among the more successful circus men of the time was George F. Bailey—nephew of Hachaliah Bailey—who married Aaron Turner's daughter and ultimately took over Turner's circus operations. By 1858, George Bailey was in control of three separate traveling circuses whose operations—continuing until 1880 and the rapid ascent of P. T. Barnum and James Bailey (no relation)—made him an exceedingly prosperous man. Another notable included Richard Sands, who took his own equestrian show to England in the 1840s, where audiences found his performances the equal of those of Astley and other Europeans. Sands originated the color circus poster and would later join with veteran Italian maestro Henri Franconi and Flatfooter Seth Howes to build a successful hippodrome in New York in 1853. By the time Howes retired in 1870, he was said to be worth $20 million, making him the most successful circus man to that point.

Of course, any number of novelties and advancements appeared in the world of the circus during the Flatfoot period. Showman W. C. Coup credited George Bailey with the invention of a wheeled tank large and sturdy enough to transport a hippopotamus. A hippo was often billed as "the blood-sweating

Behemoth of Holy Writ" and a creature, Coup declared, that "made several men wealthy."

This was also when that fabled circus archetype, the lion tamer, made a debut. Isaac A. Van Amburgh was born in 1801 not far from Hachaliah Bailey's Westchester farm. As the legend that developed around him has it, the young man, at nineteen, was so fascinated by the biblical tale of Daniel in the lion's den that he determined to become a lion trainer. He talked his way into entering a cage belonging to the Zoological Institute that contained a number of the beasts. Van Amburgh confronted the animals with seeming ease, was able to command them with his voice, and brought forth thunderous applause from the gathered audience. By the time he was twenty-three, he was traveling with his own menagerie, and in 1838, Queen Victoria herself summoned the troupe to London so that she could see for herself what was immortalized in popular song:

> *He sticks his head in the lion's mouth*
> *And holds it there a while;*
> *And when he takes it out again,*
> *He greets you with a smile.*

Van Amburgh's reputation has taken a beating over the ensuing years for his apparent tactics of intimidation of the great creatures, but some commentators claim that his penchant for whip cracking and other theatrics that emphasized the creatures' submissiveness was deliberate sleight of hand, meant to suggest that his life was in constant peril while in the cage. Still, he was one of the most noted circus performers of his day, as well known in his own time as his successor Clyde Beatty would become in his. However real were the threats to his life inside the lion cage, Van Amburgh died in his own bed of a heart attack, in 1865, at the ripe old age of sixty-four.

SIX

READYING FOR TAKEOFF

OTHER ELEMENTS INTRODUCED DURING THE FLATFOOT ERA BECAME INEXTRI-
cable parts of the circus, including the parade, a feature of which one latter-day
commentator says, "No other lost aspect of the circus is so much regretted." The
same writer carries on:

> The gaffer who long since may have forgotten his first wife's name can still
> remember standing beside the dusty road watching the approach of the band
> with its brass instruments gleaming in the sun, the gaily painted and gilded
> cages in which lions drowsed and tigers perpetually paced, the elegant riders
> on their cavorting steeds, the beautiful ladies in strange and wonderful cos-
> tumes swaying in howdahs atop the elephants, the calliope shrilling its tunes,
> the clown stumbling along beside the horses, turning occasional flip-flaps,
> and pausing every now and then to bow right and left with impressive mock
> solemnity. A lifetime later, the man who was that boy can still smell the reek
> of animals, breathe the scent of wood and cloth and metal heated by the sun.

The very first procession that can rightly be termed a "circus parade" is said
to have taken place on May 1, 1837, when Purdy, Welch, Macomber & Company deputed a group of its musicians to mount horses and ride down the streets

of Albany playing wind instruments and trailed by two drummers mounted on elephants bringing up the rear. It was the beginning of a practice that lasted for more than a century, a form of advertising for the show that became ever more elaborate and ornate.

Wind instruments soon gave way to bandwagons, where the emphasis was on brass and plenty of it, but soon enough technological advancement supplanted even that. In 1855 came the invention of the steam calliope, an arrangement of keyboard and whistles (not unlike those on a steam locomotive) powered by a charcoal-fueled boiler. When the pressure mounted to 120 pounds, and a key was pressed, steam was released through a valve and a copper or brass whistle sounded with force enough to be heard a quarter mile away. Circus promoters were quick to see the value of the calliope (named after the Greek goddess of music, but often pronounced CAL-e-ope back in the day) and, as early as 1857, the instrument made its debut in a parade organized by the Nixon and Kemp's circus.

Given their complexity and weight—some had as few as twenty-five keys, but others as many as sixty-seven—the use of the calliope was limited. Its inventor, Joshua C. Stoddard, intended the device to supplant church bells, but soon one was installed on every paddlewheel steamboat of the day, and to stroll the grounds of a circus without the reedy wheeze of a calliope in the background meant a paltry experience indeed. To this day, calliope trills and runs appear in popular music, perhaps most notably in "Being for the Benefit of Mr. Kite," on the Beatles' album *Sgt. Pepper's Lonely Hearts Club Band*. Showboats such as the *Delta Queen* still feature calliope concerts, and a number of elaborate amusement park carousels set the whirl of bobbing ponies to calliope music. In fact, the devices are still manufactured by such entrepreneurs as the Miner Company, where one might obtain one's very own calliope for somewhere between $10,000 and $20,000.

Paddle steamers themselves became part of the mid-nineteenth-century circus when former dentist Gilbert R. Spalding, who had used river steamers to transport his company up and down the Ohio and the Mississippi, got the idea for staging the show aboard a steamer, thus avoiding a complicated on-shore setup. Spalding's first idea involved building a special steamer that would be a kind of floating circus in and of itself, but practicalities intervened. In the end, he settled for towing an enormous covered barge behind a steamer. The *Floating Palace*, as it was called, debuted in Pittsburgh in March 1852. With hot-water heat and gas lighting, the barge could seat eight hundred in its theater seats and boxes and another thousand in the circus gallery. (Note that up until that time, evening performances of the circus were illuminated by candles set in wooden chandeliers affixed to the center pole of the tent.) Spalding expanded his fleet of floating exhibitions (foreshadowing the concept of the Mississippi River showboat) all the way to New Orleans and even performed along the Gulf of Mexico to Mobile up until the outbreak of the Civil War.

Spalding also devised a means to expand Aaron Turner's ninety-foot-diameter tent into a much larger, elliptically shaped enclosure with two mid-poles flanking the center stake, thus giving birth to the possibility of the three-ring circus. He also came up with the idea for the ubiquitous "stringer and jack" bleacher seating that could be erected and transported relatively easily, which essentially characterized the seating used in big top productions to the day of their demise.

While Spalding advanced a number of significant circus business practices during the Flatfoot era—including the use of his own railcars to transport his troupe and materials—the most important circus performer of the time was America's own "Joey," a man named Dan Rice. Rice, born as Daniel McLaren in New York City in 1823, began his career in vaudeville shows and circus theater presentations, including stints as a song and dance man and as a strongman, "The Young Hercules." In 1844, he appeared with the Bowery Circus in Galena, Illinois, as an equestrian comic who blended wisecracks and musical numbers into his routine. As a result, and as it is sometimes said, a star was born.

Rice morphed the classic British skit—"The Taylor Riding to Brentford"—into a routine that was classically American. It featured the appearance of a "drunk" who wanders into the circus ring and, insisting that he can ride as well as anyone, demands the chance to be allowed to prove it. The performance is immortalized in a passage in *Huckleberry Finn*, where the young narrator gives an account of the action. When members of the circus audience demand that the "drunk" be tossed out so the show can continue, the ringmaster intervenes and suggests this troublemaker be given a chance to show what he's got. The crowd quiets and the drunk is helped onto a horse, which—though held by two circus hands—immediately begins bucking and rearing, flinging the drunk about like a rag doll, but somehow he manages to stay on.

In short order, the horse breaks free of the handlers and, in Huck's words, "away he went like the very nation, round and round the ring, with that sot laying down on him and hanging to his neck, with first one leg hanging most to the ground on one side, and t'other one on t'other side, and the people just crazy. It wasn't funny to me, though; I was all of a tremble to see his danger."

Before long, the drunk steadies himself, and, as Huck describes, "the next minute he sprung up and dropped the bridle and stood! And the horse a-going like a house afire, too. He just stood up there, a-sailing around as easy and comfortable as if he warn't ever drunk in his life—and then he began to pull off his clothes and sling them. He shed them so thick they kind of clogged up the air, and altogether he shed seventeen suits."

In the end, the drunk is transformed into a slim and handsome fellow, "and he lit into that horse with his whip and made him fairly hum—and finally skipped off, and made his bow and danced off to the dressing-room and everybody just a-howling with pleasure and astonishment."

That Twain would take the time and trouble to re-create Rice's act on the pages of what was to become an American classic is proof of the power the comic exerted upon the public consciousness of his time. Rice made as much as $1,000 a week, an unheard of amount. He also delighted audiences with his interactions with Lord Byron, the "learned pig," who (responding to the almost inaudible click of his trainer's fingernails) could answer questions by grunting responses, spell out words by nudging letter cards with his snout, and close an act with a flourish by choosing the American flag from a dozen others and waving it about in triumph.

Rice was immortalized in a most unexpected way, by dint of his favorite costume based on the American flag. His tights, shirt, and pantaloons were striped in red and white, and he crowned it all with a top hat of beaver felt. With his goatee, flowing cape, and ankle boots, Rice became the unknowing model for editorial cartoonist Thomas Nast's representation of Uncle Sam, a symbol of the United States that persists to this day.

Rice's career—including the time when he marketed his undertaking as Dan Rice's One Horse Show—continued for some forty years, though he continually bounced between spectacular success and abject poverty, plagued by suspect business acumen, poor health, a fondness for the bottle, and no small amount of bad luck. Later in life, he made an unsuccessful bid for a congressional seat in Pennsylvania and then closed his days living with relatives in New Jersey, where he died a lonely and largely forgotten man in 1900.

In 1859, two other phenomena destined to be staples of circus astonishment were introduced to the public. Perhaps the most remarkable took place on June 30, when a Frenchman who called himself Blondin indelibly imprinted the skill of funambulism—or tightrope walking—upon the American consciousness by walking a rope stretched eleven hundred feet across the chasm just downriver of Niagara Falls. Newspapers of the day covered the accomplishment in detail, including the *New-York Daily Tribune*, which led its story with, "As a mere fool-hardy exploit, this feat has seldom been equaled, and as an exhibition of nerve it stands without a parallel."

The young man, whose real name was Émile Gravelet, was a member of a French troupe of wire walkers who had been performing in the United States—in Nibo's Garden in New York City—since 1855. But nothing in their routines had ever captured the public's attention as did this stunt, which began some 160 feet above the water on the American side and culminated at a height of about 170 feet on the Canadian side.

The hemp rope upon which Blondin walked was little more than three inches in diameter, steadied by a series of guys spaced every eighteen feet and anchored to spots on one or another of the opposing cliffs. His initial intention was to stretch his rope across the very jaws of Horseshoe Falls, anchoring one end on Goat Island and the other on the Canadian shore—never minding the blinding mist and slippery spray that rose there. But he was forced to move downstream when the owners of the island refused him permission "on the plea that they would not be accessory to his death, which they regarded as assured."

Dressed in pink tights and a yellow tunic and wearing buckskin moccasins, Blondin appeared at four thirty in the afternoon before a crowd of four thousand gathered on the grounds of an amusement park on the American side. Quite a few of them were residents of town whom, a reporter noted, "are generally not roused from their customary quiescence by anything less exciting than the mortal peril of some unhappy one who has been entrapped into the upper rapids and is about to be hurled over the Falls."

Blondin cavorted in some introductory theatrics upon a small rope and chatted with the crowd until about a quarter past five, when he stepped onto the main rope. He paused, turning back to the crowd as if something had just occurred to him: "Gentlemen," he said, "anyone what please to across, I carry him on my back."

When no one took him up on the offer, the Frenchman shrugged and went on his way, at times balancing on one foot, at other times bouncing up and down or lying at full length on his back. At the midpoint, where the rope's weight caused it to sag by some fifty feet—leaving him with quite the uphill climb to safety—he dropped a long cord down to the tour steamer *Maid of the Mist* that had putted out to a spot on the river a hundred feet below him.

The ship's captain tied a bottle of wine to the cord and Blondin hauled it up, drank the wine, tossed the bottle into the river, and then bowed to the crowds on either side of the chasm before continuing on to join the eight thousand souls gathered in Canada. In all, his transit took eighteen minutes. After a brief rest, Blondin returned to the US side in about half that time, to be met with cheers and the blare of a brass band. He was acclaimed "the king of the rope." The *Tribune* recorded the daring performance, summarizing: "Thus was accomplished one of the most daring and useless feats that even this fast age has ever witnessed."

Blondin repeated the crossing numerous times that summer and in the years to come, adding somersaults, chair balancing, and other such to his routine. He astonished such luminaries as William Dean Howells and Edward, Prince of Wales. Howells found the performance so nerve-wracking that he suggested such should probably be prohibited by law. The future king of England was reported to exhale, "Thank God it is all over," when Blondin stepped down to safety. The Frenchman would continue to perform dazzling feats until 1896, less than a year before his death in London, just shy of his seventy-fourth birthday, but not before having made tightrope walking de rigueur for any circus troupe.

The second phenomenon of 1859 added to the circus repertoire was in fact a novel piece of business altogether. In November 1859, the young Frenchman Jules Léotard debuted his act at the Cirque Napoleon, moving one reporter to describe it as "reckless breakneck flights from trapeze to trapeze like some tropical bird swooping from branch to branch." There had existed in the old Spanish circus an act called "casting," where two acrobats hung by their legs from stationary bars and flung a smaller acrobat back and forth between them. The smaller acrobat, or "flier," might do flips and turns while sailing through the air—but it is an open question whether Jules Léotard had ever heard of or witnessed such a performance.

He described the origin of his act as having occurred to him one day while preparing for a swim at Gymnase Léotard, the gymnasium and natatorium in Toulouse that his father owned. He was about to enter the pool when he noticed two sets of cords dangling above the water from ventilators in the roof. A picture formed in young Léotard's mind: He could fix a wooden bar between each set of cords and swing from one, let go, and fly to grab the other. If he missed, all he would endure would be a plunge into the pool.

Soon enough, young Jules and his father had concocted a routine where father swung one trapeze toward his son, and son grabbed hold, only to fling himself through the air to catch a second trapeze, then back, and so on and so forth. He often turned somersaults and twists along the way in a process that resembled actual flight.

In place of the comforting swimming pool, padded mattresses were spread across the stage beneath Léotard in case of a fall, but soon those were replaced with a net, even though an awkward tumble into a net could prove just as fatal as an unprotected fall. Then a "catcher" was added to the routine, and the "flying trapeze" act became another inextricable part of the circus. The tight-fitting one-piece outfits that young Jules favored also entered the fashion lexicon of the world.

By 1859, then, there had come to the circus its flying trapeze artists, high-wire acts, lions and tigers, learned pigs, elephants, big tops and the possibility of three rings, equestrian majesty, clowns of Shakespearian complexity, "monsters," parades, calliope music, novel transport methods, and performance scheduling and marketing—all of it adding up to a form of entertainment that seized the imagination of the American public as it had never been seized before. There arose the possibility, in truth, of creating what could be called—without the slightest hint of a pitchman's exaggeration—the greatest show on earth.

All lay in palpable readiness, awaiting the emergence of the names that would carry this grown-like-Topsy enterprise to levels never before apprehended: James A. Bailey, Phineas T. Barnum, and the Brothers Ringling.

SEVEN

HOW THEY ROLL

OTHER THINGS THAN THE CIRCUS WEIGHED UPON THE MINDS OF AMERICANS at the time, certainly. Shortly after Blondin made his crossing and Léotard was flying above astonished audiences, even more portentous events took place. On August 27, 1859, the first oil well was drilled in Titusville, Pennsylvania, an event that would eventually put an end to the dominance of the steam engine and allow for the emergence of the automobile. And on October 16 of the same year, abolitionist John Brown laid siege to the federal armory at Harpers Ferry, leading to a brief but consequential uprising of slaves in the neighboring territories. Though General Robert E. Lee, then an officer in the US Army, quelled the uprising and Brown was hanged for treason, the incident foreshadowed the grave rending that was soon to come.

In 1859, Oregon became the thirty-third state in the Union. The following year, the count would drop when South Carolina became the first state to secede from the Union in the wake of Abraham Lincoln's election as president. Though the state of the nation seemed to be worsening, there were moments of jubilation, such as in April 1860, when the Pony Express Service began carrying mail between St. Joseph's, Missouri, and Sacramento, California, a brief-lived phenomenon that ended in October 1861 when the first transcontinental telegraph lines were strung. Customers in department stores had been moving from floor to floor on elevators since 1857, and thanks to the sewing machine, patented in 1846, ready-made clothes were among the items shoppers in those stores snapped up. Other advances such as cameras, telephones, and electricity would have to wait for a while, but milk was being pasteurized from 1856 onward, anesthesia was making dental work bearable, and antiseptics had been introduced by a Hungarian named Ignaz Semmelweis.

At the time, a laborer earned 90 cents a day on average, a quart of milk cost 4 cents, a dozen eggs was 20 cents, a pound of beef, pork, or veal went for 11 cents, and a six-room apartment might rent for about $7.50 a month. The admission charge for most circuses varied between 50 cents and a dollar, with children let in for half as much.

The US Census of 1860 counted more than 31 million people in the country—including about 4 million slaves—a rather startling increase over the 23 million citizens counted just ten years earlier. New York, with about 800,000 inhabitants, and Philadelphia, with 565,000, were far and away the largest cities (Baltimore and Boston trailed, with around 200,000). Even if much of the land west of the Mississippi was still territorial, the country extended all the way south to Florida, and to the West Coast, with California and Oregon in the fold.

The construction of the Transcontinental Railroad did not begin until 1863, but more than thirty thousand miles of track had already been laid in the United States, two-thirds of it in the Northeast. The circus, though, did not adopt rail as a significant means of transport until after the Civil War. With such notable exceptions as Dr. Spalding's Floating Palace, which was seized by the Confederates and turned into a military hospital during the war, the shows traveled by road, which in the first half of the nineteenth century meant that they moved slowly and arduously indeed.

A Canadian tax officer's statement clearing a small US circus's inventory for import gives a good idea of the nature of circus transport at the time:

Eleven wagons
One music carriage
Three buggies
Sixteen sets of double harness
Three single harness
Forty-three horses
Two ponies
One set of canvass, poles, chains and fixtures for equestrian performances
Trunks containing musical instruments, wearing apparel and
    performing dresses
On which no drawback bounty or allowances have been paid or admitted

These various components were typical of those assembled into a kind of wagon train and hauled slowly along unpaved roads that more often resembled trails that turned into impassable muck when the rains came. There were rare exceptions, such as a few improved turnpikes in Kentucky and the northeastern states. And the 620-mile-long National Road (today's US Highway 40) connecting the Potomac and Ohio Rivers became one of the first macadam, or blacktop, roads in the 1830s. Still, the notion of a comprehensive network of well-marked and maintained roadways knitting up the nation remained nothing but a fantasy.

Once a performance ended, the first vehicle to set out for the locus of the next engagement was the "telegraph wagon," which carried some member of the circus production team and a local individual hired to guide the way and leave marks behind for the wagons carrying the equipment, the animals, and the performers to follow. At an intersection, the scout wagon might stop so that a rail could be taken from a fence and laid down to indicate the correct turn to take. If the company was traveling in prairie country, where rails and wood were hard to come by, the scout might draw arrows on the ground with flour or gypsum, a far cry from GPS devices and spoken "turn by turn" navigation systems of today.

As veteran showman W. C. Coup put it, "No other human being can realize like the showman the volume of dread hardship and disaster held by those two small words, 'bad roads.'" Coup recalled more than one dispiriting experience of his troupe's heavy wagons sinking to their axles. "By the light of flaring torches, a dozen big draft horses would be hitched to the refractory wagon. Inspired by the shouts, curses and sometimes the blows of the teamsters, the animals would join in a concerted pull that made their muscles stand out like knotted ropes." And still, even a battalion of six pairs of horses might fail to start a wagon. In such a case, for the show so lucky as to have made it a practicality, the call would go down the line for the great equalizer.

In Coup's case, that was Romeo, the elephant. "In a few minutes the wise old elephant would come splashing through the mud with an air that seemed to say, 'I thought you'd have to call on me.' He knew his place and would instantly take his stand behind the mired wagon."

The creature would lean into the wagon, and then the driver would give the inimitable human-to-elephant command, "Mile up!" And "gently but with a tremendous power, Romeo would push forward, the wagon would start, and lo! The past mud would close in behind the wheels like the Red Sea."

In Coup's lexicon, about the only utterance to top "bad roads" was "lost," and as for the despair inherent in that small word, the old circus man is equally eloquent. "Just imagine," he suggested, recounting one such experience, "you have slept four hours out of sixteen and are crawling along in the face of a drenching, blinding rainstorm—soaked, hungry and dazed." The caravan has already stopped a dozen times to pull out a stuck wagon or repair a broken wheel, "but it halts again, and the word 'lost' is passed back along the line of wagons. This means retracing the route back to the forks of the road miles in the rear. Many an old circus man has wished himself dead . . . under these conditions."

The workmen who set up the show generally traveled onboard the equipment wagons, sleeping as best they could while the conveyances creaked and heaved along at three or four miles an hour. Once they reached the destination, the drivers would catch a few winks in the pallets vacated by the men raising the tents. The performers and circus workers not needed until closer to showtime might have remained behind for a few hours of rest in a hotel before setting out early in the morning for the new spot.

Depending on the distance to be covered (fifteen miles was plenty, with the "big jumps" saved for Sundays, when shows were often prohibited from playing), all the members of the troupe and the wagons might have gathered in a common lot to prepare for the parade, but just as often circumstances required the musicians, the animal cages, the horses, and the performers to halt on the outskirts of a town and do the best they could to make themselves presentable for that "spectacular" procession down Main Street.

Nor were poor road conditions and a general lack of directional signs the only hazards a traveling circus might encounter. Quite often the troupes found themselves traveling roads that stretched through desolate terrain, far from civilization. Any "highway patrolmen" they encountered likely were toting pistols, but not wearing badges. One historian notes that an often-used circus route into the South had already been dubbed "The Bloody Way," for it was the route over which riverboatmen had for several years "walked northward from New Orleans through Mississippi and Tennessee, unless they were murdered for money received for goods sold in down-river markets."

One might suppose the floating riverboat troupes on the Mississippi were safe from such predations, able to skim along the water past bandits' notorious hideouts, like Cave-in-Rock, Illinois. But once a show had tied up for a performance in that region, "a gang might come ashore from Wilson's Liquor Vault and [floating] House of Entertainment and tackle a steamboat and circus company."

By far, most of the citizenry of the rawboned nation were peaceful and law abiding, more concerned with ameliorating the difficult conditions of their own lives than with stirring up trouble, and the traveling circus constituted about the only form of entertainment that visited isolated settlements. The circus might indeed proceed through the territories without incident, but once the show was set up, the lights glittering and the music pulsing, the grounds served as a beacon for young men looking for excitement. Sometimes they were overzealous in expressing their admiration for female performers; other times, like the "drunk" immortalized by the words of Huck Finn, locals were moved to test their mettle against the circus strongman or the muscled equestrians.

When a fight broke out, the cry of "Hey, Rube!" signaled the roustabouts and workmen to grab a billy stick or a sap or whatever was handy and come running. If it was a notable clash, local papers carried some word, referring to the incident as a "fracas," which in circus parlance was a "clem." P. A. Older, a veteran circus promoter who traveled with the Mabie Circus in the pre–Civil War years, recalled, "In those days it was worth a man's life to run a show. We used to have fights with the rubes two or three times a week. All they used to think of was to clean out the circus."

For all that, it remained very much in the interest of those attached to the circus to see that the show went on without incident, for without a day's receipts, there would be no day's pay. And if there were enough such poor nights, there would be no circus whatsoever. Quite often, in rough country, it meant that some local thugs were allowed to pass into the show, entourage included, without being obliged to present a ticket. Games of chance set up in the vicinity of the big top might dispense with kewpie dolls as prizes and go straight to forms of outright gambling, so long as the circus "fixer" or advance man had assured the local sheriff that he would receive a cut of the proceeds in exchange for looking the other way. On the other hand, if the operator of a wheel or a game was suspected of fleecing a local, the victim might return with a few friends seeking reimbursement, an encounter almost certain to precipitate a spirited clem.

It was to such a rough-and-tumble world, then, that James A. Bailey was introduced in 1859, when, at twelve years of age, orphaned and already a fugitive from one foster home, he left behind his position as a stable boy and—like so many before and after him—ran away to join the circus.

EIGHT

WHAT'S IN A NAME?

ONE OF THE GREAT IRONIES OF THE FABLED IMPRIMATUR OF "BARNUM & BAI-ley" is that half that well-known stamp is in fact a fabrication, invented by P. T. Barnum's partner long before the two ever met. James A. "Bailey" was actually born James Anthony McGinnis, in Detroit on the nation's birthday in 1847, around the time when Barnum, already thirty-seven, was making a name for himself as a museum keeper and exhibitor of "oddities." Barnum's life and career have become legend, but the particulars of Bailey's early life and ascension into the ranks of circus men make for a novel themselves. In an interview with the *New York Times* on March 19, 1891, well after he had arrived, Bailey revealed his true name, explaining that he was the youngest of four brothers, all of them orphaned when he was ten years old.

Though his father had left an estate of $20,000—a considerable sum in those days—James was sent to live with family in the country who would act as his guardians. "Instead of being treated as a ward for whom comfortable provision had been made," he said, "I was made to work like a dog. On the slightest provocation I was whipped. My guardian had boys of my age. For their misdeeds I was punished. I was kept working so hard that I was always late at school, so I was continually being whipped by the teacher and kept after school. Then, for being late in getting home, I was whipped again. I stood that until I was nearly thirteen years old." As if all this was not bad enough, the woman who had been appointed as his legal custodian and who so eagerly dished out all those beatings was none other than his eldest sister, Catherine—a fact James, perhaps out of embarrassment, neglected to mention to the *Times* reporter.

James stood the abuse until one day in 1859, when he was twelve, enough had finally become enough. "I remember well now the morning that I started down the country road, determined never to return except as my own master," he said. "I wore a big straw hat, a little brown jacket, and trousers that buttoned to it and was barefooted. My only possession was a jackknife with one broken blade."

It being the harvest season, he got himself hired on at a neighboring farm, where he made $3.25 a month, plus his room and board. His job, in those days long before the advent of farm machinery, was to follow along after the scythe wielder and bind the cut wheat into sheaves. "It was very hard work for a small boy," Bailey recalled, but he complained for only one reason: "Another boy, doing the same work as I was, was getting $6 a month, which was not fair, for I was a better boy than he was. I could lick him and I did lick him."

Though it is unclear whether the hoped-for raise was forthcoming as a result of this licking, James eventually made his way to Pontiac, Michigan, where he found work as a bellhop at a small hotel, a position that also required him to lend a hand in the establishment's stables, where he took a particular liking to horses. "It was at this time that Robinson and Lake's old-time circus came along," he said. "The advent of its advance agent [Fred H. Bailey, nephew of the original Flatfoot, Hachaliah], with his big red and gilt wagon . . . set the whole country around wild and me with it. Like all the rest of the boys about, I helped to post bills, etc., in consideration of a ticket to the show. Lake took a fancy to me, and when the circus came along introduced me to Robinson. I told Robinson I was an orphan, with no friends, and would like to go with the show," and with that the die was cast.

"He took me along, making me useful where he could. I have never done anything but circus work since," Bailey declared, "and I never want to." James, in effect, became the ward of advance man Fred Bailey, and the relationship between the two became so close that James A. McGinnis eventually adopted the surname of his mentor, though it is not certain whether Fred Bailey and his wife ever formally adopted young James.

During the summer seasons, young Bailey traveled with the troupe, and during the winters, he found odd jobs, usually in entertainment-related endeavors. During the winter of 1862, Lake secured a job for him "in the express business" in the hamlet of Zanesville, Ohio, but young Bailey soon tired of driving a delivery wagon up and down the streets of that town. He made his way to Nashville, where he took a job in the city's namesake theater as an usher. Soon his experience and industriousness led to his promotion to bill poster and ticket seller.

One evening, a man named Green, who worked as a provisioner for the Union Army, offered Bailey a handsome tip if he could find him a seat in the sold-out theater. Bailey found Green a seat, but "indignantly" refused the bribe. Green was so taken with Bailey that he hired him on the spot as his clerk, something of a boon, given the hard times. Bailey spent the rest of the war in the employ of the Federal Army.

While Bailey whiled away his time as a clerk, and the circus business managed to limp along in the North during the Civil War, hostilities effectively put an end to traveling circuses south of the Mason-Dixon Line. The Robinson & Lake circus, in fact, was to begin its 1861 performances in Lexington, Kentucky, but shortly after its tents had been erected and the American flag raised up the center pole, a deputation of citizens arrived to lower the colors and advise that the troupe should best remove its operations to the northerly side of the Ohio River, and be quick about it. Even for some time following the war, northern circuses often had a difficult time in the South.

As George F. Holland, a member of the Haight & Chambers troupe, recalled in his memoir, even in 1867 trouble remained: "Down there nearly every day someone of our company was killed. At Fayetteville a band of guerillas that had not yet disbanded after the war made a raid on the circus at a night performance, in which nine of the guerillas were killed, but no one belonging to the circus was compelled to bite the dust. The management employed thirty Rangers to travel with the circus for protection, and they certainly did protect us on that occasion."

And even with the gradual erosion of such tensions, other dangers for the traveling circus were ever present, as a vivid tale told by veteran showman W. C. Coup bears out. One placid morning, as his troupe was traveling north from a small Missouri town where their performance had been especially well received, good fortune changed to impending disaster in moments:

The circus caravan was nearly a mile long, "and stretched out like a long serpent" over the treeless plains, the very picture of circus glamour: "The elaborate and gilded chariots, the piebald Arabian horses, the drove of shambling camels and the huge swaying elephants gave a touch of genuine oriental picturesqueness to the scene," he rhapsodized.

Lulled into a near-doze, he roused when he noticed oddities in the behavior of the wildlife nearby. A jackrabbit, ordinarily a timid creature, sat on its haunches at the roadside, watching the caravan progress, then began to follow along after it. Then, Coup spotted a rattlesnake curving out of the grass and past a trotting team of horses without hesitation. Typically, it would have occasioned the snake to sink its fangs into one of the horses in an eyeblink.

Soon, as if drawn by an invisible force, flocks of birds overtook the caravan, lingering low in the sky and then zooming on. The tall grasses on either side of the road were alive with rabbits and other small creatures, all of them scrambling in the same direction.

"The captive animals in the darkened cages began to show signs of unusual restlessness," Coup noted, adding, "The lions and tigers began a strange moaning unlike their ordinary roars and growls. From the monkey cages came plaintive, half-human cries."

Coup sat upright, his gaze on the open prairie behind them, searching the hazy landscape for any sign of a pack of predators that might have prompted the animals' fears . . . and then it struck him. Not haze back there but smoke. The endless grasslands behind them were ablaze.

Within moments a rider on horseback caught up to the caravan, shouting, "Whip up, man! The prairie's on fire! Move for the river straight ahead!" As quickly as he had materialized, he was gone.

There were shouted orders, and the lead wagon master laid on his team with the whip.

Coup worried that the speed of the procession would be dragged down by the camels and elephants, whose pace was notoriously deliberate, but he needn't have been concerned. The rate at which both the elephants and camels began to swing over the ground astonished them all.

"Where is the river?" one man called.

"Can we make the water?" cried another.

It was a genuine chariot race, Coup said, "in which the stake was life and the fine death by flames."

Even with the cursing and the lashing of the drivers, the wall of fire that stretched across the horizon behind them steadily advanced on the wagons. It would come to no good end, Coup thought, as he clutched a rail on the bucking wagon he rode in. Then he caught sight of the circus boss galloping up the line and past him, on ahead of the lead team, where six big white horses strained with all they had. A hundred yards in front of the caravan, the circus boss leapt off his horse and bent and struck a match to the dry grass there.

Coup was dumbstruck. Building a fire in front of the caravan? Fire behind them, fire ahead? And then the boss was atop his horse and thundering back.

"Wait till the flames spread a little," the boss called to the lead driver, jerking a thumb over his shoulder. "Then break through the line of the back fire I've started and form a circle."

This "back fire" had nothing like the volume of the wall that chased after them, and one after another, the drivers were able to force their rearing teams through the low-crawling flames the boss had set, until the whole troupe— sans the speedy cadre of camels and elephants that had long since outstripped the caravan and disappeared—found themselves inside a broad charred circle, which still smoldered and sputtered, watching the great conflagration swooping toward them.

"As the prairie fire rushed upon the huddled caravan, the lead team of six white stallions who had led the escape effort abruptly lost all reason: The driver held desperately to the reins, but it was useless: The six horses charged directly toward the oncoming wall of flame and churning black smoke, the driver giving it everything to hold them in check."

"Jump back!" cried the boss at the last instant. And jump back the driver did, just as the crazed team and the wagon vanished into the wall of black and red.

"Then came a moment which was a dizzy blank to most of us, I guess," Coup said. The men could only stare, stunned, as the deadly inferno parted as if by magic, speeding around the circular firebreak, then gathering itself to tear on ahead toward the still-unseen river.

Some of the men had fainted, and the rest were dumb with relief. No more flames, no thundering herds of fleeing animals, just a smoldering silence and the grunts and snorts and pawing sounds of the remaining horses. Circus men were scarcely true believers, but a man beside Coup finally broke the silence. "I reckon there's been more genuine praying done in circus circles in the last hour than since Noah let the elephants out of the Ark!"

In time the men gathered themselves, and Coup and some others set out over the still smoldering ground. It was not far before they encountered the axles and rims of the obliterated wagon and the blackened remains of the splendid white horses. The stallions had been the pride of the show, and the loss seemed nearly as great as if it were six people whose ruined bodies lay there. "As for myself," Coup recalled, "I could hardly keep back the tears."

As it often had and as it ever would, fire proved to be the cursed bane of the circus. And yet for all the hardships and uncertainties associated with circus life, the appeal for young men like Coup and Bailey was irresistible.

NINE

GROWING A STAKE

By 1866, about the time when P. T. Barnum thought he would leave the world of entertainment behind forever, the circus was beginning to regain its footings in post–Civil War America, and James A. Bailey, at eighteen, was happy to put an end to his clerking days. For that season, he was hired by Bill Lake as an assistant agent and bill poster for Lake's Hippo-Olympiad show, earning $50 a month, a far cry from the $3.50 a month he'd earned gathering sheaves in his first gainful employment. Bailey proved a more than able assistant and within two years was promoted by Lake to general circus agent, making $200 a month.

In 1869, when Lake's show was playing a date in Granby, Missouri, Lake was overseeing the circus entrance as an after-the-show concert was about to begin. A local tough by the name of Killian barged through the gate, disregarding the admission fee for the second show. Lake stopped Killian and pointed out that if he wanted to go inside, he'd have to buy a ticket. Killian opined that he had already paid Lake enough money for an evening's entertainment, and if he wanted to stick around for the next part of the show, he would damned well do it. Lake, as used to such provocateurs as the next circus boss, remained unperturbed. He informed Killian that he would have to leave—he could either walk out, Lake said, or, nodding to a pair of burly roustabouts standing nearby, be carried out.

Killian spat a plug of tobacco at Lake's feet, gave him a venomous look, and started away, escorted by the roustabouts. Lake, thinking nothing more of it, walked back to the gate and began chatting with friends.

Suddenly, Killian stopped, pulled a pistol from beneath his coat, whirled about, and fired a shot over the shoulder of one of the startled roustabouts. The circus boss collapsed, his hands clutching his chest where the bullet had pierced his heart, killing him instantly. Though it would be some time before Killian was apprehended, Lake's widow, Agnes, gathered the troupe together immediately and vowed to carry on. She asked only that those who wanted to leave give her two weeks' notice then and there. When no one volunteered, she broke down in tearful gratitude, and the show carried on.

In the aftermath of the tragedy, and with his long-time mentor gone, Bailey decided it was time to light out on his own. He scraped together his savings and purchased a 50 percent interest in a "concert privilege" with the Hemmings, Cooper, and Whitby show. This "privilege" gave Bailey the right to stage the same types of "after-shows" that Lake had added to his troupe's repertoire and allowed him to keep half of the profits for himself. Such shows sometimes consisted of minstrel revues and often included miscellaneous vaudeville acts, including dancers, comedians, musicians—and, at times, various "freaks" (the incredibly obese, the skeletally thin, the completely tattooed).

Though not a great deal is known about Bailey's success as a concert promoter, that next season's tour was an eventful one, for one of the main troupe's general partners, Harry Whitby, was shot to death while taking tickets, as Lake had been the year before. Despite the tragedy, the enterprise soldiered on for 1872, with the resilient Bailey now employed as an agent at the princely sum of $100 a week, the most paid any general agent in circus history.

Bailey's subsequent success in the circus business was undoubtedly founded upon those fraught early experiences as a general agent, or advance man, for the small circuses. Whereas a number of circus entrepreneurs had in the past been illustrious performers, as in the cases of Astley and Rice, Bailey earned his stripes posting bills and papering towns with advertisements in the days before the show's arrival. A goodly part of his duties also involved planning the most expedient travel routes from hamlet to hamlet, winning over local politicians and law enforcement officials, securing permits, leasing suitable venues, arranging for the delivery of food, feed, and supplies, and managing all the other details necessary for the smooth functioning of a performance—all of this heightened by the fact that most engagements started and ended in fewer than twenty-four hours, only to take place again the following day, six and sometimes seven days a week.

"In the beginning of his career," Bailey's future brother-in-law and biographer Joseph T. McCaddon wrote, "he had driven over the roads of all the Midwest and southern states, year after year, in the horse and buggy days . . . and he would familiarize himself with junctional points, distances [and] the chief industries or productions" of a given area. According to McCaddon, the circus man had a "marvelous memory" for such details, and for years after, he was relatively untroubled when an advance man proved incompetent or went off on a bender, and would quickly wade in to clear up any difficulty in the infrastructure.

In 1873, Bailey parlayed the proceeds of a profitable arrangement he had crafted for the Hemmings and Bailey Show's concessions and bought out Hemmings, thereby becoming co-owner of what was called "Cooper and Bailey Circus and Sanger's Royal British Menagerie." That show traveled successfully by wagon for three years, though its mode of conveyance had finally reached its sunset years. The season of 1868–1869 had been a particularly rainy one, driving down attendance, complicating travel, and resulting in the ruin of a great deal of equipment. One commentator estimated that no more than six of the twenty-eight shows traveling through America at the time ended up with a profit.

By that time, more than forty-two thousand miles of railway were in operation around the country, representing an increase of nearly 50 percent in the past decade, but many of those lines were isolated and many others required changing cars, owing to the widespread variances in the gauge (width between rails) of railway tracks. Until 1869, the use of rail as a means of transport for the industry as a whole was spotty indeed. But all that changed when independent circus owner Dan Castello, well aware of the push to link the coasts by rail, organized a transcontinental tour for his circus and menagerie, to be transported entirely by the railroad.

Castello's troupe left Frederick, Maryland, in the spring of 1868 and traveled as far west as Leavenworth, Kansas, before it turned south for the winter, playing in New Orleans and elsewhere until the weather improved. On May 10, 1869, when the golden spike was driven in at Promontory, Utah, Castello's show was already in Omaha, and soon after, the troupe made use of the new railway to take the circus for the first time to enthusiastic audiences in such distant venues as Cheyenne, Denver (a four-day detour by wagon), Salt Lake City, and ultimately San Francisco. On June 5, 1869, Denver's *Rocky Mountain*

News enthused: "We have never seen the streets of Denver more crowded than they are today."

Castello's tour would prompt all serious circus men to reevaluate rail as a mode of transport, but the fact that in 1872 twenty-three different gauges of track existed within the sixty-six-thousand-mile national rail system worked against the industry's easy transition (today's gauge standard is fifty-six inches). Some circus men had cars built whose wheels could be adjusted to different widths of track or whose superstructures could be switched onto different wheel bases, and some resorted to simply shifting the loads from one set of cars to another at junction points. None of those methods was particularly efficient.

By the season of 1876, however, James Bailey determined to transition the transportation of his show to rail and embarked on a tour that extended from St. Louis to San Francisco. With receipts in San Francisco regularly topping $6,000 per day, Bailey convinced his partner Cooper to undertake an even more unlikely trip.

"Let's take the show to Australia," Bailey said.

Cooper laughed. "Why, man, you're crazy."

"I'm not," Bailey replied. "They've never seen anything like it in Australia. And we can make money."

Eventually, Cooper relented, and Bailey chartered a steamship, *City of Sydney*, for $17,000, to transport him and his company, including six elephants, a giraffe, a hippopotamus, and a rhinoceros, for a series of performances added in New Zealand.

Though business boomed in Australia, Bailey encountered difficulties previously unknown in the annals of circus transport. The *City of Sydney* was battered by storms. In the first, encountered shortly after they left Tasmania bound for the Dutch East Indies, seas crashed over the ship's bow with such force that a number of the animal cages lashed to the deck broke free. As sailors and circus men struggled about the storm-lashed decks under Bailey's leadership, the cage containing the bears came loose, that containing the lions piled squarely into it, and both went overboard with all the creatures inside. There was another terrific splash when the great rhinoceros tumbled free from its enclosure, hit the ship's rail like a truck out of control, and flew into the sea. In all, nearly half of the animals were lost, and in the aftermath the giraffe was found dead of a broken neck.

According to one account, no substitute giraffes could be found in all Australia, leading to a rather bizarre workaround. When the ship docked in Sydney, the dead giraffe was gutted and stuffed, and a mechanical device installed in its chest cavity. The creature was placed in a dimly lit cage, so the story goes, where its neck and head bobbed about gently—with no one the wiser—until a live replacement could be shipped in.

Bailey eventually replaced all the animals, but his troubles were far from over. As the troupe steamed for South America, this time aboard a ship called the *Golden Dawn*, another great storm hit, a wave flattening the lead elephant with such force that it killed him. The company's new rhinoceros broke free of its tethers and charged another elephant, a confrontation that sent the entire menagerie into a chorus of frantic screaming. Bailey, it is said, strode calmly onto the scene and directed his men to get ropes and chains around the rhino and drag him out of sight. Once that bellowing beast had been subdued, the rest of the animals quietened.

Bailey was thirty-one at the time. He was of medium height, weighing no more than 130 pounds, but his poise and innate reserve, married with his willingness to step into any fray, led even the boisterous roustabouts to respect him. In an industry where owners were often called "Boss" or by a given name, in his case it was always "Mr. Bailey." And woe to anyone who might have learned of his ill-starred original path and referred to him as "McGinnis." That was a name, according to his brother-in-law McCaddon, James A. Bailey had come to despise.

The depth of that feeling is borne out by McCaddon's more fulsome account of the circumstances under which young James A. McGinnis ran away from his foster home "with only a broken jackknife in my pocket." As Bailey relayed to McCaddon, he and some friends had on the day in question gone off for a swim in the nearby Detroit River, an activity forbidden because of the dangerous currents there. When an approaching police officer spotted them, the boys fled. In his haste, Jimmy snatched up only enough of his clothing to cover himself.

Though he had eluded the police, he was certain that going home halfdressed would result in yet another beating. So he never went home, ever again. The clothes he left behind on the bank, however, suggested to the authorities—and to his puzzled guardian sister—that the disappeared young James A. McGinnis had been swept away by the fearsome currents in the river and drowned.

For his part, once James made his break from his older sister's family, he felt no interest in ever contacting them again. In our own day and age, it might seem impossible that a young boy could simply vanish from one life and walk undetected into another, but this account is evidence of how different the world of 1860 was.

In fact, no one in McGinnis's family might have ever known the truth about young Jimmy, for so many years presumed to have "drownt," had not Bailey, decades after his disappearance, finally penned a letter to his older brother Edward (Ned), the one member of his family who had ever attempted to shield him from his older sister's abuse. In this long-delayed letter, Bailey, oblivious to his family's assumption about him, explained what he had been doing over the years since leaving. He'd not only run off with the circus but also owned one now. His show was to play Detroit, Bailey explained, and he would very much like Ned to visit.

It goes unrecorded whether Ned McGinnis shared this astounding news with any other family members, but McCaddon does pass along word of what came next. (As the brother-in-law of "The Boss," McCaddon was often referred to by others in the circus company as "Joe Bailey," and feeling no need to avoid being associated with the owner of the outfit, McCaddon generally let the misapprehension ride.) Shortly after the company arrived in Detroit, McCaddon was walking across the grounds when a worker hesitantly approached with a visitor in tow. The visitor looked over young McCaddon and shook his head. "Are you Mr. Bailey's son?" he asked.

"No," McCaddon replied, equally puzzled. "I'm his brother-in-law."

"Well," the visitor replied, "my name is Edward McGinnis. Mr. Bailey wrote me that he is my brother and asked me to come here."

At this juncture, neither McCaddon nor his sister, who had married Bailey, had ever heard the name McGinnis, and though it may be tempting to speculate as to the magnitude of his surprise at Ned McGinnis's claims, it could not have been any greater than McGinnis's when he was escorted into the presence of his long-lost brother. McCaddon, in his account, however, resisted the impulse to elaborate. He had walked with Edward McGinnis to find James Bailey, and then simply said, "This gentleman says his name is Edward McGinnis and he wishes to see you."

Though we might long for more detail, McCaddon was succinct: "They shook hands, and I walked away."

TEN

CLASH OF THE TITANS

IF BAILEY SEEMS EXTRAORDINARILY NONCHALANT ABOUT HIS LAZARUS-LIKE reentry into his family's life, perhaps his behavior can be understood by considering the nature of the circus itself. In marked contrast to most business enterprises of that roughshod time, the circus stood intentionally apart. The two or three or four hours audiences spent on circus grounds were meant to be antipodal to everyday life, an exercise in wonder, an opportunity to see the impossible made real.

To actually "run away with the circus," then, meant in large part to leave ordinary life behind forever. In essence, Jimmy McGinnis had ceased to exist and had literally been replaced by James Bailey. Many individuals might find such a transformation impossible or inauthentic, but the circus world was not based in the conventional. To Bailey, his rematerialization was not so much miraculous but a simple fact.

We may never know the full particulars of what passed between James Bailey and Ned McGinnis on the day they reunited, but at the very least Bailey must have been proud of himself. Why else offer the invitation to someone you love than to say, "Come see what I've become"?

Bailey's "becoming" was profoundly influenced by that monumental tour he made on the other side of the world. He had extended that international tour by nearly two years, traveling on from New Zealand to Australia and South America, around Cape Horn, and finally returning to New York City on December 10, 1878—a trek of seventy-six thousand miles. Despite his harrowing shipboard experiences, the journey provided the company with a notoriety and influence it had never enjoyed before.

When, soon after his return, Bailey got the news that a well-respected show, the Great London Circus, founded by Seth B. Howes, had fallen on hard times during a tour of the South and was stranded for lack of funds owed to a printing company, Bailey saw another opportunity. Though he would later confide that the great ocean-based tour nearly broke him financially, with the high cost of transportation and his physical losses (he had returned to the United States some $12,000 in debt), he was able to convince the printer who held the lien on the Howes show to take a great gamble on his estimation of Bailey's abilities. The printer sold the show to Bailey for $25,000 and took a promissory note for the entire sum.

If indeed Bailey's finances were teetering, the show touring in 1879–1880 did not suggest it. Billed as "Howe's Great London Circus, Sanger's Royal British Menagerie, and Cooper Bailey's International Allied Shows," the enterprise was, according to reports, not only a success but "a worthy competitor of any of the shows of the period." Among the menagerie's ark were ten elephants, ten camels, a hippo, a rhinoceros, seven tigers, four lions, six panthers, two cheetahs, one black bear, four zebras, four leopards, thirteen "reptiles," fourteen hyenas, two wolves and their cubs, two polar bears, one gnu, two baboons, eighty monkeys, one emu, one ostrich, two cages of birds, and two hundred other "small animals."

Among other innovations that Bailey introduced that season was the use of a portable direct-current generator driven by a steam engine and mounted on a wagon. It generated enough electrical output to illuminate a series of carbon-arc lamps in and about the tents, equal, his promotional literature claimed, to the light of "35,000 gas jets." Though it took several years for the carbon-arc technology to be perfected, Bailey's use of the devices was among the first commercial deployment of such a system. The brilliant lamps persisted in public use for illumination of sporting events and other outdoor events well into the twentieth century, and carbon-arc technology was employed in movie theater projectors as late as the 1970s and 1980s.

Bailey's success propelled him to major status in the industry by the end of the 1880 season, and rival promoters understood that going up against the Cooper and Bailey show the following season would be difficult. Bailey not only had developed a reputation as a micromanaging boss with a keen eye for the profit and loss ledger but also was known to be ruthless. At one point during the South American leg of his shipboard tour, the company found itself in Buenos Aires, overextended and lacking the cash to make payroll. He was officially ending the tour, Bailey announced, and there was barely enough cash left to get the animals back to New York. There was nothing to agonize about for Bailey—the performers and support staff would have to pay their own fares home.

"I have always thought Mr. Bailey was trying us out to see if we would work our way home as dining-room stewards or at other work, as performed by several performers who had squandered their money," writes a remarkably understanding J. T. McCaddon in his memoir. "I was quite sure at the last minute he would pay our fare, and I have always thought he was pleased to find we could take care of ourselves." As to whether Bailey would have in fact stepped forward will remain ever untested—the circus people managed to find their own way back.

Part of Bailey's approach to business and to those in his employ is likely the result of his own upbringing. He was in no uncertain terms a "self-made man," one of the many who would leave their imprint in America's Gilded Age, with Andrew Carnegie, Thomas Edison, Henry Clay Frick, and John D. Rockefeller among them. This cadre of successful businessmen and entrepreneurs embodied the rags-to-riches myths popularized by writer Horatio Alger. Theirs were the triumphant tales of impoverished teenaged boys rising above their circumstances through a combination of hard work, determination, courage, and honesty, qualities usually discovered and rewarded by a duly-impressed older patron.

Though Alger's fictional protagonists were invariably grateful to have escaped poverty and were motivated to pay their good fortune forward in turn, Bailey's rise—no less unlikely than that of an Alger creation—seemed not to tax him with an excess of beneficence. His was more of the attitude that anyone could—and *should*—excel at any endeavor one put one's mind to, and there was no need for unnecessary coddling.

A part of Bailey's reserve was surely due to the fact that he experienced precious little affection growing up, and his reported tendency to fuss over the slightest details of the business—often lurking in the shadows outside the tent to keep an eye out for interlopers, and always ready to grill an employee over the cost of a pot of paint—suggests that no amount of success would have ever seemed enough to guard against the possibility of failure.

Had he been the sort to discuss his fears, Bailey might have brushed aside any psychologizing to point to practicalities, including the lingering effects of the international Panic of 1873, which had begun with a market crash in Europe that led to an immense devaluation of US railroad bonds. Suddenly, the cash that American rail companies were depending on to extend the rail system had dried up, and thousands were thrown out of work. At least a hundred US banks failed, including one of New York City's most prominent, Jay Cooke & Company, which had invested heavily in the heady railroad expansion.

It was the first "great depression" ever to strike the United States and would hold the distinction as the worst downturn until the stock market crash of 1929. In the two years following the 1873 crash, eighteen thousand businesses collapsed and 89 of the 364 railroads in existence went into bankruptcy. By 1876, unemployment stood at 14 percent. Given his upbringing and his experience steering a business enterprise through such straits, perhaps Bailey's grim stoicism can be comprehended.

By 1880, the population of the United States reached fifty million. A factory worker was making about $1.37 for a day's work, and if that same person stopped in a grocery for provisions, he might pay 30 cents for a pound of coffee or 6 cents for a quart of milk. A skilled worker such as a telegraph operator might make $1,000 a year, and a law clerk in a government office might be paid $2,000. Women were still bound up in bustles, and city-dwelling men wore high-buttoned coats and bowler caps for business, and top hats, white ties, and double-breasted tailcoats for evening wear.

The year previous, Edison had begun to market the light bulb, and in February 1880, Wabash, Indiana, became the first city to have its streets illuminated using electricity. By May, Edison was testing electric trolley cars in New Jersey, and in November, the cash register became part of American commerce. The University of Southern California opened its doors that year, the Brooklyn Bridge—begun in 1870—was still three years shy of completion, and the gunfight at the OK Corral would not take place for another year. Billy the Kid and Jesse James were still on the loose, and it would be 1881 before Clara Barton founded the American Red Cross.

In March 1880, Bailey made his own big news when he announced that the company's huge Indian elephant, Babe, had given birth, the calf described as the first ever born in captivity in the United States. "Little Columbia" Bailey dubbed the baby elephant, and he spread the news of her birth far and wide.

The announcement caught the attention of not only the public but also any number of promoters in the circus world, where such claims of exclusivity—especially when they happened to be genuine—could translate directly into ticket sales. One such impresario struck by Bailey's publicity machinations regarding Little Columbia was a seventy-year-old who had been in the circus business for almost a decade.

When P. T. Barnum, lured back into show business and traveling since 1876 with a circus that he had dubbed "The Greatest Show on Earth," got wind of what had happened, he telegraphed Bailey immediately, offering to purchase Little Columbia for the then astronomical sum of $100,000, as much as $20 million in today's dollars.

To Bailey, Barnum's telegram was a godsend. He dashed off his reply, "Will not sell at any price," and continued distributing flyers and handbills in every city on the upcoming Cooper & Bailey tour: "Come see what Barnum would pay a king's ransom for!" was the message, accompanied by a facsimile of Barnum's telegraphed offer.

For Barnum, never one to underestimate a worthy opponent, it was a watershed moment. In short order, any annoyance he might have felt toward Bailey was replaced with entirely different emotions. "I had at last met showmen 'worthy of my steel'!" he wrote, adding, "Pleased to find comparatively young men with a business talent and energy approximating my own, I met them in friendly council . . . and we decided to join our two shows in one mammoth combination."

Barnum makes the merger sound simpler than it actually was, but by August 26, 1880, the contract was signed and an association begun that would change the circus world and the American entertainment landscape forevermore. Though the new show was to be called "P. T. Barnum's and Great London Combined," that moniker was just a waystation. Barnum and Bailey had now become a team.

ELEVEN

A SHOWMAN HITS HIS STRIDE

The septuagenarian Barnum may indeed have come late to the circus party, but by the time that he was lured out of retirement in 1870—a decade before teaming up with Bailey—to join veteran circus men Dan Castello and W. C. Coup in the production of what they envisioned as a circus nonpareil, Phineas Taylor Barnum was already a legendary name in American show business.

Born in Danbury, Connecticut, in 1810, "Tale," as he was known in his childhood days, was the sixth of eleven children sired by Philo Barnum, a none-too-successful farmer and merchant whose chief capability seemed to lie in the production of children. Still, whereas Barnum was put to work on the family farm as a boy, and though his upbringing was modest, compared to Bailey's it was positively entitled.

His maternal grandfather, Phineas Taylor, was a prosperous landowner and a free-spirited type with a healthy disregard for the latter-day Puritanism still alive in early-nineteenth-century New England. Uncle Phin, as he was known, was a colorful storyteller with a penchant for practical jokes, including one in which he convinced thirteen friends returning home from a weeklong fishing excursion to shave only half their beards and delight in the comic spectacle produced. After the laughter had died down, Phin announced that he would then finish his own shave, using the only razor, before passing it around to the others. However, just as he finished, he somehow lost his grip on the razor, which flew overboard into the sea. As he had planned all along, their ship soon came to shore on a Sunday afternoon, when all the town's barbers were closed. All of his friends were forced to parade down the main street toward their homes as half-bearded dimwits.

Nor was young Tale exempted from his grandfather's shenanigans. When he was a boy, Grandfather Phin bestowed upon Tale a parcel of land known as Ivy Island, which his grandfather often described as one of the richest farms in the state. His own father and mother often reminded Tale of this fabulous bequest and expressed fond hopes that he would remember them when he reached his age of majority and came into possession of his inheritance. It was not until he was twelve years old that Barnum learned the truth. He was finally taken out to inspect Ivy Island, which turned out to be nothing but a stretch of half-submerged, unusable swampland. Asked by his father how he liked his property, Barnum hung his head. "I would sell it pretty cheap," he said. Unbeknownst to him, he had been the laughingstock of the family and his neighborhood for years.

Whether such practices instilled in Barnum the impetus to freely bamboozle others in turn is uncertain, but certainly it was a profound lesson in how easily reality could be manipulated. As he put it, "Ivy Island was a part of the weight that made the wheel of fortune begin to turn in my favour at a time when my head was downward."

Perhaps even more influential was the time he spent as a clerk in his father's grocery, where he learned the fine art of bargaining by regularly trading store goods for produce or items manufactured by their customers. "Many of our customers were hatters, and we took hats in payment for goods," he said. But soon he discovered that the hatters were not above mixing in their inferior furs with their best, selling Barnum the hats as "otter," when they might have come from rabbits. The store, in turn, "mixed our sugars, teas, and liquors, and gave them the most valuable names. . . . The customers cheated us in their fabrics; we cheated the customers with our goods. Each party expected to be cheated, if it was possible." In time, Barnum graduated from such conniving and developed something of a specialty in selling lottery tickets, not only purveying the offerings of national operations but also concocting his own drawings with store goods as prizes.

When he was fifteen, Barnum's father Philo died, insolvent, so much so that young Tale had to borrow the money for a pair of shoes to wear to the funeral.

A former Danbury resident who had opened a grocery in Brooklyn eventually came to the rescue, hiring Barnum as a clerk and ultimately entrusting him with purchasing goods for the store. Barnum enjoyed learning the ropes of the wholesale business but chafed at the fact that he was in another person's employ. "There are some persons so constituted that they can never be satisfied to labour for a fixed salary," he said before declaring, "I am one of that sort."

During the summer of 1827, Barnum caught smallpox, and following his convalescence and a stay of some months in Danbury, he returned to Brooklyn with enough saved to give himself a start in business. He opened a porterhouse not far from the store where he had clerked and within months had himself an offer to sell it for a tidy profit. He stayed on in New York for a time, working for another tavern owner and spending a goodly portion of his free time attending the theater. "I had much taste for the drama," he said, and "soon became, in my own opinion, a close critic, and did not fail to exhibit my powers in this respect to all the juveniles from Connecticut who accompanied me to the theater."

Early in 1828, Grandfather Phin wrote Barnum, offering him the use of a carriage house on the main street of the Danbury suburb of Bethel, including its living quarters, if Barnum would establish some sort of business there. The offer was enough to rouse Barnum from his man-about-town status, and soon he was back at home, converting the carriage house to a fruit stand and confectionery. He had approached several of his New York contacts to ensure a steady supply of goods at suitable prices and, as a backstop, installed a keg of ale in a corner of the shop. On his first day of business, he drained the ale keg and took in sixty-three dollars altogether, enough to send him on his way. By fall he had added a line of lottery tickets, a variety of novelty items, and to top it off was dispensing stewed oysters along with pints of ale.

The following year, at the age of nineteen, Taylor Barnum proposed to his Bethel sweetheart, a tailoress named Charity Hallet. Neither of the families were certain the two principals had set their sights high enough, and in fact the groom was perfectly in accord with the Hallets' sentiment that their daughter "was altogether too good for Taylor Barnum." Nevertheless, Charity accepted the proposal and the two were married in a November 8, 1829, ceremony— kept secret from Barnum's mother—in New York City. Following her discovery of the event, it took Barnum's mother awhile to accept her son's choice, but within a month she had softened, and from that point until the day in 1855 when he penned the first edition of his memoir, Barnum could report that neither his mother "nor any other person ever said or believed that I had not been extremely fortunate in the selection of my companion."

For a time, Barnum carried on in Bethel, expanding the range of goods sold in his store to Bibles and brandy and secular books, dabbling in real estate and becoming something of a liberal force in the Danbury area, railing against the more dour features of Calvinism and propounding "cheerful Christianity" as the proper path to follow. He started a liberal-leaning weekly newspaper, *Herald of Freedom*, and opposed any number of measures meant to squelch the presentation of various forms of entertainment on the Sabbath and prohibitions on the sale of lottery tickets, which of course formed a substantial portion of his store proceeds.

When he published an article excoriating a local church dignitary for the crime of "taking usury of an orphan boy," Barnum was tossed in jail for more than two months. He continued to publish his paper during his confinement, and news of the episode made him something of a hero among liberals in the area. When he was finally released, Barnum was carried back to Danbury at the head of a celebratory parade composed of hundreds, an occasion that may well have attuned its subject to the intoxicating effects of celebrity.

Married, and with the birth of his first child, daughter Caroline Cordelia in 1830, Barnum began to grate under the various restraints of a merchant's existence. "I wanted to do business faster than ordinary mercantile transactions would admit; hence I bought largely, and in order to sell largely, was compelled to give extensive credits—and soon had an accumulation of bad debts."

A glance at the various sums crossed out as forgiven in his ledger offers a sobering, if sometimes humorous, commentary on the range of a creditor's woes: "By death, to balance." "By running away—in full." "By cheating me out of my dues, to balance." "By failing, in full." "By swearing he would not pay me, in full." As to one account of a few dollars long past due against a well-to-do Danbury resident, Barnum remarked that the balance having stood so long, "I supposed the wealthy debtor had forgotten it, and I felt loth to remind him of his indebtedness." In the end, Barnum closed the account with the note "Too rich to be dunned."

When the Connecticut legislature went so far as to ban the sale of lottery tickets in 1834, Barnum had seen enough. He sold his store, stepped away from his newspaper, and went off with his young family to New York City, there to pursue dreams of appropriate scope. Though he may have been dreaming big, the practicalities of life in New York were daunting and no work was to be found. Finally, in the spring of 1835, Barnum came into a bit of money when some old lottery debts were finally paid to him, and he used the cash to open a small boardinghouse and to purchase an interest in a grocery store nearby. It was hardly the sort of existence Barnum had come to the center of American commerce seeking, but with a wife and child involved, ends needed to be met.

How long Barnum might have been content to rent rooms and jiggle the produce scales is difficult to reckon, for all changed on one hot day in late July, when an old acquaintance from Connecticut, a Coley Bartram, made his way into the store with a proposition. Bizarre it might have been, but still it was one that he thought might interest the ambitious Barnum. Bartram explained that he owned an interest in what he described as "an extraordinary negro woman" by the name of Joice Heth. Heth was 161 years old, Bartram continued, and she was said to have served as the nursemaid to none other than George Washington himself.

Whatever Barnum might have been making of such a story was interrupted by Bartram's getting to the point. He had recently sold out his own interest in Ms. Heth to a certain R. W. Lindsay of Jefferson County, Kentucky, who had transported Heth to Philadelphia, where he was presently engaged in exhibiting her. But Lindsay was not much of a showman, Bartram confided, and with his heart not attached to the undertaking, the new buyer was anxious to find a buyer for his specimen and return to Kentucky.

As proof of all this, Bartram handed over a copy of an advertisement from the *Philadelphia Inquirer* describing some of the particulars of Ms. Heth's history and mentioning various "proofs" of her claims, including the original bill of sale filled out by Augustine Washington, the former president's father, when he disposed of Ms. Heth to his sister-in-law Elizabeth Atwood for "thirty-three pounds lawful money of Virginia." According to the document, this transfer was made on February 5, 1727, when Ms. Heth was described as "aged fifty-four years."

In truth, word of the remarkable Philadelphia exhibition of Ms. Heth had already appeared in New York newspapers, and Barnum found it at the very least an astonishing coincidence that here was a man standing in his own grocery store ready to sell him the rights to exhibit such an amazing creature. It was enough to put Barnum on a stagecoach for Philadelphia for a look and a consultation with Mr. Lindsay.

At the Masonic Hall in Philadelphia, Barnum made his inspection of Ms. Heth, whose appearance seemed in keeping with everything he had heard: "She might almost as well have been called a thousand years old," he said. She was blind and too feeble to do much more than wave one arm from the divan where she lay, but she was a voluble conversationalist, able to sing a number of Baptist hymns, and provided detailed accounts of her care of "dear little George," whom, she said, she was the first ever to dress.

Lindsay showed Barnum the glass-encased bill of sale, which to Barnum "had every appearance of antiquity," and his response to Barnum's wonder that the existence of such a person had not been made known years ago was the verbal equivalent of a shrug. She had been lying in an outhouse of the Bowling family of Kentucky for many years, Lindsay explained, and no one knew or seemed to care who she was or how old she might be, only that she had come from somewhere in Virginia. A son of Mr. Bowling ran across the ancient bill of sale while researching some other business in the Virginia records office, Lindsay said, and after making inquiries locally, became convinced of Ms. Heth's identity.

By this point, Barnum had heard enough. Just how much might Mr. Lindsay want from him in order to transact business? Three thousand dollars was the response, but Barnum had not been fooling when he haggled over all those hen's eggs and phony otter hats years before. He left Philadelphia with an option to purchase Ms. Heth at any time over the next ten days for the sum of $1,000, and he was heading home for one simple reason: "I did not possess more than five hundred dollars in cash."

In short order, Barnum divested himself of his one-half interest in his grocery store and returned to Philadelphia with enough cash to consummate his purchase. He arranged with Lindsay to carry on the Philadelphia exhibition of Ms. Heth for a week and then hurried back to make arrangements to bring what was now *his* show to New York. Taylor Barnum was no longer an anonymous grocery store clerk—he had entered the world of show business.

Back in the city, he approached a well-known tavern owner, who just months before had turned down Barnum's application as a bartender, and explained what he was up to and what he would need. Soon enough, he and William Niblo were partners, with Niblo providing exhibition space in what had shortly before been the parlor of his own home and covering the costs of printing, advertising, ticket takers, and utilities. Barnum supplied Ms. Heth, whom posters described as "The Greatest Natural & National Curiosity in the World." The take was soon averaging $1,500 a week, and the course of a career was irrevocably set.

Missing from many accounts of Barnum's momentous acquisition is the observation that Barnum was in essence engaging in the slave trade. He may have reasoned that he had simply purchased an "exhibit," and there is evidence that Ms. Heth saw herself as a performer with Barnum her manager, but for all practical purposes he had become the owner of another human being. This assessment is of course easier to make from a twenty-first-century perspective. By the 1830s, the abolitionist movement had gained traction in the United States (Nat

Turner's rebellion came in 1831), and violence was often directed in northern cities at freed Black people and their supporters, but there was little outrage directed at Barnum or the Joice Heth exhibit. The interest of the public focused primarily upon the astounding prospect of her age and her purported connection to the nation's Founding Father.

"Her appearance is very like an Egyptian mummy just escaped from its sarcophagus," wrote the *New York Evening Star*. The *Sun* chimed in: "This renowned relic of the olden time has created quite a sensation among the lovers of the curious and the marvelous; and a greater object of marvel and curiosity has never presented itself for their gratification."

In New York the exhibition took more or less the same form as Barnum had witnessed in Philadelphia. After an introduction covering her history, Ms. Heth answered questions about her age and her relationship with the beloved Washington in a manner that was by all accounts convincing, pausing from time to time to sing hymns that derived from long-forgotten editions of the Baptist prayer book. From New York, the show moved to Providence, and then Boston, which Barnum had never before visited. Bostonians were so intrigued that the room Barnum engaged at the city's concert hall was overrun, forcing the exhibition of a Mr. Maelzel and his "automaton chess-player" out of the grand parlor.

Maelzel took his eviction with equanimity, however, opining that Barnum was likely to make a successful showman. "You understand the value of the press, and that is the great thing," the venerable Italian said. "Nothing helps the showmans like the types and the ink. When your old woman dies," he said, waving a hand at the recumbent Joice Heth, "you come to me, and I will make your fortune. I will let you have my 'carousal,' my automaton trumpet-player, and many curious things which will make plenty of money."

As to money, Barnum was already making plenty. The show went on to tour most every other city of size in Massachusetts, then Hartford, New Haven, Newark, and return engagements in New York and so far as Albany, where Barnum spotted a juggler performing at the city's museum. Signor Antonio, as he was billed, was Italian-born and had arrived in Albany via London and Canada. His act, which included plate spinning, stilt walking, balancing the points of bayonets on his nose, and the like, had never been seen anywhere else in the United States. Thus, when Barnum departed Albany, he took two acts with him, Ms. Heth and the Italian juggler of crockery, whom he rechristened from Signor Antonio to a "more foreign-sounding" Signor Vivalla.

It remains an imponderable as to how much of the humbuggery surrounding Joice Heth Barnum ever believed. In the 1855 edition of his autobiography, he says, "The question naturally arises, if Joice Heth was an impostor, who taught her these things?" (Her familiarity with ancient psalmody, the minute details concerning the Washington family, and the like.) Barnum's response: "I do not know. I taught her none of these things."

The less evasive answer might have been: "She looked good enough to convince most people, and that was enough for me." In fact, as attendance began to taper off in Boston, there appeared in one of the local papers an indignant letter to the editor, wherein an individual identified only as "A Visitor" (Barnum, in actuality) contended that "Joice Heth is not a human being." Rather, said the writer, the display was "simply a curiously constructed automaton, made up of whalebone, India-rubber, and numberless springs," a contraption brought to a simulacrum of life by a ventriloquist. As Barnum describes it, and without assuming any responsibility for the letter's placement: "The consequence was, our audiences again largely increased," this time swelled by those wondering if they could detect the fakery. For Barnum, who had turned the skepticism surrounding Ms. Heth to his own advantage, the bottom line had little to do with "authenticity," so long as audiences were entertained: "If the simple truth was told with regard to the exhibition, it was really vastly curious and interesting."

The question of Joice Heth's age was finally put to rest in February 1836, when Ms. Heth, sent to recuperate from exhaustion at Barnum's half-brother Philo's house in Bethel, abruptly passed away. Philo had the body sent by sleigh to Barnum in New York, and Barnum made good on a promise he had given a noted surgeon who had asked permission to perform a postmortem on Heth should she die under Barnum's protection. At the autopsy, attended by several other physicians, medical students, and newspaper editors, the surgeon made a careful examination of the relative ossification of the arteries leading from Ms. Heth's heart. The surgeon consulted with several of his colleagues who were present and then, after the room was cleared, delivered his opinion: Joice Heth had been no more than eighty when she died.

As Barnum recalls the moment, he protested to the surgeon that he had hired Joice "in perfect good faith, and [he had] relied upon her appearance and the documents as evidence of the truth of her story." The doctor's response might have been expected—even he had found Joice's appearance suggestive of extreme longevity: perhaps the documents had been forged, or else they applied to some other individual.

The revelation prompted an editorial in the following day's *Sun* penned by Richard Locke, who had been present at the examination: "Dissection of Joice Heth—Precious Humbug Exposed" was the headline. It did not end there, however, for an assistant of Barnum's, one Levi Lyman, saw the situation as the perfect guise to play a practical joke on *New York Herald* editor James Gordon Bennett. Lyman visited Bennett's office and told him that the autopsy itself had been the hoax. In fact, Joice Heth was still alive, Lyman said, and was presently being exhibited in Connecticut. The autopsy had been performed on an anonymous Black woman whose corpse was procured from a morgue in Harlem. To scoop the rival *Sun*, Bennett published a near-verbatim account of the tale that Lyman fed him, only to discover incontrovertible proof of Ms. Heth's demise and that he'd been made a fool of.

Months later, Bennett ran into Lyman on the street and lit into him with a blistering tirade for his stunt. Lyman professed great chagrin and apologized to Bennett, promising a way to make it up to him. The pair retired to Bennett's offices, where Lyman dictated what he claimed was the "true story of Joice Heth," a tale that featured Barnum's discovery of the old woman in a shed in Kentucky, having all her teeth pulled, and coaching her in the story of her 161-year heritage. All of it was published by Bennett in a series of articles in the *Herald* that September. It is that fictitious account supplied by Lyman, Barnum said, that was often taken as the facts of the matter. It was a "ridiculous" story, Barnum claims in his memoir, but in the end—echoing Mr. Maelzel from Boston—he seemed philosophical about it all: "Newspaper and social controversy on the subject (and seldom have vastly more important matters been so largely discussed) served my purpose as 'a showman' by keeping my name before the public."

Reading Barnum's account of the Joice Heth episode provides something of a counterpoint to the image of the showman as a cynic and a charlatan often purveyed. In his own eyes, he'd given good weight in mounting the show of Joice Heth, and if those who felt they'd been duped were moved to make a continuing spectacle of their gullibility in public, he was hardly to blame.

TWELVE

FIRST TOUR OF DUTY

With Joice Heth gone, Barnum fell back on Signor Vivalla as his mainstay, even becoming a second banana of sorts, often coming onstage to toss the juggler his props and offering a running, breathless commentary upon the skills needed to hop about the stage on one stilt and the like. At one of Vivalla's performances in Philadelphia, a local juggler by the name of Roberts heckled Vivalla, claiming that he could perform rings around the Italian.

Rather than have Roberts thrown out, Barnum sensed an opportunity worthy of a bit of Philadelphia showmanship: the fictional Apollo Creed's calling out of the local Italian Stallion in *Rocky* many decades later. Barnum summoned Roberts backstage and suggested a "grudge match" between the two jugglers, with a prize of $1,000 to go to Roberts if he could indeed duplicate all of Vivalla's tricks. Roberts proved more clever than Barnum gave him credit for, however.

"You don't expect me to perform *all* of Vivalla's tricks, do you?" Roberts asked.

Barnum replied that he did not expect that outcome for a moment. "But if you do *not*, of course you will not win the thousand dollars."

Roberts protested that he was a far better juggler but had no idea how to walk on stilts, and Barnum sensed his plan about to fall apart. Forget the thousand dollars, he told Roberts, suggesting an alternative: "I will give you thirty dollars if you will perform under my directions one night at the Walnut Street Theater, and will keep your own counsel."

The result was a cooked-up rivalry between the two performers to be settled by a contest to be held at the Walnut. As Barnum describes it, "Suitable 'notices' were inserted in the papers, bragging that Roberts was an American and could beat the foreigner all hollow." Roberts declared that if he should win the still-advertised $1,000 prize, as he fully expected, a portion of it would go to charity. On the appointed night, Barnum recalls, "The pit and upper boxes were crowded to suffocation," and the rigged "contest" went off precisely as scripted, the duel going on for about forty minutes before Roberts—faced with the need to spin two plates at once, one in either hand—pronounced himself beaten. Roberts then performed a spirited denouement in which he demonstrated various impressive feats that he *could* do, which earned him great applause.

When even Vivalla came onstage to offer his compliments on Roberts's skills, the latter immediately challenged Vivalla to a subsequent match the following Tuesday, with a wager of $500 on the line, bringing cheers and stomping from the crowd. All of this had been laid out by Barnum, of course, and given that the promoter had cleared $200 on the evening, the "contests" between Vivalla and Roberts carried on for an ensuing month.

Though these duels between jugglers drew crowds and lined Barnum's pockets, the novelty eventually faded, and as the summer of 1836 approached, Barnum found himself finally completing the transition to minor circus life when he signed on with a former Danbury neighbor named Aaron Turner, who headed a traveling show. In addition to bringing Signor Vivalla to the bill, Barnum would serve as the troupe's secretary, treasurer, and ticket seller, for which he would receive 20 percent of the net profits. The show opened in Massachusetts (circus performances being still illegal in Connecticut) and traveled through the summer about the East Coast and all the way southward to North Carolina.

At that point, and having amassed some $1,200 through his labors with Turner, Barnum decided to strike out on his own, touring the South through the winter with a vaudeville-like show entitled "Barnum's Grand Scientific and Musical Theater," which featured Vivalla and an African American minstrel singer-dancer named James Sandford. All went well enough until the troupe reached Samford, South Carolina, where Sandford abruptly quit the show. With half of his headliners missing, Barnum was in something of a quandary. It was nothing a dedicated showman couldn't see through, though his method would doubtless not go over so well today.

"No one of my company was competent to fill his [Sanford's] place; but being determined not to disappoint the audience, I blacked myself thoroughly, and sung the songs advertised." As he reported, "To my surprise, my singing was applauded, and in two of the songs I was encored!"

It was not the last time Barnum would find himself pressed into service as part of the show. He also employed a magician and ventriloquist by the name of Joe Pentland, and at one performance, Pentland's diminutive assistant, who was usually crammed into the bottom of the magician's table to help with the "transformation" of various objects passed through trap doors on the tabletop, was nowhere to be found.

Though he barely fit into the hidden compartment, Barnum agreed to take on the chore. For a time, all went well, with Barnum supplying the balls, cups, scarves, and other accouterments that the script called for. The summa of Pentland's act called for him to receive a gold watch and chain passed up from someone in the audience. It would become Barnum's job to pull the watch down and then wind its chain around the neck of a live squirrel which had been ensconced in a tiny cage in the cabinet along with him. Once all was done, Barnum would shove the watch-bedecked squirrel back up through the trap door and Pentland would turn to present this fabulous assemblage to those gathered.

At the appropriate time, Pentland made his call for a watch, and one was produced by an unsuspecting audience member. Pentland placed the watch on the table, covered it with a vase, and rapped smartly, the signal for Barnum to open the trap, secure the watch, and do his work. When Barnum withdrew the squirrel from its cage, however, the animal promptly sank its teeth into Barnum's thumb.

In agony, barely able to move, much less dislodge the creature from his thumb, Barnum began to shriek and thrash, kicking until the flimsy wood of the cabinet burst apart, leaving Barnum rolling in the splinters, finally able to wrench the squirrel from its hold. As Pentland gaped, Barnum dashed behind the stage curtain, blood trailing from his hand. Meanwhile, the squirrel disappeared into the rafters with the watch still wound about its neck.

Whether or not the audience saw it for the disaster that it was or took it as all part of the show can never be ascertained. But as Barnum put it, "If ever there was hooting and shouting in a mass of spectators, it was heard that night."

In such a ragtag way, Barnum's show toured through the South until making its way to Nashville by May 1837. He spent the summer resting at home in Connecticut, then set out for another winter tour of the South, even selling his horses and wagons and moving his show up and down the Mississippi by steamboat, but he had indifferent success. Soon he was back in New York City, vowing never again to adopt the life of an itinerant showman.

Barnum had $2,500 in his pocket, which he determined to invest once and for all in a solid business undertaking of some kind. After entertaining a cast of charlatans and quacks, including one touting a perpetual motion machine, he settled upon a German with a fledgling business in the manufacture of allied products including bootblacking, waterproofing paste for leather, cologne water, and bear grease. It took a little more than two years for the business, headquartered in the Bowery, to go under and for his partner to abscond, leaving Barnum, at thirty, with little choice than to assume his former travels as a showman. He struggled along, often with little more than an Ethiopian dancer and a fiddler to tout as a "show," until the spring of 1841, when he returned to New York City, which was still suffering the ravages of the economic crash of 1837.

If there was an upside to the generally gloomy business climate Barnum found surrounding him, it was that values of any number of formerly notable properties had been greatly diminished by the crash, placing them within the reach of ordinary mortals. One such that interested him was John Scudder's American Museum, housed in a five-story building on Broadway at Ann Street near the City Park. Housing an array of stuffed birds, fossils, shells, and mineral fragments, the ten-year-old institution had been in steady decline since 1837, and though Scudder, since deceased, had sunk about $50,000 into the collection, it was being offered for $15,000.

The figure was approximately $15,000 more than Barnum had at the moment, but he was again smarting from his disappointments on the road, as well as from a brief stint as a publisher of Bibles and another as a freelance public relations writer. To top it off, he had just received a letter from a creditor in Danbury who held a mortgage of $500 on a property Barnum owned in the town. "He wrote to say that he was satisfied that I would never lay up anything until I could 'invent a riddle that would hold water,' and as that was not very likely to occur, I might as well pay him now." The letter so disheartened the thirty-one-year old that he lay it aside with a resolution to himself: "Mr. B., no more nonsense, no more living from hand to mouth, but from this moment please to concentrate your energies upon providing permanently for *the future*."

He had been visiting the American Museum regularly and, as he put it, "I saw, or believed that I saw, that only energy, tact and liberality were needed, to give it life and to put it on a profitable footing." Despite the preposterous nature of his declaration, Barnum set himself upon the task to make the museum's ownership his. When he confided his intentions to a friend, he was met with incredulity: "*You* buy the American Museum? What do you intend buying it with?"

"*Brass*," Barnum replied, unfazed, "for silver and gold I have none."

For the absent cash Barnum substituted unadorned honesty. He sent a letter to the owner of the museum's building, a retired merchant named Francis Olmstead, proposing that Olmstead purchase the contents of the museum and sign them over to Barnum, who would make a series of yearly installments until the debt was repaid. Olmstead found Barnum's earnest energy appealing, and the merchant asked if he had any references.

Barnum produced a series of individuals willing to attest to his character, including William Niblo, with whom he had originally partnered in the exhibition of Joice Heth. Finally, Olmstead was convinced sufficiently to yield, though there was one final condition: "If you only had a piece of unencumbered real estate that you could offer as additional security," Olmstead suggested.

Barnum thought hard—he had several properties in and around Danbury, but all were mortgaged to the hilt. And then it struck him. There was one fabulous holding he could offer.

"I have five acres of land in Connecticut which is free from all lien or encumbrance," he told Olmstead.

"Indeed!" Olmstead replied. "What did you pay for it?"

"It was a present from my late grandfather, Phineas Taylor," Barnum said, "given me on account of my name."

It was desolate Ivy Island Barnum was talking about. But as he watched the features of merchant Olmstead begin to soften, he understood that with his offer of that stretch of dreary swampland, the deal for the American Museum was done. At long last, the joke was no longer on Tale Barnum.

There was a bit of angst at the last minute, when a rival museum submitted a higher bid to Olmstead, but the ever-enterprising Barnum did some digging and learned that his new rival was nothing but a syndicate formed to purchase distressed properties and resell shares to unsuspecting investors at a profit. The syndicate had no intention of turning a hand upside down concerning the operation of the American Museum, whereas to Barnum the place was a gold mine waiting to happen.

To fend off the eleventh-hour competitors, Barnum was off to the contacts he had made in the New York press during the Heth exhibitions. He explained to them the situation and asked if they would let him place a series of columns in their papers exposing the intentions of the syndicate. The editors went along, and Barnum's persuasive columns put a damper on the plans of the syndicate, which, with none of the expected share sales having materialized, began to dither. When the syndicate—thinking that no one else would be interested in the property—allowed the purchase deadline to pass by a day, Olmstead declared their $1,000 deposit a forfeit and executed his contract with Barnum.

Six months or so after his purchase, Barnum was in the museum's ticket office at noontime, hastily wolfing down a plate of corned beef and bread he'd brought from home for his lunch. Olmstead came by to visit and shook his head. "Is this the way you eat your dinner?" he asked.

"I have not eaten a warm dinner since I bought the Museum except on the Sabbath," Barnum told him. "And I intend never to eat another on a weekday until I am out of debt."

Olmstead found this funny indeed and clapped Barnum on the shoulder. "Ah, you are safe. You will pay for the Museum before the year is out," he said, pointing at the line for the afternoon admissions already beginning to form outside.

Survivors outside the flaming big top, Hartford Circus Fire of 1944.
Courtesy, The John and Mable Ringling Museum of Art.

Grim firefighters and responders at the Hartford Circus Fire.
Courtesy, The John and Mable Ringling Museum of Art.

Philip Astley's London Amphitheater in 1777. Courtesy, The
John and Mable Ringling Museum of Art.

Blondin crossing
the Niagara Gorge
in 1859. Photo by
William England.

Pawnee Bill's Wild West Show ca. 1900—showing not much had changed in the wagon shows over three quarters of a century. Photo by Frederick Whitman Glasier, The John and Mable Ringling Museum of Art.

P. T. Barnum with 14- year-old George Washington "Commodore Nutt," 29 inches tall at the time (General Tom Thumb, then 24, had skyrocketed to 35 inches).

Portrait of James A. Bailey
from the digital collection of
the New York Public Library.

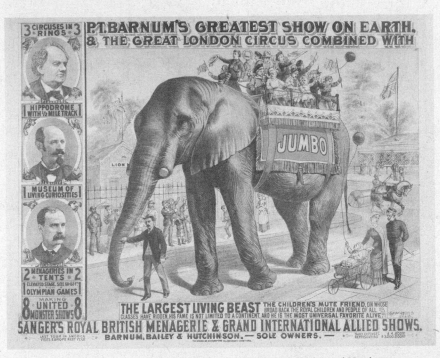

Poster touting the exhibition of Jumbo the Elephant by the Barnum, Bailey, and Hutchinson
combined shows in the early 1880s. Courtesy, The John and Mable Ringling Museum of Art.

Poster depicting the mammoth rail car operation of the Ringling Bros. and Barnum & Bailey combined shows. Courtesy, The John and Mable Ringling Museum of Art.

Portrait of John Ringling by Savely Abramovitch Sorine, 1927. Courtesy, The John and Mable Ringling Museum of Art.

Barnum & Bailey ticket wagon, 1903. Glasier Collection, courtesy, The John and Mable Ringling Museum of Art.

Early-twentieth-century parade wagon from the Hagenbeck Show, on display at the Ringling Circus Museum. Courtesy, State Archives of Florida.

THE CATCH

Copyright by
T.V. GLASIER 1907

2?3

Dramatic 1907 Glasier shot of "Queen of the Air" Maude Banvard. Glasier
Collection, courtesy, The John and Mable Ringling Museum of Art.

The ringmaster and his love,
Fred Bradna and equestrienne
Ella Bradna, in 1910. Glasier
Collection, courtesy, The John and
Mable Ringling Museum of Art.

Lillian Leitzel, far left, with her mother and aunts, the aerialist
troupe, "The Leamy Ladies," in Germany, 1905.

THIRTEEN

MUSEUM MASTER

Barnum's interest in making a success of Scudder's museum did not arise completely out of thin air, for the roots of such establishments in the United States extended back to 1791 when the Tammany Society organized in a building on King Street an exhibition of various "curiosities," including a stuffed bison, an eighteen-foot yellow snake from somewhere in South America, a lamb with two heads, assorted American Indian relics, some African ornaments, Chinese war weapons, and even a model of a guillotine featuring a beheaded wax figure. In keeping with the intended educational aims of the institution, the first American flag raised over New York City following the departure of the British in 1783 was also on display.

That original Tammany exhibition also included a modest menagerie displayed on the outdoor grounds, but it was not the only circus-oriented exhibition in Manhattan. In 1821, three Flatfoot promoters from Westchester County—John June, Lewis Titus, and Caleb Sutton Angevine—struck upon a unique solution for housing their traveling menagerie stock during the winter season. Instead of searching out a series of countryside barns and cellars where their charges could be kept safe during the off-season—and with rent required—why not find an appropriate venue and exhibit the animals in the city during the winter and make money rather than lose it?

All this was fodder for the superior exhibitions Barnum intended to bring to his newly acquired building at the corner of Broadway and Ann. As part of his arrangement with Olmstead, he housed his family, grown to four with the birth of daughter Helen in 1840, in a ground-floor apartment attached to the building and drew a stipend of $12 per week from admissions to support them. (Daughter Frances would be born in 1842, joined by Pauline in 1846.) The arrangement afforded Barnum even more time to pour into his efforts at the museum, which at the outset focused on the all-important "notoriety."

He quickly installed a series of large flags representing the world's nations along the roofline of the building, attracting notice for blocks around and imparting an air of authority. Along with the flags, he mounted on the roof the first spotlight ever seen in the city, its beams washing the skies as well as the nearby sidewalks nightly. He also had all of the hundred or so windows on the upper stories of the building covered with color paintings of the various creatures on display inside, including polar bears, elephants, kangaroos, lions, seals, and giraffes, thus creating a kind of five-story variegated billboard for passersby. The whole spectacle formed a kind of Times Square, overload-of-the-senses experience for the time. By the following spring, he had also installed an outdoor garden atop the building, where guests could stroll, enjoy refreshments, and listen to the strains of a brass band. There were hot-air balloon ascensions from the roof by day and fireworks displays at night, and soon enough there was a hundred-jet fountain geysering atop the building as well.

All this hubbub was intended to lure the curious inside, of course, and although the highlight of the original collection had been the various taxidermy specimens, Barnum realized that once a visitor had gazed for a bit upon a stuffed bison or bear, there would be little cause to repeat the experience anytime soon. Thus, to attract repeat visitors, he began the importation of a series of live acts deriving straight from the circus, including "industrious fleas, educated dog, jugglers, automatons, ventriloquists, living statuary, tableaux, gipsies, albinos, fat boys, giants, dwarfs, rope-dancers, caricatures of phrenology . . . pantomime, instrumental music, singing and dancing in great variety, (including Ethiopians)."

There were also "dioramas, panoramas, models of Dublin, Paris, Niagara, Jerusalem . . . mechanical figures, fancy glass-blowing, knitting machines . . . dissolving views, American Indians, including their warlike and religious ceremonies enacted on the stage," with Barnum intent upon including something for every taste.

As it turned out, Olmstead's declaration of faith in Barnum's abilities as a showman proved accurate. Before 1841 was out, Barnum had paid off every penny of his $12,000 loan from the proceeds of his enterprise. By the following year, he was once again in a bit of hot water, however, owing to his propensity for valuing an exhibition for its entertainment value as much as for its authenticity. "If I have exhibited a questionable dead mermaid in my Museum," Barnum was huffing in public statements, "it should not be overlooked that I have also exhibited cameleopards (giraffes), a rhinoceros, grizzly bears, orang-outangs, great serpents, etc., about which there could be no mistake because they were alive."

The reference to the "questionable dead mermaid" derived from Barnum's decision in June 1842 to partner with a rival museum keeper from Boston named Moses Kimball in the exhibition of what was purported to be an embalmed mermaid. The Feejee Mermaid, as Barnum dubbed the attraction, was in fact a carefully stitched-up assemblage of the back half of a sturgeon-like fish attached to the torso of a female orangutan capped with the head of a baboon. So far as Barnum was concerned, the purported authenticity of the thing (as in the case of Joice Heth) was of secondary importance. "Assuming, what is no doubt true, that the mermaid was manufactured," he contended, "it was a most remarkable specimen of ingenuity and untiring patience."

When he consulted his own resident naturalist about the matter, the scientist admitted that he could not detect just how the thing had been manufactured. "Then why do you suppose that it is manufactured?" Barnum asked.

"Because I don't believe in mermaids," replied the naturalist.

Barnum scoffed. "That is no reason at all," he said, "and therefore I'll believe in the mermaid and hire it."

Though some seven years had passed since the exhibition of Ms. Heth, Barnum was well aware that any mention of his name with the advertised unveiling of the Feejee Mermaid would discount a great deal of the public's interest in the phenomenon, so he set about creating an elaborate myth. According to a series of letters he cooked up and had sent to New York papers from friends of his in distant cities, the mermaid had been brought to this country by a "Dr. J. Griffin," an English naturalist from London's Lyceum of Natural History. Griffin was in fact Barnum's old coconspirator in the Joice Heth affair, Levi Lyman, sporting a goatee and a British accent. The good doctor announced that though he had not wished to exhibit his mermaid publicly, he had come to feel some considerable pressure from the naturalist community to do so. Barnum, meantime, had ginned up a "scientific" pamphlet supporting the authenticity of mermaids and had ten thousand of them sold about the city at a penny apiece (half what they had cost him, he complained).

In due course it was announced that Dr. Griffin had at last agreed to exhibit the animal, "taken near the Feejee Islands," and *positively for one week only*," at the concert hall on Broadway, with admission set at twenty-five cents, the same as that charged at the museum. When the doors of the hall opened on August 8 and the throngs poured in, Barnum looked on from the wings, concerned lest some visitor might recognize "Dr. Griffin" as the curator of Joice Heth, but his fears proved unfounded. About the only difficulties arose from the occasional red-blooded young man who took offense that the hideous, desiccated creature ensconced in a three-foot-tall glass vase bore little resemblance to the gorgeous bare-breasted and life-sized representations of mermaids adorning the entrance to the concert hall.

Following the weeklong run at the concert hall, Barnum announced that he had arranged with Dr. Griffin to have the creature moved to the American Museum, where visitors could view her "without extra charge." The take at the concert hall more than satisfied Barnum, but over the four weeks the Feejee Mermaid was exhibited at the museum, the gate tripled to more than $3,300. "Thus was the fame of the Museum," Barnum later wrote, "wafted from one end of the land to the other."

To the charge that his museum was nothing but an exercise in "humbug," or deception, Barnum turned philosophical. Though he did not employ this exact metaphor, he might have referred a complainant regarding the Feejee Mermaid to the example of a novel: Everyone understands that a novel is a construct meant to seem *like* life, but never to be mistaken for life itself. In fact, a goodly portion of the pleasure to be taken from the reading of a novel derives from one's appreciation for just how artful an author has been in enticing the willing suspension of disbelief. The sheer dexterity of the artist is to account for an appreciation of the whole. And it would be the rare reader, indeed, to mistake anything between the covers of, say, *The Da Vinci Code* for the written testimony of the Apostles. And of course there are novels that fail to convince their readers, just as there are showmen unable to mesmerize their audiences.

Furthermore, aside from the inarguable pleasure that derives from *being taken*, Barnum went to great lengths to distance himself from outright swindlers and charlatans, including those selling useless patent medicines, cheating at shell games, purveying worthless parcels of land, or masquerading as spiritualists or anointed prophets of the Almighty. Far from deceiving his customers at the museum, Barnum insisted, "when they came inside and paid to be amused and instructed, I took care to see that they not only received the full worth of their money, but were more than satisfied."

He took pleasure in comparing how the numbers of visitors to his museum consistently outdid those visiting the British Museum (where admission was "free of charge" to boot) and touted the decency of his offerings in a way that Walt Disney would have approved of a century later. "I abolished all vulgarity and profanity from the state, and I prided myself upon the fact that parents and children could attend the dramatic performances in the so-called Lecture Room, and not be shocked or offended by anything they might see or hear."

In addition, he took credit for the regular production of what he called the "Moral Drama," including such titles as "The Drunkard," "Uncle Tom's Cabin," "Moses in Egypt," and "Joseph and His Brethren." It was all based on a simple concept, part of his vision when he determined that he *would* acquire the museum or die trying. Barnum was certain that he could present "such a variety, quantity and quality of amusement, blended with instruction, 'all for twenty-five cents, children half price,' that my attractions would be irresistible, and my fortune certain." He did not believe in duping the public, he maintained, "but I believe in first *attracting* and then pleasing them."

Barnum often referred to such attractions as Joice Heth and the Feejee Mermaid as "skyrockets," special features that would draw attention—and visitors—to the museum, where any grousing concerning the makeup of the headliners would be more than compensated for by the whole of the experience. However, soon after his museum had begun to flourish, he was to encounter the skyrocket of all skyrockets, a personage whose "curiosity index" was to be matched only by his innate substance and talent. The encounter would not only enrich Barnum beyond his dreams but also establish him as a master showman for all time.

FOURTEEN

GENERAL TOM

IN NOVEMBER 1842, BARNUM WAS CALLED AWAY TO ALBANY ON A MATTER OF some importance, and as he readied himself for his return to New York, he learned that the Hudson River was frozen tight. With passenger boats unable to travel, he would have to take the Housatonic Railway back, and, as that line passed through Bridgeport, Connecticut, he decided to stay over a night at the Franklin Hotel there, where his brother Philo was the inn-keep.

As the two were talking, Barnum, thirty-two at the time, recalled having heard of a remarkably small child who lived in Bridgeport. Yes, that would have been the son of a Bridgeport carpenter named Sherwood Stratton, Philo responded, and offered to have the child brought to the hotel. "He was the smallest child I ever saw that could walk alone," Barnum recalled, following their meeting. "Not two feet in height, and weighed less than sixteen pounds."

The child, in Barnum's words, "was a bright-eyed little fellow, with light hair and ruddy cheeks, was perfectly healthy, and as symmetrical as an Apollo," meaning that he was an example of proportionate dwarfism, or in circus parlance of the time, a midget. "He was exceedingly bashful," Barnum said, "but after some coaxing he was induced to converse with me, and informed me that his name was Charles S. Stratton, son of Sherwood E. Stratton."

After a bit of further conversation, during which Barnum learned that Charles had not grown at all beyond the age of seven months, he began to understand that this nearly five-year-old child was no mere "curiosity" but an individual with extraordinary potential—providing he did not simply begin to grow again. In short order, Barnum had arranged a contract with the child's parents for an exhibition tour of four weeks, at $3 per week plus expenses.

When Charles arrived in New York on December 8, he discovered that he was being billed as General Tom Thumb, an eleven-year-old boy just come to the state from England. Those bits of fiction were necessary, Barnum explained, because Americans were far more fascinated by Europeans than their counterparts, no matter how talented; and as for the sudden increase in Charles's age, it was necessary to convince audiences that he really was a dwarf and not simply a small child. "And in *this*, at least, they really were not deceived."

Barnum ensconced Mrs. Stratton and her son in an apartment on the fifth floor of the American Museum and began a series of training sessions with the young general, who proved as adept a pupil as their initial meeting had suggested. The two had a ready affection for one another, and Barnum schooled the child on grown-up manners and speech, and had him practice a number of one-line comebacks drawn from the hoary traditions of vaudeville. "He had native talent and a love of the ludicrous," Barnum observed, coming to regard the boy as "the most interesting and extraordinary natural curiosity of which the world has any knowledge."

At the end of the first month's engagement, Barnum handed over a $50 tip to Tom, along with an extension of the contract to a full year, at $7 per week, with the understanding that he would undertake periodic traveling tours, accompanied by his parents, with all expenses paid. Before that year was out, Barnum raised Tom's pay to $25 per week, and by the time the contract ended, Barnum had paid off his notes on the American Museum and raised Tom's pay to $50 per week, with plans for a tour of Europe looming.

By all accounts Tom never felt sorry for himself concerning his size, seeming to understand that somehow this "limitation" had given him opportunities he might never otherwise have enjoyed. When he and Barnum—usually identified as "The Doctor"—appeared onstage together, Barnum would often begin by calling for a young boy from the audience to come up so his size could be contrasted with Tom's. That was the cue for Tom to pipe up in his pipsqueak's voice: "I'd rather have a little miss." It was a variation on a tried-and-true theme, propelled by this version of a manlike creature the size of a doll who could easily perch on a dainty, feminine arm.

"You being a general, perhaps you will tell us what army you command?" the Doctor might ask.

"Cupid's artillery," Tom would reply, eliciting laughs.

"But there are so many generals in the army," the Doctor would protest. "Perhaps you will tell us whether you are a major general, a brigadier general, or an adjutant general?"

"I'm a quartermaster general" was the comeback.

"Really? How do you make that out?"

"Because I look out for the quarters" came the squealed reply.

★★★

It was January 1844 when Barnum and his prodigy embarked for Europe for a tour that would end up of three years' duration, and the unfailingly upbeat Barnum recalled the occasion with considerable emotion: "My name has so long been used in connection of incidents of the mirthful kind, that many persons, probably, do not suspect that I am susceptible of sorrowful emotion," he said. Still, he insisted that the "melting mood" was heavy upon him as he prepared to leave family and friends behind, "and when the band struck up 'Home Sweet Home,' my tears flowed thick and fast."

Barnum and the young general endured a nineteen-day voyage to Liverpool, where Tom was smuggled off the boat past waiting crowds disguised as an infant in his mother's arms. Though Barnum's principal objective was to receive an audience with Queen Victoria, he had no established contacts that would guarantee such a thing and was indeed flying by the seat of his pants in that regard.

During a brief engagement at a Liverpool theater, a London theater manager came down, duly impressed, and arranged a three-day engagement at the Princess Theater in London. The response in London was as enthusiastic as it had been in Liverpool, and though he was offered a reengagement, Barnum had a better idea.

He rented a furnished home in an aristocratic neighborhood in the West End and invited influential newspaper editors and members of the gentry to visit. Word soon spread of Barnum's remarkable charge, and soon the American ambassador Edward Everett had called, later inviting Barnum and Tom to dinner. Soon enough Everett had passed word to the queen herself regarding the amazing Tom Thumb, and shortly after Barnum had booked a second hall in Piccadilly for Tom, the long-awaited word came. Queen Victoria indeed wished to have Barnum and Tom Thumb come by Buckingham Palace.

Both were "prepped" for their appearance, and though little was required of Tom, save for the need to "back out" when leaving the queen's presence, it was made clear to Barnum that under no circumstances should he presume to speak directly to the queen. Any questions she might have for him would be relayed through a second party and his responses were to go through the interloper in turn.

On the night appointed, Barnum and his charge entered the palace and were escorted to the Picture Gallery, where the doors were thrown open to reveal a group of twenty or so nobles, including Prince Albert, at the distant end of the room, surrounding the queen herself. Undaunted, Tom Thumb—"looking like a wax doll gifted with the power of locomotion," in Barnum's words— "advanced with a firm step, and as he came within hailing distance, made a very graceful bow, and exclaimed, 'Good evening, *ladies and gentlemen!*'"

With that, the ice was shattered, and as the laughter subsided, the queen took Tom Thumb by the hand and led him about the gallery in conversation. Tom proclaimed that her gallery was "first-rate" and wondered aloud where the Prince of Wales might be, because he was looking forward to meeting him. The prince was resting, the perfectly charmed queen replied, but assured Tom that indeed the two would meet and soon. After an hour more of Tom singing, dancing, and doing impersonations of Napoleon and others, he and Barnum departed, their backing out of the huge room interrupted only by the sudden charge of one of the queen's small dogs. The spectacle of Tom's expert parrying of the dog's charge with his tiny cane added the final touch to what Barnum understood to be a triumph beyond his wildest expectations.

News of this command performance spread widely, requiring that Barnum find a larger hall for Tom's performances, and leading to a second visit to Buckingham Palace eight days later, when his wish to meet the Prince of Wales was fulfilled. During that visit, seven-year-old Tom opined that the Yellow Drawing Room, where they were hosted, was in fact a more handsome room than the Picture Gallery, adding, "That chandelier is very fine." He regaled those present with a rendition of "Yankee Doodle" and graciously accepted a souvenir from the queen, telling her, "I will keep it for as long as I live."

Soon, Barnum estimated that the daily gate at the theater in Piccadilly was $500, and sometimes more. He had a tiny, Thumb-sized carriage built for Tom pulled by four ponies, with an attendant and driver who were actually children themselves, the whole assemblage an unparalleled rolling advertisement when paraded down the London streets. And though Tom Thumb was unquestionably the most popular exhibit in the great city, Barnum was constantly on the prowl for other acts that he thought might be imported to the United States.

He was particularly smitten when he encountered a group of Irish bell ringers, "the most extraordinary and beautiful musical exhibition I ever saw or heard," as he wrote. Forty or fifty bells of various sizes and timbres were placed on a long table, and the group of seven players behind the table manipulated their "instruments" to produce, as Barnum put it, "any tunes they please with an accuracy, precision, softness and harmony unsurpassed by any orchestra in the world." Soon he had signed them up for an American tour, explaining with typical Barnum reasoning in a letter to old friend Moses Kimball, "I have made them 'Swiss,' procured *Swiss dresses*, got out a lithograph representing them in *Swiss costume*." (When the men protested that they spoke only English and that this ruse would never fly, Barnum assured them that if they continued to speak only in the same thick brogue that was natural to them, no one in America would be the wiser.) The group would have its own US concert tour and was to be folded into the offerings at the American Museum only when proceeds began to decline.

There was another brainstorm to be embraced when Barnum realized that in a hall adjacent to that where Tom Thumb was appearing, the American artist George Catlin seemed to be veritably printing money by selling his Western-themed paintings displayed among a florid setting of American Indian pottery, weapons, costumes, and even a huge wigwam. Within six months, Barnum had arranged for an entire troupe of American Indians to be transported to London, where he and Catlin would partner in an exhibition of native dances and ceremonies.

Another bolt of inspiration struck, when, after a tour of Stratford-upon-Avon, it occurred to Barnum that he might buy the house where Shakespeare was born and have it disassembled and packed up for shipment to the States, where he was certain it would make for quite the attraction. Only when the plan became public did a group of civic-minded Brits intercede to outbid Barnum and present the home to a newly formed Shakespeare Association.

Eventually, after extending General Tom's tour from London to every town of size in England and Scotland, and including forays to Belfast and Dublin, Barnum and his young charge took their show to France, where they appeared before King Louis Philippe at Tuileries Palace on four separate occasions, including a private audience. The overall reception in France was even greater than in London, with Barnum mentioning that it had become as much of an effort to tamp down advance enthusiasm as build it in order that the venues not be swamped (though he also complained bitterly about the entertainment taxes levied upon the act, which sometimes rose to half the proceeds). There was even a play written for Tom, *Le Petit Poucet* (*Little Thumb*), in which he popped up from a huge pie and slid downstage through the legs of a line of chorus girls.

The tour continued about France and thence into Belgium, where King Leopold and his family were as charmed by the young general as everyone else had been. If nothing else about the young phenomenon was notable, his continued display of humility and innocence might have been most remarkable of all. As Barnum said, "In spite of the extraordinary attention and unbounded petting the little General received . . . he was in no sense a 'spoiled child,' but retained throughout that natural simplicity of character and demeanor which added so much to the charm of his exhibitions. He was literally the pet of Paris."

The tour returned to London, where Barnum—never one to pass up an opportunity—commissioned an English-language version of *Le Petit Poucet* entitled *Hop o' My Thumb* that enjoyed a long run at the Standard Theatre, interrupted only by tours to various resorts and venues around the country. After a final trip to Ireland and a farewell performance at the Rotunda Hall in Dublin, where Barnum tallied the day's receipts at $1,305, the pair decamped for home after three years abroad, arriving back in New York in February 1847.

FIFTEEN

EST ARRIVÉ

Barnum had left the United States in 1844, with his museum note redeemed, a bit of money in his pocket, and in the company of a young star he believed to be of limitless potential. Things may have boded well when he left his native land, but all was still potential.

When he returned in 1847, Barnum was no longer a seeker. He had become an important man. As he walked about his museum, he said, "I found eyes peering and fingers pointing at me, and could frequently overhear the remark, 'There's Barnum.'" One day, he was sitting in the ticket booth reading a newspaper as the attendant handed over a ticket to a patron.

"Is Mr. Barnum in the museum?" the man asked.

The ticket taker pointed. "This is Mr. Barnum."

Barnum lowered his paper, assuming the man was there on some sort of business.

"Is this Mr. Barnum?" the man demanded of the ticket taker.

"It is," Barnum assured him.

The man stared at Barnum for a moment and finally tossed his ticket aside. "It's all right," he told the bewildered ticket taker. "I have got the worth of my money." And away he went, without having entered the museum.

As for the young general, he spent a month at the American Museum upon his return, before record crowds. Then, before his tours about the country resumed, he spent a month among his family and friends in Bridgeport, all of whom marveled at the transformation that had taken place in the formerly bashful young man. Now eight years old, and without having grown an inch, they found him "abounding in foreign airs and native graces."

"We never thought Charlie much of a phenomenon when he lived among us," one citizen remarked, "but now that he has become 'Barnumized,' he is a rare curiosity."

To Barnum, there was little mystery about it. He had seen the changes in his young charge take place incrementally. "The General left America three years before a diffident, uncultivated little boy; he came back an educated, accomplished little man. He had seen much and profited much." In fact, Tom Thumb had become a rich little man and he and Barnum were to settle upon a new contract, as equal partners.

Tom's father used $30,000 of the general's earnings (as much as $6 million in today's funds) to build the family a resplendent mansion near Bridgeport, and Barnum was soon following suit in establishing roots, looking forward to a time "when I could withdraw from the whirlpool of business excitement and settle down permanently with my family." He chose a seventeen-acre site in Fairfield County, close to Bridgeport, where he built "Iranistan," a Turkish-Oriental-themed palace modeled after the Pavilion of George IV in England. In November of 1848, following two years of construction, he and his family hosted a housewarming party for a thousand guests in the three-story dream-like structure, decorated with elaborate grillwork and a multitude of minarets and towers. Truly, it resembled nothing ever built in the country previously and was described by one guest as "a little of Joice Heth, a sprinkling of Tom Thumb . . . the tail of the anaconda . . . and a monstrous slice of the two last giants."

Featuring burglar and fire alarms, the building was heated by forced air from Barnum's own gasworks, and its bathrooms all sported hot and cold running water. Barnum had his own retreat, a satin-walled study connected to a bathing suite with a shower and multiple tubs. On the third floor was a billiard and entertainment room linked by a spiral staircase rising inside a great central dome that commanded a view of the countryside.

Barnum, almost forty, took great pride as well as pleasure in his new estate, but in truth he was no more capable of setting aside his natural impulses as an impresario than the proverbial leopard was of rearranging his spots. So it was that an unlikely project began to occupy his thoughts late in 1849: the possibility of bringing Jenny Lind, the singer who as the "Swedish Nightingale" had so captivated Europe with her otherworldly voice and phrasings. US newspapers and magazines carried reports of the "Jenny Lind mania" that had swept the Continent over the past several years, and she was described as the "favorite" of Queen Victoria, but there had been no stateside appearances or talk of any.

"I had never heard her sing," Barnum admitted, but the great stir over her talents suggested there could be but one result in arranging a US tour for the twenty-nine-year-old diva: "immense success." And there might have been a bit of pride to account for Barnum's interest in this particular phenomenon, for as he put it, "Inasmuch as my name has long been associated with 'humbug,' and the American public suspect that my capacities do not extend beyond the power to exhibit a stuffed monkey-skin or a dead mermaid, I can afford to lose $50,000 in such an enterprise as bringing to this country . . . the greatest musical wonder in the world."

Barnum set about his planning with his typical care and zeal and soon an emissary—a British horn player of Barnum's acquaintance—was on a ship bound for Europe with an offer for Ms. Lind of $1,000 per night, for as many nights as she might wish to contract, with all expenses paid, including those of her musical director and accompanying baritone. Ms. Lind was at first hesitant, being the recipient of several competing offers from US promoters, including one who cautioned her that Barnum "would not scruple to put her into a box and exhibit her through the country at twenty-five cents a head!"

Friends that Barnum had made in London managed to put Ms. Lind's fears to bed, however, and soon the agreement was announced. Jenny Lind would deliver a 150-night concert tour of the United States. That good news was counterbalanced only by one reality: the cost to Barnum would be $187,500, a sum that would have to be placed in the hands of a London bank as a guarantee.

To an individual who was used to paying his expenses from the previous night's receipts, the amount was daunting, but by this time, Barnum was intent. He raked up all his cash, took out a mortgage on the museum and his new home, and borrowed $20,000 from the London bankers who would serve as trustees. He was still a bit short, though, and stinging from a rebuke from one of his New York bankers: "Mr. Barnum, it is generally believed in Wall Street that your engagement with Jenny Lind will ruin you." Indignant, Barnum left the banker's offices, put up a few pieces of property for cash, and secured the last $5,000 he needed from an old friend, the Reverend Abel C. Thomas of Philadelphia.

On his way by train from Philadelphia to New York, Barnum opened the morning paper to find that his contract with the famed singer had been leaked to the press well ahead of any attempts he might have made to "Barnumize" the matter. The train's conductor, an old acquaintance, noticed Barnum's agitation and wondered if something were the matter.

It was nothing, Barnum assured the conductor. It was just a story about his making an engagement with Jenny Lind and that she would surely visit this country the following August. He stared at the conductor, wondering how this news flash might strike him.

The conductor nodded. "Jenny Lind!" he exclaimed. "Is she a dancer?"

★ ★ ★

If the conductor's response was not exactly what Barnum had been hoping for, it may have been part of the impetus for the work that he put into prepublicizing Ms. Lind's arrival in the country, including reams of "puff" delivered to newspapers, the reprinting of reviews of recent triumphant concerts in Europe, and the prepping and plying of dignitaries in cities far and wide to extend previously unknown levels of hospitality to this rare bird.

It more than paid off, however, for as Ms. Lind's steamship *The Atlantic* docked at the foot of Canal Street on September 1, 1850, there were said to be somewhere between thirty thousand and forty thousand gathered to get a glimpse of her. Barnum had spent the night at a friend's home on Staten Island so that he might spot her ship and be transported onboard before it docked.

Shortly before noon, the ship hove into view and within minutes, as Barnum described it, "I was on board the ship and had taken Jenny Lind by the hand."

After a few opening pleasantries, Barnum said, Ms. Lind got down to an important point. When and where was it that he had first heard her sing, she wondered?

"I never had the pleasure of seeing you before in my life," Barnum replied.

It was scarcely what she expected, but she gathered herself. "How is it possible that you dared risk so much money on a person whom you never heard sing?"

The answer was one that could have conceivably sunk the metaphorical ship, but it was adroit and perfectly in character. "I risked it on your reputation," Barnum said, "which in musical matters I would much rather trust than my own judgment."

If she wondered just what she might have gotten herself into, the wonders did not soon abate. After guiding her past the throngs at dockside and helping fend off the hundreds of bouquets thrust at her, Barnum got her into his carriage and himself took a seat on top beside the driver to guide them to the Irving House—finest in the city at the time—where another ten thousand awaited the songstress. The crowd outside the hotel remained undiminished through the day, and at midnight, two hundred musicians from the New York Musical Fund Society arrived to serenade her, escorted there by three hundred red-shirted firemen, all bearing torches to illuminate the scene.

At an auctioning of tickets for opening night, the winning bid was submitted by John Genin, the hatter whose store sat next door to Barnum's museum. The amount paid was $225, a sum that made Genin a national celebrity (the cheapest regular ticket went for $4.50). The news was also trumpeted that Barnum had torn up the contract he had negotiated between the two: in addition to the $1,000 promised for each of her performances, he would henceforth split the net proceeds of each event with the singer, a gesture that prompted Ms. Lind to vow that she would sing for Barnum anywhere, "for as long as you please."

On the night of September 11, the first of six New York concerts was held at the Castle Garden, a waterside auditorium at the foot of Manhattan, with some six thousand in attendance, and as one reporter said, "For once, anticipation had not outrun reality." She appeared, the reporter said, "like a sweet voiced bird, warbling to its mate, or to the still night, for very love of music. . . . Ere the last note died into an echo, the enthusiasm was indescribable." Even Barnum was called up from the crowd to receive kudos for "the rich treat he had been instrumental in procuring," and when he announced that Ms. Lind was donating her share of the evening's proceeds—about $10,000—to various local charities, the news brought the house down.

Some modern-day commentators have quibbled as to whether Ms. Lind was indeed the best singer of her day, and even a critic writing in the *Herald* of September 14 noted "little deficiencies in execution, in ascending the scale." That writer concluded, however, by saying, "She has an individuality in her musical character that places her apart and above most of her contemporaries. If she does not do some things as well as others, she does that which no other vocalist can do."

Certainly, and though Barnum may have outdone himself in creating a frenzy of anticipation for her appearances, there is little doubt that she was very good indeed, talented enough to turn her tour into a wild success, with the pair netting just under $1 million for the endeavor, with about $500,000 going to Barnum and $350,000 to Ms. Lind.

Ahead of one March 1851 stop in Havana, Cuba, locals had been complaining for some days at the announced cost of tickets for performances, with one paper calling Barnum a "Yankee pirate." Barnum, for his part, was annoyed at the fact that the venue where Ms. Lind would appear had demanded $1,000 a night in rent. He kept word of all this from Ms. Lind, however, who innocently took her place onstage before a full house of five thousand on opening night at the Tacón Theater. According to a review in the *New York Tribune*, "Some two or three hundred persons clapped their hands at her appearance, but this token of approbation was instantly and peremptorily silenced by at least four thousand five hundred, cold, calculating, decided and palpable hisses." According to the *Tribune* account, Ms. Lind's countenance changed instantaneously "to a haughty self-possession" as she realized that for whatever reason, she had an audience to win over. The result, the writer said, was "a bursting of the soul" on the performer's part that ended with "such a tremendous shout of applause as went up was never before heard."

Barnum never made it clear whether he came clean to Ms. Lind about the reasons for her initial reception, but he did report that following her fifth encore that evening, he rushed to the stage to congratulate her on her triumph: "God bless you, Jenny, you have settled them."

By May 1851, the tour had wound its way up the Mississippi and the Ohio and back to New York and Philadelphia, tallying more than ninety performances in all. By that time, certain individuals close to Ms. Lind had begun to plant the notion that she was in essence being exploited by Barnum and that she had no need of him in continuing to perform on her own. Barnum, tired of fending off such efforts over the past several weeks, and having made a fortune from the tour already, was ready for the end. On the evening of their ninety-third performance, Ms. Lind presented him with a note terminating their engagement, and with that, Barnum's most ambitious undertaking to that date was over.

SIXTEEN

RICHES TO RAGS, AND BACK AGAIN

WHILE BARNUM WAS CONTENT TO SPEND THE FOLLOWING SUMMER RESTING at Iranistan, Ms. Lind continued her travels about the United States, and in Boston in 1852, while still on tour, she married Otto Goldschmidt, the German pianist who had been performing with her. According to Barnum, he and Lind remained friends and visited together backstage at her farewell concert later in 1852. She told Barnum that she did not expect to sing a great deal upon her return to Europe, except for charitable purpose, given that she now had "all the money which I shall ever need." Lind ended up living in London, bearing three children, and keeping to her word by performing only rarely. In her later years she would become a professor of voice at the Royal College of Music.

Barnum, of course, would not rest for long. He was soon back full force at the museum, where he introduced such features as the country's first public aquaria and a display of remarkable serpents—anacondas and rattlesnakes among them—and installed a "moral lecture room," which was really a kind of cleaned-up theater where such titles as *Uncle Tom's Cabin* and *The Drunkard*, a thinly disguised tale of Barnum's own conversion to teetotalism in the late 1840s, became popular.

He also added to his repertoire of human curiosities such as Madame Josephine Clofulia, "the most heavily bearded woman ever presented before the public," and the Lucasie Family of Holland—mother, father, and daughter—three striking albinos billed as of "black Madagascar lineage." He organized annual beautiful baby contests, fattest baby contests, flower shows, dog shows, poultry shows, and a beauty pageant he dubbed the "Gallery of American Beauty." For a year, he dabbled in publishing as the editor of a pictorial weekly called the *Illustrated News*, a venture he gave up once he understood the immense effort required to keep it going.

In 1854, Barnum began what would prove to be one of his most valuable and lasting enterprises, that of crafting his memoir. *The Life of P.T. Barnum*, published in December of that year, sold 160,000 copies by the time the following Christmas rolled around, earning its author a neat $75,000 in royalties. The book, undergoing periodic revisions for the rest of Barnum's life, was rarely out of print and flew off the shelves at the museum (and later at his circus), easily surpassing one million in sales. The original edition remained the most reliable account of a remarkable life.

To be sure, some critics found Barnum's offhand candor off-putting, just as they might have dismissed the appeal of his museum: "Its conceited coarseness, and the disgusting way in which it glories in shameless frauds upon the public have astonished us," wrote one, but others, including Mark Twain, found Barnum's honesty and wry humor irresistible. In truth, what might have been the overblown braggadocio of a supremely accomplished entertainer remains an eminently readable history and analysis of American entertainment.

Over the course of the 1850s Barnum became involved in a number of business schemes having nothing to do with entertainment, including investment in something called the "Fire Annihilator," a device purported to produce enough steam vapor to extinguish a blaze without the usual attendant ruin brought about by water damage. The Annihilator was itself soon slain by a lack of public confidence, nicking Barnum for less than $10,000, but other investments would prove more costly.

In 1851, Barnum became involved in land speculation, developing a 174-acre parcel known as East Bridgeport on the east side of the Pequannock River. As part of his efforts to lure industry to the area, Barnum agreed to secure a number of loans to the Jerome Clock Company of New Haven in return for the promises of Chauncey Jerome, president of the company, to relocate to East Bridgeport. Barnum's liability was to be limited to $110,000, according to the agreement.

All seemed to go well until early in 1856 when Barnum got word that his credit was in question. When he investigated, he found that in fact his name had been used to secure nearly half a million dollars in loans made to the clock company, which itself was entering bankruptcy. The failure took Barnum down with it and elicited glee from those who had always found his enterprises distasteful. "All the profits of all his Feejee Mermaids, all his . . . Joice Heth's, negroes turning white, Tom Thumbs and monsters and impostors of all kinds . . . are all swept away, Hindoo palace, elephants and all," wrote longtime newsman and adversary James Gordon Bennett. "It is a case eminently adapted to 'point a moral or adorn a tale.'"

Barnum, gone from Iranistan, scrambled to stay afloat, transferring the lease on the museum building to his wife's name and selling off the museum collection to John Greenwood Jr. and Henry D. Butler (though he realized almost no cash in the latter transfer). An industrialist investor in the East Bridgeport project offered him an interest-free loan to help pay off some of the outstanding clock factory notes, and other friends offered similar assistance, but Barnum was adamant in wishing to pull himself back to his feet.

In that regard, no offer of help could have been more providential than came in a letter of May 12, 1856, from an old friend: "I understand your friends, and that means 'all creation' intend to get up some benefits for your family. Now, my dear sir, just be good enough to remember that I belong to that mighty crowd, and I must have a finger (or at least a 'thumb') in that pie." The words were those of General Tom Thumb, offering to join with Barnum on a reprise of their wildly successful tour of Europe in the 1840s.

The pair toured England, Germany, and Holland in 1857, the crowds as healthy as ever, with Barnum chipping away at his debts and keeping a low profile lest creditors try to storm box offices or otherwise interfere with his plans. Eventually, Barnum returned to the States for the October wedding of his seventeen-year-old daughter Helen, but even that happy occasion was soon overshadowed by further tragedy. Boarded up and awaiting sale to satisfy creditors, his beloved Iranistan caught fire on the evening of December 17, after a workman forgot his lighted pipe inside. The home, worth in the neighborhood of $150,000 and with only $28,000 of insurance, burned to the ground. Ultimately, Barnum would sell the land for $50,000, with all of the proceeds going to his creditors.

In early 1858, Barnum returned to England and embarked upon a tour of Scotland and Wales with General Thumb, by then in his twenties but still as popular. At the suggestion of some American friends living in London, Barnum worked up a lecture entitled "The Art of Money Getting," and despite his protestation that perhaps he should call it "The Art of Money Losing," he booked himself into a hall in Piccadilly just before the New Year to give it a shot. As it turned out, the three-thousand-seat hall sold out and reviews of the motivational speech were enthusiastic. He went on to deliver this Tony Robbins–like presentation at more than a hundred venues about England, and by the time he returned to the United States, nearly all of the debt he had amassed was retired. In early 1860, he was able to secure a loan to satisfy the last $20,000 in claims, and on March 24, a few months shy of his fiftieth birthday, he signed the contract to reassume the ownership of the American Museum.

Barnum brought any number of curiosities to his revamped establishment, including a display of whales and a retinue of Native American chiefs and even a brief six-week engagement in late 1860 of the famous conjoined "Siamese" twins, Chang and Eng. The pair, joined at the stomach and born in fact near Bangkok, Siam, were show business veterans, nearly fifty by the time they came to work with Barnum, and were remarkably distinct individuals: Eng a teetotaler, Chang a resolute drunk; the former quiet and deferential, the latter loud and irascible. They were married to women who themselves fought vehemently, and together they owned a plantation in the Blue Ridge Mountains of North Carolina with thirty-three slaves who worked it. All of this augured against a compatible relationship with Barnum, who, though an astute businessman, had become a devout supporter of the Union cause and, following the Civil War, a staunch defender of African American freedoms.

While the engagement of Chang and Eng at the museum was a financial success, the stress surrounding them was ever present. One night there was a frightful disturbance heard in the museum apartment where the two were housed, and the door was broken down to reveal Chang atop Eng, choking the life out of him. While the two were calmed and the show would go on, the agreement was not extended, and the twins were to return to their home shortly before South Carolina's secession and the onset of the Civil War.

Though by 1869 Barnum would issue a revised edition of his autobiography in which he professed that the Joice Heth exhibit had been "the least deserving of my efforts in the show line," characterizing it as something "which by accident came in my way and seemed to compel my agency," there is other evidence that Barnum's early attitudes toward slavery were suspect. In 1844, he wrote a letter printed in the *New York Atlas* in which he claimed not to be an "apologist for slavery" but added that "the rabid fanaticism of some abolitionists is more reprehensible than slavery itself." There is even some evidence that Barnum— the matter of Joice Heth aside—was inarguably a slave owner, if only for a short time. A sketch published in the *Atlas* in 1845 reported that during one of his travels in the South in the late 1830s he purchased a slave to serve as his valet and at another point received a "negro woman and child" as partial payment for a boat that he sold. He sold the three a short time later, but not before he reported having given the valet fifty lashes for theft.

Such evidence alone suggests a lamentable dichotomy in Barnum's attitude toward Black persons, but his decision to mount an exhibition of the individual he billed as "The What Is It?" was perhaps one of his most egregious. Purporting to have found "the missing link" between man and ape, a fantasy conjured up in the wake of Charles Darwin's *On the Origin of Species* (1859), Barnum in February 1860 placed on display a creature described in a *New York Tribune* advertisement of March 1 as a four-foot-tall, fifty-pound creature "supposed to belong to the orang-outing [*sic*] species, but having all the appearance of a human being." The "it" was in actuality an African American dwarf born with microcephaly that resulted in a small, misshapen head and a mild degree of mental disability. Even with "its" scientific probability discounted almost immediately, the appeal of this exhibition was immediate and persistent.

Although there is some doubt as to whether he was the original "It," performer William Henry Johnson appeared in his role until his death in 1926, having been viewed according to some estimates by "one hundred million people." Whatever he may have thought of Black people in his heart of hearts, Barnum's treatment of his employees was equitable. By all accounts, he and Johnson developed a genuine friendship over the years, with the promoter making Johnson a partner and buying him a house in Bridgeport.

When the war broke out, there was little doubt that Barnum stood firmly with President Lincoln and the Union, blasting secessionist sympathizers in and around Bridgeport, and staging a number of dramas and exhibitions at the museum in support of the Union cause. "If needs be I am willing to be reduced to the last shirt and the last dollar," he wrote to a British friend in 1862, "if that will help to preserve this nation as one and inseparable."

Barnum was criticized for his outspoken support of the Union cause, and a number of threats were made that his museum would be burned, along with the new home, Lindencroft, which he had built in Bridgeport. Ultimately, his stated belief, that "it always seemed to me that a man who 'takes no interest in politics' is unfit to live in a land where the government rests in the hands of the people," led him to accept the draft of the Republican Party to run for the Connecticut legislature. "I felt it would be an honor to be permitted to vote for the then proposed amendment to the Constitution of the United States to abolish slavery forever from the land," he announced, and ultimately found himself elected by a margin of 187 votes.

In 1866, he won a second term, and was appointed chairman of the state Agriculture Committee. In 1867, the Republicans put him forward for the congressional seat representing Fairfield and Litchfield Counties, but a Democratic landslide swept over the state, removing the governor and dooming a number of Republican candidates, including Barnum.

"I was neither disappointed nor cast down by my defeat," Barnum claimed, insisting that he would not miss "the filth and scandal, the slanders and vindictiveness, the plottings and fawnings" of the political scene. He came away from his ventures into politics introduced "to new phases of human nature," he said, and the lessons he had learned about the innate duplicity of politics were enough to last him a lifetime.

It was not only double-dealing and back-stabbing and compromising and the other attendances of politics that had darkened Barnum's postwar days. On July 13, 1865, as he was addressing the Connecticut legislature on a railroad expansion scheme that he opposed, he was handed a telegram advising him that his American Museum had caught fire and was burning to the ground. Barnum finished his address without a hiccup and then rushed to New York to find that indeed the results of a half-million dollars in expenditures and twenty-five years of collecting lay in ashes. He had perhaps $40,000 worth of insurance.

When he walked into the offices of Horace Greeley, editor of the *New York Tribune*, seeking counsel, Greeley was direct. "Accept this fire as a notice to quit, and go a-fishing," he told Barnum. And Barnum might have taken that advice, he said, if it had not been for the 150 employees who depended on the museum for their livelihoods, and for his conviction that the museum was important to New York. In the end, he decided that "a-fishing" would have to wait. He leased the former Chinese Museum buildings farther uptown, at 535–539 Broadway, and on November 13, 1865, Barnum's New American Museum opened for business.

Among the many improvements he planned for the second iteration of the museum was the installation of a permanent menagerie, and to that end he entered into a partnership with the Van Amburgh Menagerie Company, whereby that troupe would continue its summer travel exhibition and schedule but bring all the wild animals back to New York for display over the winter. As Barnum described it, the menagerie was "superior in extent to any other similar collection in America," including a small African elephant and what he claimed was the only living giraffe then in the United States. "The collection of lions and royal Bengal tigers was superb," he added.

In addition to the menagerie, he constructed a much larger lecture room, and, given the crowds, he added an adjoining building to the complex. All of this provided Barnum with the impetus to investigate the establishment of a true national exhibition hall, which he envisioned as an American counterpart to the British Museum. His establishment would become, he said, simply "the nucleus of a great free national institution."

Barnum presented his plans, endorsed by Horace Greeley and a group of prominent citizens, to President Andrew Johnson, who lent his approval to the project, and soon Barnum was making the rounds in Washington promoting the establishment of a National Museum in New York City.

As to what became of such a grand vision we will never know, for on the evening of March 2, 1868, fire once again came calling upon Barnum, consuming the whole of his new establishment and taking with it the lives of nearly all of the animals in the menagerie. To Barnum, who had lost one home and two businesses to fire, to the tune of about $1 million, it was enough. "I therefore at once dissolved with the Van Amburgh Company, and sold out to them all my interest."

SEVENTEEN

THE CIRCUS COMES CALLING

For a time, Barnum hewed to Greeley's advice. Just two weeks after the second museum conflagration, his eighty-three-year-old mother Irena died in the small family home in Bethel that she had never left, a further suggestion to the inveterate businessman that his future was not infinite. At the same time, his wife Charity's health had begun to decline, and with her doctor suggesting that living near the shore might improve her constitution, Barnum sold Lindencroft in Fairfield, the second of his grand homes, and moved to an interim residence near a parcel of land he had purchased on Long Island Sound in what is now Bridgeport's South End. "We found the delightful sea-breeze so bracing and refreshing that the season passed like a happy dream," he said, and by the fall of 1868 he was engaged in the building of a new home on the water nearby that was to be called Waldemere, or Woods-by-the-Sea. It would be both a home and a giant guesthouse, Barnum proclaimed, and if he had little interest in actual fishing, it would be a place of glorious repose.

Yet being idle was not in the fifty-eight-year-old Barnum's repertoire. As he put it, "Nature will assert herself. Reading is pleasant as a pastime; writing without any special purpose soon tires; a game of chess will answer as a condiment; lectures, concerts, operas, and dinner parties are well enough in their way; but to a robust, healthy man of forty years' active business life, something else is needed to satisfy."

He tried traveling, but scarcely had he gotten to Salt Lake City than he was conferring with Brigham Young about the possibility of exhibiting the polygamist Mormon leader, along with a number of his wives and a suitable number of his many children, in New York. Barnum suggested to Young that the enterprise might net them about $200,000 a year, and although Young expressed something of an interest, nothing came of the idea. In San Francisco, Barnum encountered a dwarf "more diminutive than General Tom Thumb was when I first found him," and soon "Admiral Dot" was out on tour under the arrangements of the inveterate showman, at the same time that the little general was undertaking a new world tour, also under Barnum's aegis.

In 1869, Barnum's imagination was captured by the "discovery" of the so-called Cardiff Giant on a farm near Syracuse. In reality, the ten-foot-long specimen was nothing more than a statue carved out of gypsum in the likeness of a man, its surface pocked with needle holes to suggest pores, but soon it was being exhibited as an example of a "petrified man" from some previous age. Barnum offered to buy the object, and when rebuffed, had his own copy made and placed on display at an acquaintance's museum in New York, calling his own specimen the "real" giant and the one being shown in Syracuse a fake.

In response to his discovery of Barnum's poaching, David Hannum, the leader of the Syracuse syndicate displaying Cardiff Giant no. 1, made the remark that has become legendary: "There's a sucker born every minute." Hannum was simply using a familiar phrase of the time to disparage anyone foolish enough to pay to view a copy of what was a fake to begin with, but over time that utterance became conflated with Barnum himself.

Assuredly, Barnum had openly stated that there were a great many people who, in the context of entertainment, enjoyed being fooled *if* the humbug was fresh, clever, and imaginatively presented. However, the degree of disdain contained in that supposed "quote of all Barnum quotes" simply is not in keeping with Barnum's character. Above all else, he wanted audiences to feel that they had gotten their money's worth, that they had been genuinely entertained, and he was as critical of outright swindlers as anyone. In fact, in 1865 he published a volume entitled *Humbugs of the World* in which he went to great lengths to distinguish between such frivolities as Joice Heth or the Feejee Mermaid and the truly perverse and harmful predations of spirit mediums promising to connect the dead with agonized loved ones or auctioneers offering just-unearthed Old Masters at prices too good to be true.

In 1869, Barnum also brought out a revised and expanded edition of his autobiography and toyed with various other schemes, including one whereby he might "fence in a bit of the East River" for the purpose of exhibiting a squad of sea lions to be captured off the coast of San Francisco. No sea lions ever materialized in the East River, but it was evidence that Barnum was losing all patience with "a-fishing." Thus, it was no surprise that in the fall of 1870, when William Cameron Coup came calling with a business proposition, Barnum was in the mood to listen.

From this end of history's telescope, it might seem a surprise to learn that it was the circus that approached Barnum and not the other way around, but that would discount the amount of respect that he had amassed in the world of popular entertainment by that time. In his autobiography, Barnum suggests that he was nonetheless primed for the overtures. He had managed to divert himself with travel and hunting and any number of passing "sensations," he said, but given that suitable diversions were simply not forthcoming in sufficient number, "in the autumn of 1870, to open a safety-valve for my pent-up energies, I began to prepare a great show enterprise, comprising a Museum, Menagerie, Caravan, Hippodrome, and Circus of such proportions as to require five hundred men and horses to transport it through the country."

But the truth is that W. C. Coup, who had been knocking about circuses since 1853, when he was sixteen, provided the inspiration for Barnum's momentous career turn. Coup, who had survived that terrifying prairie fire in the 1860s, had run the sideshows for a couple of the so-called mud shows, small outfits that traveled the often unpaved roads of small-town western America. By 1869, he had finally worked his way up to the position of assistant manager of the Yankee Robinson Wagon Circus, when his wife finally convinced him to give up the circus life in favor of what she thought was a more reasonable existence breeding livestock on a farm in Wisconsin.

Coup gave animal husbandry his best shot, but the farm where he practiced happened to be located near Delavan, a town in southern Wisconsin, where a number of small shows kept their winter quarters. When one of Coup's old friends, seasoned performer Dan Castello, arrived back in Delavan after touring the West Coast with a small show of his own, the two soon hatched plans to charter a steamer, load Castello's troupe aboard, and, as Dan Castello's Great Circus & Egyptian Caravan, begin playing the burgeoning lumber camp towns strung along nearby Lake Michigan. The two did well enough, and by the time that winter closed down their travels, they had convinced themselves that they were simply one bold stroke away from fame and fortune as circus men.

In 1852, Coup, then fourteen, had worked for a season as a roustabout for a traveling show in which Barnum had an interest. Coup had seen firsthand the drawing power of the Barnum name, and the experience gave him the confidence in 1869 to actually approach Barnum with his bold idea. If Barnum was willing to bring his name, his financial backing, and his genius for identifying talent into collaboration with their expertise in managing circuses, so Coup and Castello reasoned, they could together create the greatest traveling show ever known.

It was to Coup and Castello's great good fortune that they came upon Barnum when he was desperate for something to do. At first Barnum professed no interest, but Coup persisted—all they were asking for was the use of the great man's name in the title of their show. Later, Coup would write that Barnum finally agreed to invest $100,000 with them but still hesitated about getting fully involved.

The matter was finally settled, Coup said, on an afternoon when he had traveled to Barnum's offices to once again press his suit. The two were playing a game of checkers, according to the story, and were talking about various possibilities for the proposed show. A bystander to the interchange tendered a jab at Barnum, saying, "I thought you were a man of leisure."

At this, Barnum jumped from his chair. "I thought so, too," he said, as checkers rattled to the floor.

Coup looked up. "Barnum," he said, "it's time to decide this thing. You've got $100,000 in it. If you want to get out, all right."

"Well, I'm in it," Barnum replied, waving his hand. "The checkers can lay where they are."

On October 6, 1870, Barnum wrote Coup from Bridgeport to advise that he was all in with the proposal provided that his son-in-law Samuel Hurd was retained as the company treasurer. For a modest 3 percent of the receipts Barnum would back the show and allow the use of his name; he also advised that he would add certain key attractions to the troupe, including tiny Admiral Dot, his copy of the Cardiff Giant, and several other curiosities to be borrowed from the museum of his friend George Wood. He would also advise the pair on the preparation of advertising materials, playbills, and cages and the like. In Delavan, Coup and Castello busied themselves assembling ten carloads of animals and other circus performers and paraphernalia that would be shipped to New York.

On April 10, 1871, "P.T. Barnum's Great Traveling Museum, Menagerie, Caravan and Hippodrome" opened beneath three acres of canvas tents, the largest ever assembled, on a field in Brooklyn. Ten thousand spectators attended that opening, with thousands more having to be turned away. The show went on the road from Maine to Kansas, returning to New York City in November, where it played at the ten-thousand-seat Empire Rink through the Christmas holidays, closing only to ready itself for the upcoming season.

Barnum's enhancements to the show were many: for the menagerie, he insisted on including camelopards (he intended two, but one expired on the voyage across the Atlantic) and noted, "As no giraffe has ever lived two years in America, all other managers had given up any attempt to import them, but this only made me more determined."

He also sent off representatives to Alaska in search of a posse of sea lions and seals and discovered an Italian-trained goat named Alexis who could ride on the back of a horse and jump through hoops and over rails without losing her place. Perhaps the topper was the group of "four wild Fiji Cannibals, ransomed at great cost from the hands of a royal enemy, into whose hands they had fallen, and by whom they were about to be killed and perhaps eaten."

The animals and curiosities that Barnum made available were invaluable to the show itself, but as they had foretold, the knowledge Coup and Castello held about how to tour and manage a traveling circus was equally vital to the success of the partnership. "As far as the technical details of the show were concerned," Coup said, "Mr. Barnum was absolutely ignorant, but in its place he possessed an amount of commercial daring and business sagacity, that which amply atoned for his other shortcomings."

For one thing, Coup was a master at advance publicity, often posting bills as far away as fifty miles from the towns where the show would play. One estimate has it that Coup "hung as much paper" in a week as some shows did in a year. Another innovation Coup claimed credit for was the use of the train to move the circus, an undertaking that Barnum resisted early on. As Coup put it, "I was . . . mentally fatigued by my partner's opposition and his requests to abandon the scheme; but . . . I determined to stick it out to the end."

If in fact Barnum had to be convinced about using the train, he soon became enthusiastic, noting that it was clear that the ever-burgeoning show could not continue to be transported by wagon. Even using rail, he said, required "sixty to seventy freight cars, six passenger cars, and three engines . . . often traveling one hundred miles in a single night to hit good-size towns every day, arriving in time to give three exhibitions, and the usual street pageant at eight o'clock A.M."

It was the speed of the train that allowed the show to bypass smaller venues in favor of larger cities where the receipts would tally twice or three times as much. An associated idea that Coup almost certainly came up with was the use of "crossover plates" laid between cars of uniform height so that cages and equipment could be loaded at one spot—the rear of the train—and then rolled forward through car after car, much as a train traveler would move from the sleeper to the diner. In this way it was no longer necessary to laboriously roll cages alongside the tracks to each car for loading. Barnum would have understandably been unaware of such details, given that he did not travel with the show but usually dropped in for a few days during some parts of the tour and then returned home.

"Now we had Pullman cars for the artists," Coup said, "sleeping cars for the laborers, box cars for the extra stuff, palace cars for the horses and other large animals . . . and platform cars for wagons, chariots, cages, and carriages."

The show itself was presented in three separate tents: one for the menagerie exhibition, a second for the museum, and a third for the performance arena itself, which seated somewhere between five thousand and seventy-five hundred. The so-called museum was a traveling version of Barnum's former Broadway enterprise, containing a mixture of genuine educational items, oddities, and outright humbug, such as the Cardiff Giant.

Admiral Dot indeed joined the sideshow, usually appearing alongside the "French Giant," Monsieur Joseph, said to be eight foot ten. Also among the oddities was one Anne E. Leake, who had been born without arms but nonetheless entertained spectators by sewing, crocheting, drinking, and employing a knife and fork at dinner, all with the use of her toes.

Whereas the blithe exhibition of so-called biological rarities seems offensive today, it is important to consider these undertakings within their historical context. During the nineteenth and twentieth centuries, "freaks" themselves often viewed themselves as "special," if not superior to the masses who came to gawk at them, and for many, a well-paying job as a performer was far preferable to a life of joblessness and isolation in the "normal" world. The freak show was simply an accepted part of British and American popular culture well into the mid-twentieth century.

As Barnum biographer Robert Wilson points out, many in our contemporary culture find it difficult to consider the actions of those who have lived even centuries before in their historical context. "It is an ahistorical age," he says, "one that is quick to condemn historical figures using the standards of the present." Thus, certain instincts that made Barnum a genius of his time have subjected him to scornful dismissal by some today, an absolutist approach that can lead to short-sightedness.

In any case, in addition to human oddities, various marvelous mechanical automatons were displayed: an automatic trumpeter, a "Sleeping (and breathing) Beauty," a flock of fluttering, warbling birds, and seven lifelike bell ringers. There was a monkey violinist, a tambourine-playing rabbit, and a life-sized rendition of *The Last Supper*, wherein the figures of biblical history ate, drank, and seemed to converse with one another. If the last seems an unlikely spectacle, consider that the Laguna Beach "Pageant of the Masters," where famous works of art are brought to life onstage, has been playing to sold-out audiences for more than eighty consecutive summers.

In addition to this array of the fantastic were added such attractions as Egyptian mummies, various wax figures, a series of stuffed exotic animals, the massive jawbone and teeth of a whale, and a goodly array of Oriental weaponry. One popular natural specimen was the cross section of a California redwood tree, its innards hollowed out so that twenty people could stand inside to have their picture taken.

The menagerie included camels, lions, zebras, two elephants, kangaroos, a rhino, leopards, monkeys, and all conceivable else, amounting to about thirty cages worth of wildlife. The sea lions eventually made it in from Alaska to be exhibited in tanks, requiring far and away the most attention of all the animals, including three hundred pounds of fish per day to satisfy their appetites.

To all this was added the sixty arena performers and another seventy-five individuals involved in the production of the show—all of it requiring about $2,500 a day to maintain. It was an outlay that seemed astounding to other circus men, who were sure the undertaking was madness. Still, "amazing" was what Castello and Coup had come calling for, and that is what the imagination of Barnum gave them. And by the end of the first season's tour, everyone could relax—as Coup would tell a reporter for the *Atlanta Constitution*: "We made an even half million."

Following the 1872 tour, Barnum purchased a building on Fourteenth Street in Manhattan where he intended to present a winter season version of the traveling show, but the operation was underway for less than a month before fire made yet another appearance in Barnum's life. This one burned the building, most of the animals, and the elaborate wardrobes of the performers. As was his way, however, Barnum sent out an immediate call for replacements to his menagerie and the show was back on the road for the summer of 1873.

For that year, an innovation arrived that seems to have been a joint decision. Given that the main tent had grown to an elongated shape under which thirteen thousand could be accommodated, audiences seated on the ends would often leave their seats to rush ringside to better see the intricacies of some performance. When Barnum consulted with Castello as to a solution, the latter came up with the idea of mounting two simultaneous performances in adjoining rings. It was a feature not always endorsed by the human performers, for it meant that the attention of audiences was unavoidably divided. For most audiences, however, it seemed a value-added feature, for how could one complain when there seemed to be twice as much going on for the money?

In April 1874, Barnum finally arrived back in New York to preside over the opening of the new Great Roman Hippodrome, a replacement for the fire-destroyed venue that had been erected over the preceding winter on the site where one day Madison Square Garden would stand. The hippodrome could seat ten thousand, and the arena floor was large enough to permit a jaw-dropper of a closer: a reenactment of a Roman chariot race.

That summer a robust-looking, sixty-four-year-old Barnum bade farewell to the hippodrome as Coup took the show out on the road. As it turned out, there was good reason for Barnum to be looking chipper, for it was soon discovered he was planning to be remarried in the fall. The bride was to be twenty-four-year-old Nancy Fish, the daughter of long-time friend John Fish of Lancashire, with whose family Barnum had spent considerable of his days while regathering his spirits following his wife Charity's death.

Barnum's union with Nancy Fish was formalized in a September ceremony, little elaborated upon in his memoirs: "In the autumn of 1874 I married again. . . . After a brief bridal tour, our wedding receptions were attended at Waldemere." In truth, there was good reason for Barnum to have treated the occasion in matter-of-fact style, for documents discovered long after his death reveal that he and Ms. Fish had actually been married in a Valentine's Day ceremony earlier in 1874, not three months after Charity's death. If there is any defending Barnum in this matter, it is that Charity had been essentially a recluse and an invalid for a number of years, often having, in Barnum's words, "prayed for death to come as an angel of mercy to take her 'home.'"

While Barnum and his new wife remained in Waldemere, the elaborate hippodrome show was back on the road in 1874 and 1875, along with a second show that more closely resembled a typical circus, emphasizing lions and clowns and acrobats over chariot races and dramatic spectacles featuring balloon ascensions and Indian horsemen charging after stampeding buffaloes and the like. It all became too much for Coup and Castello, who sold out their interests to Barnum and went back to profitable exhibitions of their own.

Barnum finally divested himself of the permanent exhibition in New York and placed all his showman's energies in the traveling show that continued on through the decade, even as he spent a one-year term as the mayor of Bridgeport and resumed a thirty-stop lecture tour about the country for the Redpath Lyceum Bureau. The 1876 edition of the traveling show was conceived of "to provide a Fourth of July celebration every day," closing with the singing of "America," with the entire audience joining in the chorus, and the nighttime program including a fireworks display, all this in conjunction with Samuel Hurd and four new partners, all of them experienced Flatfoot circus men: Avery Smith, John J. Nathans, Lewis B. June, and George F. Bailey, the nephew of the original employer of the circus elephant, Hachaliah Bailey.

For doing little more than advisement and lending his name, Barnum raked in 50 percent of the profits of the newly organized show, generally exceeding $50,000 a season, though in the last year of his partnership with the Flatfoots, Barnum's share was $87,500, or as much as $17.5 million in today's dollars. Barnum also profited handsomely from sales of his autobiography, which went for $1.50 a copy, "reduced from $3.50." By that time, the volume held nine hundred gilt-edged pages bound in muslin and accompanied by one free admission to the show.

The principal engine of this success was advertising and publicity, undertakings at which Barnum had few equals. He was a pioneer in the use of vivid color lithography, featuring posters ten feet tall and fifty feet wide, and one of his more imaginative traveling displays consisted of a sixty-four-foot-long "Advertising Coach" car, with his portrait emblazoned on either side, along with dramatic representations of the show's featured animals and performers.

The coach served as the nerve center for the advertising and public relations corps and often arrived in the larger venues days ahead of the show, both an impressive visual herald of the colossus that was soon to arrive and a practical operations base for the hard-working publicity crew. In a typical year, the outlay for advertising and publicity for the show was around $100,000, about one-third of the show's total budget.

By this time, Barnum's name had become legend. During a meeting with retired US president Ulysses S. Grant, Barnum remarked, "General, since your journey around the world, you are the best-known man on the globe."

But Grant would have none of it. "No, sir, your name is familiar to multitudes who never heard of me. Wherever I went, among the most distant nations, the fact that I was an American led to constant inquiries whether I knew Barnum."

Indeed, Barnum's contract with the Flatfoots required that he appear no less than a dozen times at stops to be mutually determined, and it is said that more than one young visitor to the circus was heard to inquire of a parent, "Where's the cage that Barnum's in?"

EIGHTEEN

MR. B, MEET MR. B

In a later edition of his autobiography, when self-aggrandizement had begun to rival good-natured self-deprecation, Barnum wrote that "up to 1880, no travelling show in the world bore any comparison with my justly-called 'Greatest Show on Earth'" (he had begun to use the sobriquet in the later 1870s). Other show managers boasted of owning equally impressive shows, he said, but he estimated the value of his competitors' operations as $20,000 or even $50,000, "while mine cost millions of dollars." It might cost a competing showman $300 to $700 a day to stage a show, whereas Barnum's costs were upward of $3,000 per day. "The public soon discovered the difference between the sham and the reality," he insisted, before admitting to the existence of one exception.

"My strongest competitors," Barnum allowed, "were the so-called 'Great London Circus, Royal British Menagerie and Grand International Allied Shows.'" This, of course, was the grand undertaking piloted by James A. Bailey, the very same enterprise that had nearly gone full fathom five more than once during the tour of Australia and South America. If Barnum thought highly of Bailey's sagacity, however, he was hesitant to say so. "Its managers," he said, "had adopted my manner of dealing with the public, and consequently their great show grew in popularity."

Nothing, however, struck Barnum about his competitors' prominence more than the news of the birth on March 10, 1880, of what he called "The Baby

Elephant." Following that blessed event, Barnum said, "the managers so effectively advertised the fact that the public became wild with excitement. . . . Naturalists and men of science rushed in number to Philadelphia, examined the wonderful 'little stranger' and gave glowing reports to the papers of this country and of Europe." To P. T. There-Is-No-Bad-Publicity Barnum, the crush of media attention focused on Little Columbia's birth constituted an insurmountable advantage for Bailey and his partners. Irked by the fact that the Great London was now advertising imminent performances in his own, formerly sacrosanct Bridgeport, Barnum stewed for two months before sending the fateful telegram offering to purchase Little Columbia that Bailey turned into a marketing bonanza.

Having surmised that indeed Bailey and his associates were "foemen worthy of my steel," Barnum went assiduously and pragmatically to work. By October 1880, the *New York Clipper* was reporting that James Bailey had bought out the interests of his partner James Cooper in the Great London Circus, and shortly thereafter came word that P. T. Barnum had dissolved his partnership with the four Flatfoots.

Soon, the startling news was announced: the shows of Cooper, Bailey & Company would be combined with those of P. T. Barnum, with a series of "monster" consolidation performances to be given in New York in the spring. It was reported that following those exhibitions, one of the shows would undertake a five-year European tour while the other played domestically. At the end of the five-year term, the positions would be swapped, and no competing exhibitions would be scheduled for a period of twenty years.

With Cooper out of the picture, the new team would consist of Bailey, Barnum, and James L. Hutchinson, Bailey's former concessions manager, who would serve as chief financial officer for the new concern. Barnum was a 50 percent owner in the new show, with Bailey and Hutchinson dividing the other half. Barnum estimated that daily expenses for the new enterprise would run at $4,500, a figure that once again brought scoffs from competing showmen. No show could hope to recoup profits on such an outlay.

Though plans in fact were laid for the Great London Circus to travel to England in the coming April under Barnum's supervision, that tour had to be scuttled when Barnum fell ill on November 16, diagnosed with an intestinal blockage. Unable to eat and in excruciating pain, his weight fell from 215 to 144 within the month, and for a time his doctors feared the worst. Finally, he began to improve, and doctors sent him off to Florida to convalesce.

Meanwhile, planning for what was to come for the new proprietorship fell to Bailey, who announced that the two shows would be folded into one, P. T. Barnum's and Great London Combined, with a grand tour of the United States to take place in 1881. Bailey told a reporter for the New Haven *Sunday Union* that three shows daily would be performed at each stop, given that families and school groups were especially fond of morning performances. He claimed that the menagerie that accompanied the circus was more comprehensive than any other in the world, with the possible exception of the London Zoological Garden and its counterpart in Paris.

The whole of the production, indoors and out, he said, would be bathed in electric light, and much of what Bailey obviously found claptrap—wax figures, stuffed animals, panoramas, and the like—would be removed from the museum exhibitions. Perhaps most momentous was his announcement that, in order to display all the talent assembled and meant to be divided between two discrete shows, the new production would be carried on in three rings, for the first time ever. The 1881 show, Bailey said, would be remembered "in the amusement records of America as the greatest artistic success of the times."

As if on cue, Barnum, who had been slowly recuperating in Florida, returned for the opening of the new show in late March, which was preceded by a spectacular torchlight parade through the Manhattan streets. To tout the undertaking, Barnum and Bailey issued invitations to a hundred top newspaper editors from around the country and transported them to New York to view the opening performance at Barnum's Hippodrome on March 28, 1881. "It was a very costly piece of advertising," Barnum noted, "which yet yielded us a magnificent return."

It was not only the opening of an unrivaled new partnership but also the first time that performances were carried on in three rings simultaneously. Of this unprecedented mode, the *New York Herald* said, "The only drawback . . . was that the spectator was compelled to receive more than his money's worth . . . while his head was turned in one direction he felt he was losing something good in another."

The show traveled by train, of course, and in turn, Barnum continued a practice that Coup had begun: the booking of excursion trains to bring circusgoers from miles around the various stops, thus often swelling the size of the crowds to several times the total population of a given town. As he noted with satisfaction, "Frequently the public and private schools, as well as manufactories, were closed on 'Barnum Day,' school committees and teachers recognizing that children would learn more natural history by one visit to our menagerie than they could acquire by months of reading."

Beyond the scope and the glamour that the merging of the two entities brought to the very concept of the circus, Barnum and Bailey themselves were to bring a degree of respectability to the enterprise. The teetotaling Barnum, with his emphasis upon the "moral character" of the various pageants and dramatic performances within his shows, had always been a favorite of religious groups and their associated media. And though Bailey, not a drinker himself, would have scoffed at the idea of presenting himself as a moral exemplar or delivering a temperance lecture, he was scrupulously honest, disgusted by the various "privilege" sales, or franchising of operations ancillary to the circus performance itself, that other circus managers practiced. Quite often robbers and pickpockets traveled with shows, having paid for the "privilege" of plying their trades in stops along the way, and others paid handsomely for the rights to set up various games of chance on circus grounds. Of course, the only "chance" that those who played the games had was that of losing, but some operations were glad to protect the various grifters in exchange for a cut of the take.

Another practice that Bailey found unacceptable was the advance sale privilege, where agents bought up any number of tickets prior to a show's arrival in a town, with the aim of reselling them for as much over the 50-cent face value as they could get. Ordinarily, an agent paid a 10-cent premium for each ticket, and anything they got over 60 cents was theirs to keep. Even Barnum, previous to his joining up with Bailey, regularly sold the rights to "outside sales," for as much as $10,000 a season. Though he never was accused of selling the "clothesline privilege," where robbers took advantage of circusgoers' absence to strip their clotheslines of drying laundry, it was standard practice to extend "privileges" to such enterprises as the running of the cook tent, the candy stands, the lemonade stands, program sales, and the side shows.

B. F. "Tody" Hamilton, a long-time public relations writer for Barnum and Bailey, estimated that owners of the outside sales rights might clear as much as $25,000 a season on their investments. Nor was deception and outright thievery limited to the criminal element. Hamilton relates the story of one stop at a small city in the West, where the chief of police showed up in Bailey's office one morning shortly after the company had arrived.

"Good morning, Mr. Bailey," the chief enthused, come to deliver the bottom-line news. "Everything goes here for $500."

Bailey fixed the man with a bland stare. "I have nothing to 'go,'" he replied. "Good morning, Mr. Chief of Police."

The disbelieving chief was heard muttering as he made his way out of the office, "Nothing to go? This is a hell of a show."

Given his rigid code, with their merger, Bailey insisted upon bringing all the privileges under the show's own umbrella. Salaried employees conducted every single business transaction related to the show, with nothing rented or sold. "Ticket speculation was abolished at one swoop," Hamilton wrote. "And so was the general mess of scoundrelism that was, even under the best circumstances, incidental to the former system."

In all, the 1881 show, featuring such attractions as Chang Yu Sing, the seven-foot-six-inch "Chinese Giant"—who often appeared with General Tom Thumb at his side—Zazel, "The Human Cannonball—"fired" out of a spring-loaded, smoke-belching "cannon" to grab a trapeze bar sixty to eighty feet away—and Salamander the Fire Horse—who galloped about the ring leaping through "burning" hoops, traveled more than twelve thousand miles during its thirty-three-week season, playing a final date in Arkansas before returning to Bridgeport in November for the winter.

All of this might have been a sufficient platform by itself for a resounding follow-up season of 1882, but once again Barnum was to top himself. He had long envied the London Zoo for its most prized possession, a giant African elephant named Jumbo, the name thought to have been derived from "Mumbo Jumbo," an outsized figure in indigenous myth. Over the years, the elephant had grown to nearly twelve feet in height, weighing about thirteen thousand pounds, and it had become something of a British national treasure, having carried thousands of children about the zoo on its back.

African elephants, however, are more cantankerous than their Indian counterparts, and even though Jumbo had been in harness for nearly twenty years, one of Barnum's European agents got wind of rumors that the creature had been throwing some unusually willful tantrums of late. With the zoo concerned as to its liability should something happen while a bevy of children were underfoot, the agent thought there might be an opening. After some investigation, the agent cabled Barnum that an offer of $10,000 might in fact swing the deal. Barnum fired back his answer. He would gladly offer $10,000 but believed the zoo would not sell. Two days later, Barnum's offer was accepted, and Barnum immediately had a man on a steamer to London with a check.

The outcry that resulted in Great Britain was unprecedented. Newspapers decried the sale, British children wrote piteous letters to Barnum, and the *Daily Telegraph* sent Barnum a telegram asking that he simply name a price for which he would cancel his contract and permit Jumbo to remain at the London Zoo.

Barnum wrote back that by now "Jumbo-mania" had overtaken the United States. It was a frenzy, he said, that "makes Jumbo's presence here imperative. Hundred thousand pounds would be no inducement to cancel purchase."

After a successful defense against the quashing of the sale brought by one of the principal stockholders of the zoo against its management, all seemed decided. But then Jumbo himself got involved. When the gigantic cage constructed for his transport was wheeled into the gardens, Jumbo refused to enter. Prodding by his long-time trainer Matthew Scott did no good. Jumbo simply bellowed in protest and then lay down.

Eventually, the elephant returned to his old cage, leaving the humans to their own devices. In time, a solution was struck upon whereby a transport cage was brought up against the door to Jumbo's quarters, with sliding doors at either end. The cage acted as a kind of hallway through which the elephant became accustomed to traveling when it wanted to go out. And then one day, as he was making his passage, the doors at either end of the smaller cage were slammed shut, trapping Jumbo in the new cage, which could be moved to the docks for transport. Matthew Scott agreed to enter Barnum's employ and accompany Jumbo to America, and eventually Jumbo was placed aboard the *Assyrian Monarch*, bound for New York.

The ship arrived on April 9, and Jumbo immediately went on exhibition in the menagerie of "Barnum's & London" at Madison Square Garden. The creature might have cost him $30,000 in all, Barnum said, but the increase in receipts for the next two weeks more than covered the acquisition.

NINETEEN

ON MASSIVE SHOULDERS

OVER THE ENSUING FOUR SEASONS, BARNUM CONTINUED TO ADD TO THE REP-
ertoire of acts for the show, including oddities such as Jo-Jo the Dog-Faced
Boy, in truth a sixteen-year-old from Russia named Fedor Jeftichew, whose face
indeed was covered with a thick and silky growth of fine yellow hair, giving him
the appearance, the *New-York Tribune* said, "of a Skye Terrier." Though one of
Barnum's brochures claimed that the boy had been found in a cave in central
Russia where he had been living with his father, subsisting on wild berries and
game, the truth was that Jeftichew's father had himself toured Russia for most
of his life as a similar oddity, adding his son to the act when he was old enough.

There were also the remarkable Portuguese child cyclists, the Elliots, aged six
to sixteen, whose appearances brought Barnum up before the courts on charges
that he was endangering the health and safety of children. The charges were
quickly dismissed by a panel of judges after they watched the Elliots in action,
but not before the well-publicized proceedings provided the show with a fortune in free publicity.

The show traveled with a greatly scaled-down museum and side show and
two menagerie tents through which audiences passed on the way into the main
tent, there to be seated in an immense oval surrounding the three-ring extrav-
aganza. Separating the rings from the stands was the broad hippodrome track

that was used for the entry parade as well as for races of all kinds: chariot races, clowns-riding-ostrich races, camel races, giraffe races, elephant races, races pitting ladies drawn from the crowd, and so on. The most popular "legitimate" acts continued to be the equestrian performers, and the Barnum & London's William Dutton was considered to be the best such going.

Barnum had also secured a fabled "white" elephant from Burma (it turned out to be primarily gray with some pale and pinkish splotchings) and in 1884 conceived of an exhibition that's deeply cringeworthy from today's perspective. The "Grand Ethnological Congress of Nations" consisted of a kind of United Nations parade about the hippodrome track of representatives from "the uncivilized nations," including Zulus, Nubians, Hindus, Todas Indians, Polynesians, Australian aborigines, and Sioux. If it seems beyond ill-conceived today, the spectacle was of real interest to the highly cloistered American public of Barnum's time, earning respectable reviews from the *New York Herald* and others who viewed it as a commendable display of humanity's diversity.

Still, for three and a half years, Jumbo the elephant, pried at such great cost from the London Zoo, was the unquestioned star of the Barnum & London's show. As his keeper Matthew Scott put it, "I have seen them by thousands, when they couldn't find fifty cents to get into the show, ready to pay a quarter of a dollar to just go inside and have one peep at Jumbo. 'It's all we want to see, and we won't look at anything else; we don't care about the balance, but oh! Let us see Jumbo.'"

Of course, Scott's accounts may be somewhat colored by the unquestioned bond that existed between him and his charge. The great elephant was said to bellow and stomp if Scott was a few minutes late for the accustomed feeding or exercise time and would put up with the rattle and stress of train travel between stops only if Scott would sleep in his car with him. "The shaking and jar of the train, the worrying noises, etc., keep him in a constant ferment of nervous excitement, and he gives me little chance of sleep. I no sooner get just nicely off into a doze than his trunk is groping into my little bed, feeling all round my body to find my face, to ascertain if I am there, so as to awake me to talk to him."

His tone suggests that Scott found such harassment more endearing than anything else, and there was one occasion when Jumbo surely made up for any trouble he caused his keeper. During a stop in Ottumwa, Iowa, in October 1883, after the tents were erected and the afternoon show was about to begin, Scott had just entered Jumbo's special tent when he heard a sound like a sudden peal of thunder. He ran to pull the tent flap aside only to find the company's remaining herd of elephants—all thirty of them—charging his way. Whatever had panicked the pack, they were out of control, broken chains flapping from mighty legs like snapped shoelaces.

"In a moment," Scott said, "they rushed into our tent. If death ever stared me in the face it did at that moment. On came the black mass of mad animals, and I thought there was no escape . . . when Jumbo came to the rescue.

"He twined his trunk about my body like a flash," said Scott, "and placed me out of harm's way between his legs; then stood firmly and stretched out his trunk, as rigid as the limb of a large tree, and permitted not an elephant to get past it." In moments, Scott said, Jumbo had succeeded in stalling the entire charge, leaving the herd to stomp and fume harmlessly until the keepers arrived to peel them away.

Given that the oldest elephant ever, Lin Wang, died in 2003 in the Taipei Zoo at the age of eighty-six, there is no telling how long Jumbo might have reigned supreme with Barnum & Bailey, save for what took place at St. Thomas, Ontario, on the evening of September 15, 1885. As was usual, when the circus train pulled into the Grand Trunk Railroad yards there, it was shunted onto a siding, this on the south side of the main line, separated from it by a few feet of gravel roadbed. On the north side of the main track, a steep embankment fell away about six feet to the vacant fields where the circus tents would be set up. On the siding, workers uncoupled the circus train in the middle, making a passageway there so that animals and equipment wouldn't have to walk completely to the ends of the train to get around and cross to the north side of the tracks.

That night, as the show was concluding, twenty-nine of the elephants completed their "military drill," and keepers herded them back to the train where they could be loaded for transport to the next stop. According to his testimony at a subsequent hearing, St. Thomas depot operator Fred R. Armes had warned the animal handlers that a westbound express train was due to pass through that night, and that they should plan to delay crossing back over the tracks with the elephants until 9:55 at the earliest. The crossing was to be attended by a railroad yard crew and to take place at a spot close to the station house, well up the tracks from the site where the show tents were erected.

Perhaps all that was communicated to the handlers in charge of the elephants, and perhaps it wasn't. In any case, it was hardly 8:00 p.m. when the elephants had completed their work, and, following their departure from the big top, the handlers—valuing efficiency above all else—marched the herd directly south toward the tracks. There, they dismantled a section of the right-of-way fence and prodded the elephants up the steep embankment and across the main line toward their cars parked on the siding.

Back under the big top, the two remaining elephants, gigantic Jumbo and a comic dwarf clown specimen named—what else—Tom Thumb, were going through their popular closing routine, Jumbo's ponderous foot easily lifting the whole of tiny Tom at the opposite end of a teeter-totter, and so forth. When the two had finished, trainer Scott guided his charges out of the tent and toward the crossing that his predecessors had taken.

As Depot Master Armes had pointed out, westbound Grand Trunk Special Freight no. 151 was an express train and would not stop at St. Thomas. In fact, there was a downgrade coming into St. Thomas from the east, and the diamond-stacked locomotive would be doing all it could to pick up speed as it barreled through.

Indeed, that was exactly what engineer William Burnip was trying to do that night. As he picked up speed approaching the St. Thomas station, the illumination coming off the kerosene lantern mounted above the engine's cowcatcher didn't amount to much, but even if he'd had better, it wouldn't have helped a great deal. An average freight train pulling a hundred cars and moving at fifty-five miles an hour takes about a mile to stop after the brakes are pulled, and that is with modern air brakes. On Burnip's train, every car had its own brake wheel, which had to be turned individually by the brakeman.

By the time Burnip was sure of what he saw in front of him—two *elephants* plodding squarely down a set of tracks toward his train in rural Ontario—all he could do was slam the engine into reverse and give three short blasts on the whistle, the signal for the brakeman to fly to work. Sparks showered from the wheels of the great locomotive as the wheels churned backward, and screams issued from frozen boxcar wheels in turn.

When Scott, walking behind Tom Thumb and Jumbo, heard the whistle blasts, he turned to a nearby flagman in alarm. "What line is that train on?" he asked warily.

The flagman was stunned. "My God, it's on our track." He ran toward the bobbing kerosene lamp of the engine, waving his own lantern in desperation.

Scott, stuck with the animals between the steep embankment on one side, and the immovable circus cars just feet away of the other, somehow managed to get the animals turned around. "Run, Jumbo, run!" he cried.

He tried to guide the huge animal to the right, down the steep slope, but Jumbo was having none of it. The great creature kept to the middle of the track as if he meant to outdistance the train at his back, and even with his great bulk, was outpacing the short-limbed Tom Thumb.

If they could reach the end of the parked train beside them, Scott thought, there would be room to veer away from the tracks, but as the awful commotion grew at their backs, he realized there was little hope. Still, there was that breach just ahead, where the circus train had been uncoupled in its middle. If they could make it to that spot, he might be able to turn the elephants aside into that opening, and the train would roar harmlessly past.

It was possible, he thought, and the possibility gave him hope. "Run, Jumbo," he called. "Run."

And then there was the scream behind him as the locomotive's cowcatcher rammed into Tom Thumb, breaking one of his legs and tossing him over the side of the embankment as if he were made of fluff. Scott turned from the sight to see that he had reached the gap where the circus train had been uncoupled. He dodged off the main track and into the breach, imploring Jumbo to follow him.

"Jumbo! Jumbo!" Scott cried, but in some ways the massive train and the mammoth animal were alike. Jumbo's momentum carried him two cars past the gap before he could stop. And that is when the locomotive—as Burnip and his brakeman bailed out from the cab—piled into the huge elephant.

The impact dropped Jumbo onto his knees and sent the locomotive hurtling off the tracks, its cars spilling over the embankment after it. Jumbo was sent sliding off the tracks to the other side, his head jammed violently under the wheel carriage of a circus car. One of his enormous tusks was driven backward into his brain. Terrible as that might sound, it might also have shortened his agony.

The stricken Scott ran to Jumbo, realizing he was still conscious. Scott crawled under the car to comfort his companion of more than twenty years, and with his last breaths Jumbo took Scott's hand in his trunk. Moments later, while Scott wept uncontrollably, Jumbo died.

★★★

It took 160 men with ropes and timbers and prybars to remove Jumbo from beneath the train car and move his corpse across the tracks to the side of the embankment, and soon there were swarms of photographers and reporters on the scene. Worse yet were the mutilations of the corpse by souvenir hunters wanting a piece of Jumbo's hide. A furious Scott kept vigil over the body for as long as he could but eventually fell asleep while lying atop his old friend. When he awoke to find a chunk of one of Jumbo's ears hacked away, he went into a frenzy. The St. Thomas police came to mount a twenty-four-hour watch over Jumbo's remains.

Back in New York, Barnum was reportedly struck when he heard the news, blurting to a reporter, "The loss is tremendous." But he soon had recovered sufficiently to begin his inimitable gift for making chicken soup out of something decidedly less.

By September 18, he was writing from Bridgeport to publisher Harper Brothers in New York proposing a book memorializing Jumbo: "Would you like to publish for the holidays, *The Life, History, and Death of Jumbo, with Many Incidents & Anecdotes not heretofore Published*?" he wondered. A clue to his approach to the material was contained in a letter of October 20, 1885, to William A. Croffut, a journalist and travel-writer friend, whom he pressed to write up and place accounts of the tragedy: "It is proved beyond question—not only by Jumbo's keeper Scott & four of our reliable showfolks . . . that when the great, noble beast first saw the deadly train approaching, he immediately seized the trick elephant Tom Thumb, threw him over the track to a place of safety, then instantly pushed Scott out of danger." It being too late to save himself, Barnum said, Jumbo then "charged the locomotive and was crushed to death in 3 minutes by being pressed between a heavily loaded freight train standing still on a sidetrack & the incoming freight train."

Barnum also saw to it that Jumbo's hide was removed and stuffed and his skeleton repaired and reassembled so that these items could be carried on display. Little Tom Thumb in fact recovered from his injuries and carried on with the circus, featured as the fellow creature whom the world's largest elephant gave his life to save. Barnum also acquired another elephant named Alice from the London Zoo, she who had been mistakenly characterized by the British press as a forlorn mate of Jumbo. Alice was scarcely the physical specimen her supposed mate had been, but she traveled for two years with the circus, displayed alongside Jumbo's stuffed self, suggesting that she continued to mourn her loss.

After Barnum's death and until it was destroyed by fire in 1975, the stuffed Jumbo was displayed for many years at the Barnum Museum at Tufts University, where athletic teams eventually became known as the Jumbos. The former

African bush elephant's impressive skeleton remains to this day in the holdings of the Museum of Natural History.

And Jumbo lives on in other ways. A life-sized statue was erected in 1985 upon the centennial of his death in St. Thomas, Ontario, and Walt Disney paid homage in naming his famous flying elephant's mother "Mrs. Jumbo." Perhaps most pervasive of all is his impact on our language. Before his forays and his spectacular demise, there was no such superlative for "the biggest" as what he brought: including jumbo jet, jumbotron, and "Jumbo those fries, please."

TWENTY

THE GREATEST SHOW

WHEN THEY WERE NEGOTIATING THE TERMS OF THEIR PARTNERSHIP BACK IN 1880, James Bailey had issued a rather startling declaration: "Mr. Barnum," he said, "I don't care for your name; I want your capital. My name as a circus man stands above yours; but I need more money, and you've got it. That is the only reason I am entering into this partnership."

Though no one had likely ever come to the circus grounds asking to see the cage where Bailey was on display, he was nonetheless on solid ground when he ranked himself above Barnum as strictly a circus man, one who knew the ins and outs of that business. Barnum may have been a world-renowned celebrity, but it had been many years since he had labored in the trenches, laying out routes and work schedules, writing copy, and directing workers at all levels. Bailey, however, was a micromanaging workaholic who personally called employees to get them out of bed on Saturdays and relished the oversight of the slightest detail of business operations.

To one journalist who succeeded in getting him to sit down to talk for a few minutes, Bailey—said to chew nervously on rubber bands when he was upset—explained that after he finished up a typical twelve-hour day in his office, he would go home to think about the circus and then, after finally falling asleep, to *dream* about it. As his brother-in-law Joseph McCaddon recalled, working for Bailey meant learning to obey orders. "If he directs you to post a bill upside down, be sure you understand correctly and don't argue about it. Do as you are instructed." Even Barnum, it was said, never referred to his partner by any other name than "Mister" Bailey.

Such intensity does not come without cost, especially when entering into the partnership with Barnum both expanded the scope of operations exponentially and required the folding of Barnum's million and one ideas about what would constitute a bigger and better show into the mix. By the close of the 1884 season, Bailey, three years short of his fortieth birthday, was exhausted, tottering on emotional collapse.

The problem, Barnum declared in a letter to Bailey's wife, was "too much thinking." Barnum was seventy-five, twice Bailey's age, and though he had at times worked himself to the point of exhaustion, he had found that the only sure cure was "a season of *brain-rest* and not *thinking*." Bailey should not so much as *think* of the show during the 1885 season, Barnum reassured Mrs. Bailey, for "it is all moving like good machinery."

Ultimately, Bailey was forced to absent himself from daily operations. In fact, Bailey's leave persisted for two years, with Barnum and Hutchinson turning to long-time Chicago circus man W. W. Cole and Bailey's old partner James Cooper to undertake the daily management of the show, and while operations limped along, Barnum was able to understand just how much of a consummate manager Bailey had been. In October 1887, the two agreed that Bailey should return to the newly reorganized undertaking that would tour in 1888 for the first time as the Barnum & Bailey Greatest Show on Earth.

Things began on a less than auspicious note on November 20, when fire broke out at the winter quarters of the show in Bridgeport, with only the great proportion of the elephants surviving, along with a single lion. Alice, Jumbo's purported widow, died in the flames, as did the somewhat "white" elephant Barnum had acquired. Gracie, one of the other elephants, escaped the flames by swimming out into the frigid waters of Long Island Sound while the fire raged, but she later died of exposure while being towed back to shore.

Nimrod the lion, the only other creature of note to survive, was nowhere to be found when the flames subsided and was at first assumed to be a casualty buried somewhere in the ashes. The lion, however, was later found in the barn of a nearby farm. He was discovered by the farmer's wife, who entered the barn at first light and saw a shadowy shape bent over the lifeless forms of a cow and her calf, gnawing away. Assuming it was a large dog, she began to beat the creature with a broom. When the unperturbed creature momentarily raised its head from its meal, the poor woman realized the true nature of her adversary and ran away shrieking.

Eleven days after the fire, Barnum said, he found Bailey in his office, riffling through a stack of telegrams and letters, making notes all the while. When Barnum asked what he was up to, consummate manager Bailey answered coolly, "I am ordering a menagerie."

"All in one day?" Barnum asked.

"Certainly," Bailey replied. "In six hours we shall own a much finer menagerie than the one we lost." Accordingly, the Greatest Show was on the road in 1888, having not lost a step.

Following the close of the 1889 season, with Barnum aged seventy-nine, the Greatest Show on Earth returned to England for a hundred-day engagement, with both Jumbo's stuffed likeness and his skeleton in tow. Though Barnum had some concerns about this first return since he'd nabbed Jumbo from the national zoo, they proved unfounded. The 1,240-performer show, capped by a mammoth grand finale entitled "Nero, or the Destruction of Rome," played to packed houses at the twelve-thousand-seat Olympia auditorium, and each performance featured a carriage tour of the hippodrome track with the great showman doffing his hat and proclaiming, "Wa-al, I'm Barnum," to cheering spectators. Following that tour, he returned to Bridgeport, where, while remaining active in business, he spent his time quietly. In November 1890, he suffered a stroke and on April 7, 1891, he died.

According to one account, his last words consisted of a request to know what the receipts had been that day for the show at Madison Square Garden. In its obituary, the *Times* called him "a man of genius" and also observed: "He early realized that essential feature of a modern democracy, its readiness to be led to what will amuse and instruct it." His final tour, said the *Times*, lacked only a Carlyle to come forward with a discourse upon "the Hero as Showman." Biographer Wilson says, "Barnum embodied some of America's worst impulses, but also many of its best . . . and he did so with a sense of humor and a joy in living that is rare in today's public figures." And American drama critic Louis Kronenberger wrote that, with the exception of Karl Marx and Sigmund Freud, the individual with the greatest impact on American lives was P. T. Barnum.

★★★

In the aftermath, the *New York Times* proclaimed, "One of the most modest little men that ever lived has been forced to the front by the death of P.T. Barnum," a little less than two weeks following Barnum's passing. "Everybody knew Barnum," the paper continued. "Comparatively, nobody knows Bailey, and few would ever have known him if Barnum had outlived him."

Still, the paper said, Bailey could be called the creator of the modern circus, and it credited him with lifting the entire enterprise "to a standard that renders almost ridiculous the laws that once were so necessary for its regulation." He had rid the circus of the various disreputable elements that traveled in its orbit and "has surrounded the circus with conditions that justify its classification as an institution."

It left Bailey at the head of the largest of the "big seven" circuses, all of which traveled by rail. The Greatest Show on Earth traveled in 65 cars in 1891; Adam Forepaugh's shows, with which there had been a brief association in the 1880s, traveled in 52 cars; the Sells Brothers had 42 cars; John Robinson used 35; and William Main used 27. The two smallest competing companies, the Great Wallace and the Ringling Brothers, each employed 20 cars.

But if the position of the Ringling Brothers at the bottom of that list provided James Bailey some comfort, it was to be short-lived indeed. Within a few years, Bailey discovered that all of the concerns that had plagued him over his years in the circus business faded into insignificance when matched against the brothers from Baraboo and he who would become foremost among them, John Ringling.

TWENTY-ONE

UPSTARTS

AMERICAN NOVELIST HAMLIN GARLAND WROTE LYRICALLY OF THE MYTHICAL power of the circus upon his Iowa boyhood of the 1870s: "In those days, even the 'colossal caravans' did not travel in special trains, but came across the country in the night and bloomed out in white canvas under the rising sun, like mysterious and splendid mushrooms, seemingly as permanent as granite to the awed country lads who came to gaze timidly from afar.

"To go from the lonely prairie or the dusty corn-field and come face to face with the 'amazing aggregation of world-wide wonders,'" Garland said, "was like enduring the visions of the Apocalypse." To him and his compatriots, the spectacle of the parade was "a glittering river of Elysian splendors, emptying itself into the tent.'"

In accordance with such reckoning, it is generally agreed that the fascination of John Ringling with the circus began in the summer of 1869, when he was four years old, hauled along by his four older brothers, Albert, August, Otto, and Alfred, to witness the arrival of a steamboat-borne circus in McGregor, Iowa, then a boomtown on the Mississippi. P. T. Barnum was almost sixty at that time, still without any substantial connection to the circus, and James Bailey, at twenty-two, was a lowly assistant on a traveling show with his boss about to be shot by an irate customer. Though John Ringling had no connection to Hamlin Garland, there was in fact a distant familial relationship to Mark Twain on his father's side. Whether Ringling ever thought much of the

similarities between his adventures and those of his fictional downstream counterparts Tom Sawyer and Huck Finn has never been documented.

What does survive is the journal entry penned by brother Alfred describing the arrival in McGregor one idyllic summer day of what most believe
was Dan Rice's Brilliant Combination of Arenic Attractions, known to have
stopped in the town on June 21, 1869. The party of five Ringlings—it was
still spelled in the Germanic Ruengling then—led by eighteen-year-old Albert, made their way to the boat landing well before dawn, waiting on the
mist-shrouded shores until lights of the circus boat became visible around a
bend just upstream. As the boat approached the shore, a series of chromatic
whistles—precursor to the steam-driven calliope—sounded.

"There were no screeching tones," Alf writes, "none of the ear-splitting
screams that the calliope of today sends out to rattle against the windows and
walls of a city street. The old river calliope made music that was sweet . . . as
soft and soothing as a cradle song."

As the boys watched, the boat was tied up and what passed for a circus parade in those days began: first the nondescript tent wagons were dragged off and
hitched to six-horse teams, followed by the far more exotic red and gold circus
wagons and their snorting, stamping traveling teams. Next came the menagerie, which to a group of callow McGregorites would have seemed like the un-
burdening of the Ark itself: there were a deuce of bears, each led by a ring in its
nose; a spitting, beady-eyed camel; the sturdy broad-backed equestrian horses;
and finally, the elephant, a great gray creature who raised its trunk to sample
the air of this unlikely destination, then at last lifted up one foreleg to test the
strength of the gangplank leading to shore.

Alf admits that as the elephant made its way grudgingly down the plank, the
mists billowing off the river surely distorted the scene. Still, all of the Ringling
boys insisted for the rest of their lives that it was the biggest such creature they
had ever seen. In any case, there was but one topic of conversation as the five
walked back home: one day they would have a circus of their own.

★★★

It was not idle chatter, for in the Ringling home, any notion that promised a
bit of extra income was not to be summarily discarded. Though the boys' father
August was an accomplished harness maker and carriage trimmer who had fled
from a fractious Germany in 1848, his record as a businessman was spotty.
August first settled in Milwaukee, where in 1852 he met and married Marie
Salome Juliar, who had come to the United States with her French parents seven

years earlier. The couple moved in 1852 to Chicago, where August plied his trade and their first boy, Albert, was born. In 1854, they went back to Milwaukee, where second son August Jr. was born. In 1855, the family relocated to the village of Baraboo, Wisconsin, where third son Otto was born, roughly concomitant with an advertisement placed by August in the town's *Republic* announcing the opening of "The One Horse Harness Shop." A notice the following year advised that the concern had grown into the "DOUBLE HORSE Harness Shop."

Such prosperity was not to last long, however, for in 1858, the *Republic* carried August's announcement that "in consequence of the Hard Times, he is selling out his entire stock of Double and Single Harness, Saddles, etc. At Cost." In 1860, the Ringlings made the move to McGregor, where Alfred, Charles, John, Henry, and lone sister Ida were born.

Although August Sr. was able to secure a comfortable frame house in McGregor for his ever-burgeoning family, there were many mouths to feed, and his harness making had proven over time to be a largely subsistence endeavor. Thus, in addition to the thrill of duplicating the wonders of Dan Rice's show in the minds of the Ringling boys was also the very practical prospect of extra income flowing into the family coffers.

Most of the boys (Albert was eighteen, Otto fourteen, Alf T. eight, Charles seven, and John five, with August, sixteen, opting out and Henry far too young at two) persisted with their plans, and soon, in a "mammoth arena" constructed in the family yard of canvas scraps, castoff carpet, and old blankets, they presented their first show, charging a penny for admission. Today, the population of McGregor, which sits roughly halfway along a line drawn on a map between Chicago and Minneapolis, is 838. In 1870, the Ringlings realized, according to Alfred's careful figures, $8.37 for their series of performances, which suggests that either McGregor was massively larger a century and a half ago or that the boys succeeded in attracting a relatively enormous number of their friends and neighbors during that first season. In any case, they were sufficiently buoyed by their success to plow the bigger part of their take back into the business, purchasing a huge sheet of muslin with which to construct a serviceable tent.

Planning and practice for the 1871 season provided a substantial diversion for the Ringlings during the intervening upper-midwestern winter. As the day of the first performance dawned that following year, McGregorites were treated to the first circus parade in Ringling history, an entourage led by oldest brother Albert driving a wagon pulled by a mustang pony bedecked in the finest leather harness work by A. Ringling Sr. Albert played bugle from his seat while his brothers trailed behind, playing washboard, snares, and other instruments, all of them wearing plumes that matched that bobbing atop the sorrowful pony's head. Also part of the parade was sixteen-year-old Otto Ringling leading the family goat, Billy Rainbow.

Otto had spent much of the preceding winter months working hard with Billy, who had acquired enough of a repertoire to leave his ordinary goat status behind and be reclassified in the program as a "hippo-capra." All this was enough to entice a sizable crowd to follow along to a vacant lot where the new muslin sheeting was draped from a fresh-cut pine center pole, topped by a snapping American flag and a series of pennants the boys had scissored from felt. A sign by the entrance announced the opening of the "Ring-Ling" Circus and advised that admission had risen to 5 cents.

More than a hundred handed over their nickels to the ticket-hawking Otto and filed inside to gather about the sawdust center ring, gawking as nine-year-old Alfred, riding atop the ridge-backed pony and billed as "The King of the Sandwich Islands" in an old Union officer's dress uniform, a scrap of quilt for a cape, and a crown cut from cardboard, led the grand entrance of the performers (the "Spec"—short for *spectacular*—in circus lingo). The other brothers followed, wearing dyed and beribboned long underwear in place of tights, and finally came John, aged five, painted up in clown face and leading the doleful "hippo-capra" by a rope.

There was a smattering of applause as Alfred dismounted and bowed to his audience with a flourish. And although John Ringling would forever disavow any intentions, what happened next presaged a career marked by uncanny judgment regarding the essence of entertainment.

Alfred recounted the story thus: As he made his glorious bow to the crowd, young John's grip on Billy Rainbow's rope loosened, and the "hippo-capra" charged, his aim unerring. The goat's head met Alfred's bottom squarely and sent the King of the Sandwich Islands flying face first into the sawdust.

Acts to follow had actually been rehearsed, including brother Al's more or less successful plate-juggling routine; Charles's bareback riding of the pony, tumbling, and trapeze work; John's hamming it up as a singing clown; and even Billy Rainbow and Otto's return to the ring for some scripted activity. But nothing could top the sight of the King of the Sandwich Islands taking flight and plowing into the sawdust, the screamingly hysterical impact of the unexpected scarcely lost on John Ringling.

The production, unintentionally comic as much of it was, nonetheless marked the beginning of a life of showmanship for the Ringlings, who would ever after date their seasons from that day in McGregor.

★★★

Meantime, the career of August Ringling Sr. enjoyed little success. In the fall of 1872, August took what promised to be a secure job at a carriage factory across the Mississippi River, in Prairie du Chien, Wisconsin. Hardly had he begun his work than the factory burned to the ground and an ensuing economic downturn ensured it would never reopen. Nevertheless, August and Marie welcomed an eighth child, Ida, to the family in early 1874 and were soon on the move again, returning to Baraboo in 1876. By that time, eldest brother Albert had left home to try his luck as a performer and show manager, Gus had gone off to work as a harness maker, and Otto, twenty-five, had done the same. Alfred and Charles were helping in their father's shop, and John, then twelve, was left to make some decisions of his own.

One day, his father came home from work to find no trace of him. Morning dawned with still no sign. There was no note, no word, but these were days long before the absence of a young child—even a twelve-year-old—was a signal of foul play. August Sr. put out the word to authorities, of course, but he had his own suspicions as to what was going on.

Soon enough, word came from Milwaukee. John Ringling had made his way there and was set up in business, working out of an abandoned warehouse where he had assembled a series of packing crates into new roles as chairs, table, bed, and workbench. At the latter, he involved himself in the manufacture of what he was marketing around the streets of Milwaukee as Ringling Cleanser, abrasive powder to which he had added a bit of bluing, for the cleaning of pots and pans. As he would recall many years later, he had been doing quite well and was saddened when his parents collected him and took him back to Baraboo.

Over the ensuing years, John ran away from home at least three more times, the last when he followed after a small "hall show" that had played in Baraboo. He convinced the manager that he was sixteen and was hired on as a roustabout, general factotum, and ticket taker. His agreed-upon pay was three dollars a week, but the sum was seldom forthcoming and almost never in full. Finally, one night while the show was going on, John counted what was in the till, determined that it was about the amount that was owed him, and left while the audience was still applauding the performers in the hall. He scurried away to lose himself in St. Paul, but it was not long before his father's inquiries to the authorities bore fruit and he found himself once again back in Baraboo.

There is no telling where John might have flown to next had it not been for the fortuitous return of oldest brother Albert, who turned up in June 1882. After three years of barnstorming and managing the affairs of other peoples' shows, he was intent on becoming his own man. He was back in Baraboo to convince his brothers to reformulate their dreams. What Albert described would eventually make it onto handbills as "THE RINGLING BROS. CLASSIC AND COMIC CONCERT CO.," described as "a refined and high class entertainment," including "New Faces, New Songs, Wonderful Dancers and Noted Comedians," constituting "Two Hours of Solid Fun," and representing the troupe's "Fourth Season."

Albert arrived at "fourth season" by counting that five-cent show of ten years earlier, added to his own three years of peripatetic employment; it was but a minor exaggeration. Brothers Alfred and Charles were sick and tired of harness making and threw in immediately with Albert. As for young John, there was little difficulty in convincing him to join up. Soon, the brothers were hard at work in preparation for a tour, with rehearsals undertaken, costumes purchased, dates arranged, and handbills printed. By late November 1882, the Ringling Brothers were ready to make a run at show business in earnest.

TWENTY-TWO

THE COMING MEN

THE FIRST "PROFESSIONAL" SHOW FOR THE RINGLINGS (SANS JOHN, KEPT AT home for a bit on domestic duty) took place on November 27, 1882, in Mazomanie, Wisconsin, a little less than thirty miles south of Baraboo, and far enough away, so the boys hoped, to discourage friends from following along just to heckle their efforts. As brother Charles describes the opening concert: "From the very beginning the troupe in its entirety seemed to fly to pieces. . . . It seemed as if every note from the cornet was a blue one, every blast from the clarinet a shriek. . . . We were a confused and demoralized lot when we left the stage."

It was hardly the sort of opening that would steel a performer's nerve. "You can imagine how we felt when we had to go out and face the audience single-handed and alone to perform our specialties," Charles recounted. "But we did it."

In the end, none of the fifty-nine members of the audience got up and walked out. "They even applauded at times," said Charles. "I hope every one of them has prospered since, and may live a long and happy life. Each deserves it after such a sacrifice."

Afterward, the Ringlings counted up the house to find they had taken in $13.00 in admissions. Against this, they had racked up travel expenses of $19.90, $6.00 for the rental of the hall, and disbursed $2.00 to helpers, putting them $12.90 in the hole. Nonetheless, the take the next night in Spring Valley was more than $60, the locals applauding the dancing, singing, and juggling, and howling at every tired joke the Ringlings produced.

On December 18, in the metropolis of Sanborn, Iowa, John Ringling, aged fifteen and finally released from his domestic obligations, caught up with his brothers and made his debut with the troupe, playing comic roles in a pair of skits and closing out with a clog-shoe dance. Given that the orchestra was in need of an alto horn, John set himself to master the instrument and shortly was able to manage. In that way, the troupe continued through the wintry hinterlands of the upper Midwest, often bogged down by snowstorms, sometimes having to race from their fleabag lodgings in the middle of the night before payment was due, at other times managing to bob slightly above even and closing the season in May, when far more polished productions would begin their summer tours.

The less-than-glamorous experience did nothing to dampen the Ringlings' enthusiasm, and by the fall of 1883, they were off again, having added a circus-experienced married couple to the troupe and toting along a portable organ. This iteration was entitled the Ringling Brothers Grand Carnival of Fun. The company struggled along into the frigid winter until brother Al, who had taken a lucrative position with another company for the fall, joined them in Lincoln, Nebraska, in January 1884, bringing along with him a new wife, Louise, who would one day become an adept snake charmer and bareback rider. Al also brought a veteran circus man named Yankee Robinson, who, though fallen on hard times, had taken a liking to Al and was willing to throw in with the Ringlings for lack of better prospects.

The result, John wrote the family from the road, was the complete reorganization of the company into something that had vague resemblance to the practicable and was to be known as "Yankee Robinson's Great Show and Ringling Brothers Carnival of Comedy." On May 19, 1884, this entity gave its first performance under a newly acquired big top in Baraboo, where the white-whiskered Robinson doffed his top hat and assured the audience that despite his forty years in the circus business he had finally found the troupe with which he would die in harness. "For I can tell you," he said, his voice dipping to a note of confidential prophecy, "*I can tell you* that the Ringling brothers are the future showmen of America. They are the *coming men!*"

There were six hundred bleacher seats assembled beneath the ninety- by forty-five-foot tent, and Robinson immediately began a return on his income (one-third of the receipts from the after-show concert) when a section of the seating collapsed. He was instantly on the scene, helping folks up, dusting them off, cracking jokes, and smoothing feathers.

What those finally assembled and seated saw for their twenty-five-cent admission was hardly the stuff of a Barnum & Bailey show, or for that matter anything marking the Ringlings as "the coming men." There were twenty-one employees of the company in total, including the teamsters and roustabouts, and not a single horse in the ring. The show itself consisted of some juggling and balancing acts, tumbling, horizontal bar acrobatics, and a contortionist, all interspersed with comic skits. Brother John Ringling appeared as the company's clown. Throughout it all, Robinson reminded the audience of the concert to come and adjured them not to miss the sideshow, which featured an "educated" pig.

If Robinson's claim that the Ringlings were the coming men would one day prove improbably true, his assurances to the Baraboo audience that he would die in the traces with the boys would also prove to be prescient, and sooner than might have been expected. In August, while on a side trip to see his son performing in a nearby show, Robinson passed away in his train seat. In the Ringling route book, he was memorialized under his rightful name: *Fayette Ludovic Robinson, d. August, 25, 1884, Jefferson, Iowa.*

Immensely bettered by their brief association with Robinson, the Ringlings persevered and played on until early May 1885. After two short weeks of rest in Baraboo, they were out again, having added to their "trained animal exposition"—that is, the educated pig—a somewhat forlorn-looking hyena, billed as "the Mammoth, Marauding, Man-eating Monstrosity, Striata Gigantum." There was also a new round big top, eighty feet in diameter, and the entire company required fifteen wagons to transport.

In 1886 the show was renamed the "Ringling Bros. Great Double Shows and Congress of Wild and Trained Animals" and employed eighteen wagons for transport of a ninety-foot tent, a ticket and bandwagon, and a menagerie that had grown to include a bear, several monkeys, and an eagle. There was also added a trained animal act that consisted of a donkey named January and a Shetland pony named Minnie, bolstering a crew of twenty-three trained performers.

This contingent did battle with a rival company for the first time when it entered Vinton, Iowa, only to discover that the Reiner Brothers Great European Railroad Show had steamed into town and would play opposite the Ringlings. "Since they are a railroad show they have a big advantage over us," wrote brother Otto. "They laughed at us and were inclined to belittle us." But amazingly enough, the contest went well for the brothers. "Today we have fought and won a bloody battle," Otto crowed. "Now they will be as anxious to avoid us as we are to avoid them."

Bolstered by such success, the show doubled in size once again for the 1887 season. This installment was called the "Ringling Bros. United Monster Shows, Great Double Circus, Royal European Menagerie, Museum, Caravan and Congress of Trained Animals," with the latter consisting of an elk, the afore-mentioned bear and hyena and monkeys, two lions, a kangaroo, a deer, four Shetland ponies, and a camel, which was purchased along the road and did not live out the tour.

For the 1887 tour, the brothers made the decision to incorporate young brother Henry into the business. They would send the seventeen-year-old out as an advance man to map the routes and set up the parades at the stops, and they outfitted him with a stylish carriage and brace of trotters as would befit the representative of a group of coming circus men. On the appointed day, a hand-somely outfitted Henry set off in his carriage for Pardeeville, Wisconsin . . . and he kept right on going, fully engaged for the following six weeks in a bender of magnificent proportions which he capped off by selling first the fine carriage and horses and finally his outfits of clothes. It would take a dozen years or so for Henry to outdistance the scourge of alcohol and fully enter the Ringling part-nership, and according to nephew Henry Ringling North, his namesake never took on the larger-than-life gusto of the others.

In 1888, the Ringling circus took steps that propelled them to a new level. They acquired a new big top worthy of the name at 148 by 100 feet, and among the entities exhibited beneath it were Babylon and Fannie, a pair of elephants purchased during a sheriff's sale of a bankrupt circus for something in excess of $4,000. Also added were a pair of camels, Sampson and Queenie, as well as a zebra and an emu. And the price of admission was raised to the then-standard fifty cents for all the major shows. In this way if no other, the Ringlings had finally entered the big time.

The summer of 1888 was one of the rainiest in memory, however, depressing receipts considerably and leading the Ringlings, down to their last $100, to write home to the Bank of Baraboo to plead for a $1,000 loan. They got the money, but things became even more bleak on June 23, when circus strongman Monsieur Dialo (aka James Richardson) found himself embroiled in a scuffle between two townsmen in Webster City, Iowa. Thomas Baskett, a notoriously hot-headed barkeep, tossed a townsman named Roll Brewer out into the street, then decided it was not enough. He followed Brewer to the grounds where the

Ringling circus was set up and proceeded with a full-fledged beating of Brewer sufficient to alarm bystanders. When Brewer's daughter flew into the fracas, trying to help her father, Baskett leveled her with a punch and kicked her about the sawdust.

At this point, strongman Dialo stepped in, ready to use his talents on a worthy target. Baskett, however, proved stronger still. He pulled a pistol out of his waistband and shot the unarmed Dialo in the stomach. It would take Dialo twenty-four hours to die. Ultimately, Baskett would receive a fifteen-year sentence for the act.

Fortunately, in the following weeks, the weather took a dryer turn, and the brothers made $3,000 during the first week of July that enabled them to send the $1,000 back to their banker. "A few weeks like this will make up for the spring," they wrote. "At any rate we are even with you and will get back to Baraboo with enough to feed the elephant."

Enough to feed the elephant and more, as it turned out. For 1889, the brothers added a "Roman Hippodrome" to their repertoire, though an inkling of its true grandeur is contained in a note added a bit later to the route book: "Put in a *real* Hippodrome for 1891." That year of 1889 was also momentous for the addition of the last of the Ringling brothers to the show. Up unto that time, mild-mannered Gus had been working side by side as a harness maker with their father, but those traveling with the show finally convinced him that the future lay in the circus and appointed him as operations manager. The only down note for the season was the passing of another veteran performer of the troupe when the long-suffering and ever-unnamed hyena finally cashed in.

In 1890, the seven Ringlings took their show on the road for the first time by rail, with John Ringling in charge of the intricate task of routing, piecing together the meticulously timed routes across the multitude of rail companies and lines over which the cars would travel. The eighteen-car assembly left Baraboo in early May with fifty-four performers, three elephants, four lions, three camels, and an assortment of other creatures, quite a step up from the mud show of only six years ago. But it was still a one-ring operation, a veritable pipsqueak when measured against Barnum & Bailey, whose big top measured about 500 by 250 feet, or most of the other railroad shows.

Thus, it became John Ringling's task to navigate their enterprise about the spider's web of rail, in an effort to hit every smaller venue of any value and, especially, to avoid having to play against the larger shows. Proof of his abilities came in the form of the bottom line at season's close—there would be enough in the kitty to expand the show for 1891, one entitled "Ringling Bros. World's

Greatest Railroad Show, Real Roman Hippodrome, 3 Ring Circus and Elevated Stages, Millionaire Menagerie, Museum and Aquarium and Spectacular Tournament Production of Caesar's Entry into Rome."

It was certainly a mouthful, its name not quite matched with its size, for it could be moved about on only twenty-two cars, many fewer than most circuses of the time. As the season of 1892 began, the Ringling Brothers might have been the smallest of the so-called Big Seven and scarcely of any concern to James A. Bailey, but the odds they had overcome to reach that point were staggering, a testament most likely to the bond of common resolve that had developed among them. As descendant Richard Ringling later observed, "Perhaps it wasn't that the uncles were so smart, but just that there were so God damned many of them."

TWENTY-THREE

PUNCH AND COUNTERPUNCH

OUTSIDE THE CIRCUS WORLD IN 1892, THE UNITED STATES WAS VERY MUCH A raw, burgeoning work in progress, just beginning its ascent to unquestioned world leadership. Grover Cleveland was elected president of a country that numbered about sixty-three million. Two years earlier, Idaho and Wyoming had become the forty-third and forty-fourth states, and the same year the Wounded Knee Massacre had also taken place, effectively ending the last vestiges of Native American independence.

Also in 1892, pioneering railroader Henry Flagler pushed his Florida East Coast line down to Palm Beach, an eighteen-mile-long palmetto-covered island that he thought might turn into something one day—farther south than that in Florida was nothing. In Pittsburgh, Andrew Carnegie and Henry Clay Frick were doing their best to oust the unions from an American steel business that in fact had become world dominant, thus laying the groundwork for July's Homestead Strike, the bloodiest in all history. In California, the city of Los Angeles had grown to fifty thousand, but it had also run out of water. One developer was suggesting as a solution that the city tap a river in the mountains near Reno, a scheme that everyone found preposterous—Californians would simply have to be content with San Francisco as their top dog.

A suit of clothing in the dandy's Prince Albert style went for $12.50, a pound of steak was 26 cents, and a loaf of bread cost 7 cents. A laborer made about $2.00 a day in one of Carnegie's steel plants, but a day's work could be bought for half of that in less-organized surroundings, so for large swaths of the population, it took some pretty canny budgeting to come up with a 50-cent circus ticket.

Also, under construction in 1892 was the White City, another name for the fourteen principal buildings that would constitute the World's Columbian Exposition in Chicago, purported to be a celebration of the arrival of the Portuguese navigator in the New World half a millennium previous. At its core, however, the undertaking was conceived of as a way to demonstrate the might, the vibrancy, the singularity, and, essentially, the superiority of the United States among nations. Art, architecture, music, horticulture, manufacturing, and all manner of technical innovation would go on display, and a sprawling entertainment and carnival area would highlight the very first Ferris Wheel, more than 260 feet in diameter and holding thirty-six cars, each of which could carry forty people. The area, often referred to as the Midway, after its geographical location in Chicago, is generally credited with instigating the concept for every amusement park that followed, from Coney Island on down to Disney World.

Certainly, not a circus man in the country remained unaware of the excitement attending the approaching exposition, which would open to the public in May 1893 and run through October. Buffalo Bill would in fact transport his Wild West Show to Chicago and set up operations for the duration right outside the gates. Of course, traveling all the way to Chicago was an outright impossibility for most of the population, thus leaving a traveling circus man with a reasonably captive set of audiences to serve; but the very existence of the World's Fair served notice that all forms of entertainment simply needed to become bigger and better.

James Bailey, finally out of the shadow cast by the voluble Barnum, cemented his position at the top of the circus pyramid by acquiring the holdings of his second-most successful competitor, Adam "4-Paw" Forepaugh, who boasted that he "owned, controlled and exhibited more wild animals and individually possessed more show property than any other person in the world." If the former Philadelphia meat and horse dealer had always been rough about the edges—after Barnum brought his sacred white elephant from Ceylon, Forepaugh simply had one of his own whitewashed and called Barnum's a fake—he nonetheless had fared well, said to be worth $5 million when he died in 1890.

Bailey purchased the Forepaugh show from surviving partner James Cooper and kept it traveling through 1894, with his brother-in-law and future biographer Joseph McCaddon at the helm, though it never fared as well as it had with Forepaugh running things. When Bailey finally shut down the 4-Paw, he transferred much of the equipment to Cody's Wild West Show, in which he had also purchased an interest.

For the Ringlings, who continued to stick with the strategy of avoiding conflict with Bailey and the other major shows wherever possible, their chief competition was the Sells Brothers operation, the largest concern left standing after the Bailey-Forepaugh merger. Like the Ringlings, Lew Sells favored touring the smaller towns of the Midwest and Plains states, which often led to the two shows playing the same venue on dates of close proximity. The Ringlings might roll into a town to play a date ahead of Sells, only to find out that their competitor's advance men had already blown through, distributing "rat sheets" everywhere.

"WHY WASTE YOUR MONEY ON A BUNCH OF FAKES, WHEN SELLS BROTHERS CIRCUS GIVES YOU TWICE AS MUCH FOR THE SAME PRICE" might read a headline on such a handbill, with subscripts such as "The Ringlings are cheap crooks who try to inflate their Pitiful Third-Rate Show by extravagant FALSE claims, as shown below."

"Below" would be found columns of commentary filled with the muckraker's poetry: "Ringlings' Claims—Millionaire Menagerie. The Truth—It is a collection of two sick lions, three small elephants, and a few other miserable creatures which would not bring $500 on the auction block, where they soon will be."

For all this, any true circus man felt a much greater kinship with any other circus man than with an outsider. At one juncture during the decade of the 1890s, when the Ringlings found themselves often pitted against Buffalo Bill's Wild West Show, a message arrived in Baraboo from the old sharpshooter himself: "Tell John Ringling he'd better stay out of my way or he'll bitterly regret it."

Ringling responded to the messenger, "Give Colonel Cody my compliments and tell him I'm not very worried. In fact, the next time I see him I'm going to throw him down and scalp him."

When the two finally did run into each other in a bar in Philadelphia during a period of dueling engagements, the only argument that ensued was over who was going to stand whom to the drinks.

Nonetheless, the economic competition with Sells escalated through the 1894 season, with Sells going to extraordinary lengths in Texas, Iowa, and

Minnesota, where they dropped admissions for their shows in half, to twenty-five cents. The Ringlings were forced to meet the price, but it meant that both shows would operate at a loss. In the South, however, both shows kept admissions at a half dollar, and the Ringlings ultimately returned from the season's tour with a profit.

They would use their available cash to expand the show to forty-four cars, the brothers decided at their winter summit, a step that would put them on a par with Sells. In addition, they would open their season with a splash, in an indoor coliseum, in the metropolis of Chicago.

It was a momentous step for the brothers, quite a notch up from a backyard show with the family's goat the featured attraction. They rented out Tattersall's, a barn-like structure often used for horse and cattle auctions, and gave it a thorough makeover, replacing the bleachers with folding seats, hanging all manner of flags and bunting from the rafters, and laying out banks of potted plants and flowers, replacing the antiquated lighting system with electric lights.

Three days before the show opened came a torchlight parade through the Chicago streets, with a fifty-five-piece band, several hundred performers on horseback, the menagerie caged in horse-drawn wagons, clowns cavorting about it all, and of course, the necessary squadron of elephants. The show itself featured equestrians, aerialists, animal acts, and a four-horse chariot race, as well as living statue displays that might have been even more racy save for the fact they were billed as representations of classical sculpture. The showstopper was delivered by a daredevil named Speedy, who dove eighty feet from a perch in the building's rafters into a tank the size of a kiddie pool three and a half feet deep.

The show played to standing-room-only crowds and moved from Chicago to St. Louis and on to Boston, often following immediately after Barnum & Bailey and Buffalo Bill's Wild West Show but drawing equally well. By the end of the 1895 season, the Ringling Brothers had been transformed from second-tier wannabes to a show on virtually equal footing with the Sells Brothers and Barnum & Bailey.

The number of rubber bands James Bailey was nervously chewing through is nowhere recorded, but it had to be prodigious. The success of the Ringlings led him to purchase a half interest in the Sells Brothers show, and in 1896 he booked that troupe, along with Cody's Wild West Show, up against the Ringling show in every city possible, leading to a plethora of rat-bill campaigns, sometimes violent skirmishes over billboard space, and incessant negative public relations battles.

The contest was so wearying that both sides pulled back for 1897, agreeing that there was plenty of room in the burgeoning nation for the existence of more than one top-notch circus. Only once during that season did the Ringlings and Barnum & Bailey clash directly, when both were booked into Minneapolis on the same dates. The Ringling Brothers route book recounts that by the time their advance team arrived in the city, there was no billboard or wall space to be had, leaving them little recourse but to rely on banners, small postboards, and newspaper ads. Still, they were drawing as well as they might have hoped, the route book adding, "Turned people away each performance."

Circus historians still debate the reasons for Bailey's next move. For the season of 1898, he announced, he would take the Greatest Show on Earth back to London and thence to the European continent, leaving what had become known as Forepaugh-Sells and Buffalo Bill's Wild West Show to play in the United States. Some say that the move was in essence a retreat by a wearied Bailey from the battle with the Ringlings, but others say that Bailey simply recognized that there was great hay to be made by taking his show across the Atlantic. There is no question that Bailey's return to the Continent resulted in spectacular success for his operations—in the end, he would remain in Europe for the next five years. And while Bailey was conquering the Old World, the Ringlings were steadily building their position as the premier circus operation in the United States.

TWENTY-FOUR

BUILDING A LEVIATHAN

WHILE BAILEY WAS OFF BEING TOASTED BY THE CROWNED HEADS OF A DISTANT continent, the Ringlings were hard at work conjuring new and improved elements for their domestic show. One of the additions for 1897, especially effective for the parades and big top processions, was that of a mounted band, thirty brass players in red and gold uniforms atop a set of pure white horses. Another was the so-called Bell Wagon, a twelve-bell carillon mounted on a wagon drawn by eight horses and rivaling the bells of St. Mary's as it rumbled by. There was also added the English Derby Day Pageant, a procession of notable models of horse-drawn carriages—Victorias, landaus, phaetons, and coaches—all of them peopled by models dressed in the latest elegant fashions, a forerunner of the exotic motor-car concourses of today.

By 1901, the embellished Ringling show was crisscrossing the nation and beyond, with stops from Boston to San Diego, from Montreal to Yazoo City. And at every stop, the stages of fascination were the same: the arrival and unloading of the equipment train at dawn, observed by half the parents and children in the town; the hauling of seats, poles, and canvas to the grounds to be followed by a faultlessly efficient erecting of a ten-thousand- to fifteen-thousand-seat arena in a few hours; and then the arrival of the performers, the curiosities, and the animals for the parade down Main Street toward the big top, a spectacle described by one reporter in mind-boggling terms: "Den after den of the grand menagerie . . . the side-show band in glaring uniforms of red, richly embla-zoned and heavy with gold; the famous English Derby Day section . . . ponder-ous war elephants hauling cannon . . . the Arabian Caravan; the representatives of the standing armies of the nations of the world . . . each of the thirty separate sections of the grand spectacular street pageant, bewilder the eyes of the throng with their very magnificence—a mile and a half of marvels."

In the eyes of the Ringlings, and for all but the most jaded circus men, the mounting of such spectacle and pageantry was in reality far more than a Hertz versus Avis contest to fill the seats and squeeze the last dollar out of a gullible public, but indeed an undertaking of significance. As Henry Ringling North wrote of his illustrious uncles, they and other showmen like them were con-vinced of the special value of their enterprise. The circus "contributed some-thing of real value to American life," North insists, echoing the wonderment chronicled by Hamlin Garland, "introducing scenes of comparatively sophis-ticated magnificence and beauty to a public that, especially in the small west-ern cities, hungered desperately for the thing which they had read of but never seen."

During his time in Europe, Bailey relied upon Buffalo Bill's Wild West Show and the Forepaugh-Sells Circus—both of which he had controlled since the mid-1890s—to maintain his place at the table in the States, but without his presence, those shows provided at most holding action at best. When Bailey finally returned home in November 1902, he understood the need to make his a grand reentrance. Accordingly, he expanded his show to the point that moving from location to location strained even his legendary management capabilities.

Ninety cars would be required to transport the expanded Barnum & Bailey show, which required seven tents in all: the big top and the menagerie tents each had six center poles, the baggage stock stable had four, the side show tent three (along with the ring stock stable and dining tent), and the dressing room tent had two poles. Bailey gave special attention to the street parade, designing as a centerpiece the largest and most ornate circus wagon ever constructed. The Two Hemispheres Band Wagon with elaborate carvings depicting various acts and animals measured twenty-seven feet in length, eight and a half feet in width, and thirteen feet high, outdoing the height of a Greyhound bus by about a yard. The wagon was pulled by a team of forty matched bay horses. The opening pageant inside the big top was entitled "Cleopatra" and included a cast of 1,250.

In addition, Bailey had secured the services of two performers who would become legends of the circus world. While in Europe, the long-time circus man found himself bowled over by the talents of the lovely equestrienne Ella Bradna, generally recognized as the finest in the world at the time. Bailey persuaded her to join the Greatest Show and with her came her husband and sometime performing partner Fred Bradna, a former German cavalry officer.

In his memoir, *The Big Top*, published in 1952, Bradna described attending a circus performance in Paris as a young man where a beautiful young bareback rider was thrown from her mount only to land in his lap. Bradna was so taken with the lovely Ella that he made a vow then and there: he would marry this beauty and he would join the circus. And after his army enlistment was up in three years, that is exactly what he did, eventually suffering banishment from his illustrious brewing family and renouncing his own family name (Ferbere) to marry her.

An able amateur athlete, Fred Bradna followed the path of so many others who married circus performers: he first gained skill as an acrobat on the horizontal bars, then joined his wife in an equestrian act. The engaging and adept Bradna would eventually become equestrian manager and ultimately the longtime ringmaster of the Greatest Show on Earth, earning the sobriquet as its "Field Marshall."

During his five years in Europe, the legendary micromanaging Bailey had impressed transportation experts with his efficiency in moving the circus troupe about Great Britain and the Continent. He had specially constructed sixty-seven railcars, each fifty-five feet long, and while the rail gauge was the same as that in the United States, tunnels and bridges were often narrower and their height clearances lower. To avoid bottlenecks, Bailey always sent a scout train ahead on the planned route pulling one loaded boxcar, a flat car, and a sleeper. If the scout car arrived at the ensuing destination unscathed, the remaining sixty-plus units would follow on the morrow.

Such ingenuity was not lost on European artillery commanders, and it is said that Kaiser Wilhelm himself, astonished that an entertainer would be able to outmaneuver his own highly touted ordnance experts, interviewed Bailey on his methods. Back home in 1903, however, Bailey's highly touted approach began to falter.

His new circus, designed to be bigger and better than the Ringlings', was also unavoidably much heavier. The bulk of a troupe might indeed be carried by rail from depot to depot, but to get to the circus grounds and back still required a great deal of old-fashioned horse power, the gas-powered truck and tractor having not yet been invented. Coupled with a labor shortage caused by a wave of unprecedented American prosperity, it meant that Bailey often had trouble breaking down his massive show and moving it to a succeeding venue in time to parade and then produce both an afternoon and an evening show.

In time, word began to spread that a customer could not always count on a ticket being honored for an afternoon performance of the Greatest Show, and a much lighter Ringling operation began to feed off this weakness, often darting into a venue ahead of Bailey and gobbling up business. Even the Ringlings would privately concede that Bailey had assembled a more elaborate show, but over their five years as the uncontested kings of the circus world, they had learned to present themselves as the best.

Following the 1903 season, the fifty-seven-year-old Bailey, still battling intermittent nervous fatigue, approached the Ringlings with something of a peace treaty in hand. Bailey offered them a half interest in the Forepaugh-Sells show and proposed that the three entities be scheduled without any date conflicts for 1904. The Ringlings accepted, and the Forepaugh-Sells show toured for the next three seasons under the direction of Henry Ringling.

Meantime, Bailey's attempts to regain his competitive edge led him to make a momentous change in operations. Following another obstacle-filled season of 1904, he determined to put an end to the circus parade for the Greatest Show. Though second thoughts had him waffling, early in the 1905 season he finally followed through, shutting down the street processions and sending all parade equipment back to storage in Bridgeport. He had found that European audiences often took enough satisfaction in the parades that they would forgo the purchase of a ticket to an actual show, and he tried to justify his actions to the American public in the same light, but again, the Ringlings one-upped him by continuing the practice.

Despite the mounting business pressures and his own precarious health, Bailey soldiered on. Early in 1906, he was back inside Madison Square Garden, immersed in rehearsals for the show that would kick off the season for that year. For a number of years following, no one contested what happened to Bailey was a result of those rehearsals. A great amount of topsoil was traditionally carried into the arena to prepare for the show, none of it free from the possibility of contamination in those presterilization days. Doctors who were called to attend a suddenly stricken Bailey found that he was suffering from erysipelas, a streptococcal infection, and theorized that he had contracted the disease after being bitten by a mosquito bred in the muck spread about the garden's floor.

The disease, it might be noted, is easily cured by antibiotics today, though these were not available in 1906, and Bailey, his system weakened by stress, was soon confined to his home in Mount Vernon (New York), where he died after a five-day struggle. There the matter might end save for the discovery in 1986 of the unfinished biography of Bailey written by his brother-in-law Joseph McCaddon. In this document, McCaddon contends that Bailey was not infected by a disease-bearing mosquito but rather was infected in a far less appetizing way.

Bailey had for years been afflicted with the disgusting habit of using his fingers to yank out hairs that protruded from his nostrils, often causing sores to form in the tender nasal tissues and causing painful infections. This time, however, the infection spread from Bailey's nose to both sides of his head, McCaddon said, and even down his right arm to his elbow, and the raging sepsis ultimately proved fatal. "Thus passed to his long last rest a great and indomitable spirit," McCaddon concluded.

Bizarre as McCaddon's footnote may seem, such an unlikely way of passing is right in keeping with a life that began with a drowning that wasn't really a drowning and the shucking of one identity for another. Indeed, indeed, perhaps such odd events seem strange only when judged by the standards of an ostensibly "normal" world. Within the universe of the circus, the unlikely and the outrageous take on a more ordinary hue.

TWENTY-FIVE

TERMS OF SUCCESS

BAILEY'S DEATH IN FACT TIES OFF ONE THREAD IN THIS EXAMINATION OF A PAR-
ticularly American phenomenon. With his demise came the end of the fierce
competition that had swirled to control the most spectacular indigenous form
of entertainment in a rawboned nation still expanding, still looking for the
next big thing, still ready to believe that anything was possible. Major League
Baseball was still in its infancy (Yankee Stadium would not be built until
1923), basketball had scarcely been invented, and *football* was a word virtually
unknown. Carnegie Hall had been built in 1891, and though it was already
the unquestioned national center for performances of classical music, even a
standing-room crowd numbered under three thousand, and citizens were not
lining the streets to watch the musicians parade to work.

Following Bailey's demise, while the Greatest Show struggled to operate
without its fallen general, Joseph McCaddon approached the Ringlings with
proposals to combine the Greatest Show on Earth, the Forepaugh-Sells circus,
and Buffalo Bill's Wild West Show with the Ringling operations. The Ringlings
did agree to purchase the Forepaugh-Sells show, but McCaddon's proposal for a
full-fledged merger stalled, quite possibly over the terms of future involvement
that McCaddon envisioned for himself.

However, 1907 ushered in a financial panic, and the stock in the Greatest
Show, suffering the absence of management genius Bailey, fell to eighty-five
cents a share, a price at which John Ringling began to buy it up. Henry Ringling

North suggests that of all the brothers, John was the most business-savvy and ambitious and was truly driven to secure a monopoly of the circus business in the country. And there may have been another factor in play: even during all the years of Bailey's decampment to Europe, the Ringlings had never played New York City, for all the while Bailey maintained control of Madison Square Garden, the only suitable arena there.

Whatever the case, John Ringling approached Bailey's widow and began negotiations to acquire all operations, and when he finally had his price, he came before his brothers to argue for their approval of the deal. Brother Otto— perhaps second to John in influence among the brothers—listened and was for it, and with that the others threw in. On October 22, 1907, the Ringlings, operating as the Ringling Brothers World's Greatest Shows, bought the Barnum & Bailey Greatest Show on Earth for $410,000. The two shows would continue to operate and travel as separate entities, however, and by the end of the 1908 season, their combined profits more than repaid the Ringlings for that purchase.

The routing of the two shows was handled by John, who had developed a near-photographic recall of the US railway system, combining it with an equally encyclopedic awareness of local economic conditions. To follow up on the success of 1908, he booked the Ringling show to open the 1909 season at Madison Square Garden in New York, the first time the show would play that city. At the same time, the Barnum & Bailey show was booked into Chicago. The result was middling, with the engagements butting directly against the chauvinism of the respective communities, both of which felt deserted by their favored companies. If, indeed, John or the other Ringlings had always felt slighted by not playing the Big Apple, the experiment of 1909 was enough to make them get over it.

To prove that his decision to buy out the competition had been correct, John Ringling threw himself into the oversight of the show's production with particular fervor, leaving details of the business's management to his brothers. One of the first decisions he made was to feature the equestrienne act of Ella Bradna in the big top's center ring, with no other acts ongoing to distract audiences from the singularity of her performance. Wearing a low-cut sequin top and white tights, with white kid gloves and an ostrich fan, she was paired with Fred Derrick, attired elegantly in knee breeches and a tail coat, their act every bit as enchanting to audiences as that of a high-society revue by Fred Astaire and Ginger Rogers in the decades to come.

Ella burst into the ring standing astride two magnificent white stallions, with Derrick just behind her and about to vault up to stand atop her shoulders, the horses pounding about the ring all the while. In the next moment, Derrick would back-somersault to the ground, then begin a series of vaults and pirouettes on and off one of the mounts, while Ella performed a veritable ballet solo on the other, ending with a bareback toe dance that astonished audiences. In a finale the equivalent of a fireworks closing, the two were rejoined, vaulting on and off the galloping horses in what seemed an endless Möbius strip of athleticism.

While Ella was recognized as an equestrienne nonpareil, the act was designed and choreographed with significant input from Fred Bradna, who brought his army cavalry rigor and precision into perfect complement with Ella's ethereal grace and elegance. By 1915, John Ringling had promoted Fred to become equestrian director for the Barnum show, and later for the combined shows, a post he would hold for some thirty years. As nephew North recalls, Fred Bradna was not a big man, but what he lacked in size, he made up for in presence.

Fred could curse exquisitely in nine languages, and often did so when confronting undisciplined performers. Perhaps the worst of those was Papa Leers, whose daughter Lucita was one of the most gifted acrobats Ringling had discovered. The culmination of Lucita's act had her performing a full split on a pair of Roman rings, which audiences found impressive enough. Lucita, however, then lowered the ends of a rope wound around her waist to the arena floor, where her father grabbed hold, pulled himself up, and began his own series of acrobatics, his entire weight and force supported by the rope circling his daughter's torso.

To Fred Bradna, and most spectators, whatever antics Papa Leers was engaged in were far less notable than the fact that an adult male was cavorting at the ends of a rope dangling from a young woman in a steady full split upon a pair of Roman rings! Papa Leers, however, did everything he could to draw attention to himself, a fact that sent Fred into hysterical rages, hissing vilifications and threats of murder from beneath his top hat as Papa grinned and swung about like a chimp.

Other novelties introduced by John Ringling reflected changes in the world outside the circus. Given the fascination of the public with the automobile, Ringling brought two such acts with him to the New York opening. In one, a pair of strongmen known as the Saxons lay on their backs while property men laid out a bridge framework using the legs of the two men as the sole support stanchions. Next, a touring automobile carrying six gaily dressed passengers entered the big top, and after a spin about the concourse, sped into the ring, climbed the approach to the "bridge," and lumbered on across while the Saxons lay beneath, their legs extended high and supporting it all, as the *New York Times* reported, "without a quiver."

In the other automobile act, the grand finale, one Mademoiselle La Belle Roche drove her machine to the top of a steep incline, then gunned the engine, and sped down a platform laid out below like a ski jump. At the bottom, the automobile shot off the lip of the jump with its engine whining, turned two back-somersaults in midair, and came crashing down on its tires. Mlle. Roche waved brightly to the stunned crowd from behind the wheel and sped off, the cheers resounding behind her.

The New York engagement was well enough received, with the *Times* reporting that the crowd went away "many saying they had seen the best circus of their lives," but receipts were down a bit and expenses were up, with both shows forced to travel far from their respective winter quarters for the openings: the Ringling show from Baraboo, Wisconsin, and the Greatest Show on Earth all the way to Chicago from Bridgeport. The road receipts from 1909 were also down.

Although the Ringlings were far and away the dominant force in the circus business, there was nonetheless considerable competition to deal with, given that some thirty shows traveled during that season, some of them using as few as two rail cars, in comparison to the Ringlings' eighty-four. The decline in profits and an uptick in the various unseemly competitive practices led the Ringlings to initiate the formation of a circus owners association with bonds posted to support agreements on fair trade practices, but it was a short-lived operation, most of the members finding it difficult to hew to the "Sunday-school show" standards of the Ringlings.

As to the difficulty of maintaining that wholesome image, John Ringling's long-time valet Taylor Gordon recalled the season when his boss had gathered 150 young dancers for a spectacle vaguely connected to the splendors of the court of King Solomon. "They had special cars for them, and hours to be in at night," Gordon said, with the managers issuing daily reminders: "Please don't be seen leaving hotels in the city in the daytime—it looks so crude." "Do leave the patrons alone on the circus grounds, for the business's respectability." Though most of the dancers were compliant, such was not always the case.

"One girl got really unreasonable," Gordon said. "Mr. Ringling had to take her in charge. He threatened to pay her off. She told him, 'God financed me at birth—don't worry about me,' and she bid him farewell in the most unusual words of slang. It made the long black cigar bounce from one side of his mouth to the other, and his eyes battered like a man who had been looking at the eclipse of the sun without smoked glasses."

Despite his insistence on proper moral behavior from others, Ringling was no stranger to pleasures of the flesh himself, either before or after his marriage. Of the latter, nephew Henry observes that his Aunt Mable had the good judgment not to press John about what he might or might not have done during his many excursions about the country and across the Atlantic. Things that were not ever spoken of thus simply never happened. However, says North, even during his bachelor days, Ringling scrupulously avoided any improprieties with the women in his employ, and he confined his roving eye to those he might meet elsewhere.

Ringling favored the Palmer House for his lodging when the show was in Chicago, and something of a contest began between Ringling and the house detective there. One of the primary functions of the so-called house dick was to ensure that unmarried couples were not having sex in the hotel's rooms, which was not only a criminal offense referred to as unlawful cohabitation in many jurisdictions but also a practice that most elite establishments professed to disdain. At first, Ringling was convinced the Palmer House detective was clairvoyant, for any time that he had used the most deceptive methods to smuggle a woman into his room, even in the middle of the night, the door invariably flew open just as the fireworks were about to begin.

In time, however, Ringling caught on. Once satisfied that Ringling was in his room for the night, the detective would lean a matchstick against the door. If he passed by later to find the matchstick on the ground, it was all the proof the operative needed to pound on the door and escort the interloper out. Accordingly, Ringling adapted. Once his visitor was inside, he would wiggle his fingers out beneath the bottom of the door and prop the matchstick up again.

Improprieties aside, during the first decade of the new century, time itself caught up with the Ringling operations in a number of ways. Brother Gus died in 1907, at the age of fifty-three, and Otto, the third-oldest and the partnership's financial wizard, died in 1911 at fifty-four. Though the hard-working youngest brother Henry was made a full partner in Otto's place, the loss only underscored John Ringling's position as the dominant force in operations. In contrast to Barnum, whose measure of the quality of an act or exhibit was generally limited to the amount of fanfare or business it might attract, Ringling's time in Europe, scouting for attractions, had broadened his cultural horizons. In 1914, he added a ballet to the show, featuring eighty trained ballerinas in full classical exhibition at a time when many Americans had no idea what "ballet" might actually be. He was in complete support of brother Alf T.'s inclusion of plays in the show, including numbers such as "Joan of Arc" and "Cinderella," the latter including a cast of 1,370, along with 735 horses, and—likely for the only time in that epic's history—"five herds of elephants."

Nor was John Ringling a particular fan of wild animal acts, for he considered them unpredictable and dangerous. Bears, for instance, were notoriously difficult to work with, requiring meticulous consistency in their routines and schedules and being far more likely to turn on their trainers when disrupted than big cats. Even the act of a somewhat unhinged German acrobat named Ernest Gadbin was one he tolerated more than admired.

Gadbin, who came to the show shortly before the United States entered World War I, operated under the aptly chosen stage name of "Desperado" and had cooked up a routine wherein he did a swan dive off an eighty-foot platform to land on his chest on a kind of toboggan slide slathered with a cornmeal paste to lubricate it. Gadbin would hit the slide traveling at about a mile a minute, zoom on down its length to its turned-up lip, then soar through the air to land gracefully in a waiting net. To an audience, such lunacy was thrilling, but to John Ringling it was only a reminder that cornmeal paste might one day thicken a bit sooner that one might expect.

Speaking to a magazine reporter in 1919, Ringling explained that over time he had sought to cut out what he termed "the thrillers" for a simple reason: "We discovered that at the climax of such acts, four out of five of the women and children turned away their faces and refused to look."

Whatever the "thriller index" of a particular circus organization, the years from the turn of the twentieth century until the country's entrance into the war are often held up as comprising the "Golden Age" of the industry, with virtually every one of the thirty or so traveling companies unveiling a street parade upon its arrival into towns and such shows as the Ringlings (84 cars in 1910), Barnum & Bailey (also 84), Forepaugh-Sells (47), Hagenbeck-Wallace (45), and John Robinson (42) going to great lengths to outdo each other in one or another aspect of circus splendor, physical achievement, or wonder.

Some years later, E. B. White, the creator of *Charlotte's Web*, would write in an essay: "The circus comes as close to being the world in a microcosm as anything I know; in a way, it puts all the rest of show business in the shade. Its magic is universal and complex. Out of its wild disorder comes order; from its rank smell rises the good aroma of courage and daring; out of its preliminary shabbiness comes the final splendor. And buried in the familiar boast of its advance agents lies the modesty of most of its people."

The full flowering of the circus as White exalted it was to be found in those halcyon prewar years before the many forces that would worry at its magic manifested. If human beings—or human beings in concert with animals—had learned to do something stupendous, repeatable, and real, then that achievement would sooner or later be presented in the flesh and under the big top, while hundreds or thousands, as the case might be, cheered them on.

In 1916, as the nation waited for word as to whether Woodrow Wilson would run again for president, he attended a performance of the Barnum & Bailey show in Washington, DC. Wilson had often expressed his dearest fantasy, that of riding an elephant in the show, and though John Ringling and Fred Bradna would have been glad to accommodate him, the Secret Service kept it from happening. However, on May 8, 1916, as Wilson was being escorted from the performers' entrance to the reserved seats, the band struck up "Hail to the Chief." Wilson paused to raise his hat in appreciation . . . and then slung it mightily into the middle of the center ring. While the crowd erupted, reporters rushed to find phones so they could phone in their common lead: "The President has—*literally*—thrown his hat into the ring."

Even before the war, there were precursors of the smear of progress upon the circus badge. The spectacle of teams of sweat-glistening men alternating blows of sledgehammers upon the stakes that held the guy ropes of the big top would one day be replaced by the device invented in 1904 by George Heiser: it was a wagon-mounted pile driver, its blows delivered not by John Henry look-alikes but by a four-horsepower gasoline engine. Soon the canvas of the big top itself would be mounted on huge spools and carried about on spool wagons, which could unfurl the tents in a fraction of the time that it had taken roustabouts.

Instead of using horse teams—and sometimes elephants—to pull the guys that raised and held the huge tents, tractors were employed. And the time-consuming task of erecting bleacher seating for thousands of spectators at each stop was about to be bettered by the invention of a collapsible bleacher seat wagon, whereby twenty- and thirty-foot sections of seats could be folded down onto their wheels and towed from one location to another, there to be joined in seamless harmony with their counterparts.

Time's march also continued its assault on the Ringling partnership. On New Year's Day 1916, eldest son Albert, the original performer and founder of the common enterprise—he who had amazed early audiences by, among other things, balancing a plow on the point of his chin—died of a heart attack at sixty-four. Al's passing was mourned significantly in Baraboo, for he of all the brothers had maintained close connections with the town he considered home. Just the year before his death, he had a copy of Marie Antoinette's private opera house at Versailles built as a gift for the town, though the deed was never officially conveyed to Baraboo, and subsequent bickering between the Ringling heirs would keep it from ever being turned over.

Queen the Diving Horse, a typical barnstorming act in the Barnum tradition, caught by Glasier in mid-plunge from a 40-foot platform, ca. 1905. Glasier Collection, courtesy, The John and Mable Ringling Museum of Art.

Equestrian performer practicing at Ringling Winter HQ in Sarasota. Joseph Janney Steinmetz Collection, State Archives of Florida.

Karl Wallenda starting his 5-year-old daughter Carla across a twenty-foot-high wire during a 1941 practice session in Sarasota. Steinmetz Collection, State Archives of Florida.

Emmett Kelly applying his "Weary Willie" makeup. Steinmetz Collection, State Archives of Florida.

"Weary Willie" in the flesh. Steinmetz Collection, State Archives of Florida.

"The Durbar," opening pageant of the combined shows, Madison Square Garden, 1933. Courtesy, The John and Mable Ringling Museum of Art.

Bears and lions rehearsing at Ringling winter headquarters in Sarasota. Steinmetz Collection, State Archives of Florida.

Aerial view of Ca' d'Zan, above Sarasota Bay, ca. 1936.
R. A. Gray Collection, State Archives of Florida.

The great hall of Ringling's
ornate residence on
Sarasota Bay. Courtesy,
State Archives of Florida.

The "Congress of Freaks," Ringling Bros. combined shows, 1924. Courtesy, State Archives of Florida.

Henry Ringling North with his son John Ringling North II in 1942. Steinmetz Collection, State Archives of Florida.

John Ringling North with animal collector and adventurer Frank Buck, who appeared briefly with the combined shows in the late 1930s.

Gunther Gebel-Williams, animal trainer for Ringling Bros. Barnum & Bailey Shows from 1968 to 1990.

Famed "lion tamer" Clyde Beatty in the cage, ca. 1945. Courtesy, State Archives of Florida.

Trainer Walter McClain and his elephants practicing at the Ringling Circus HQ in Sarasota, ca. 1942. Steinmetz Collection, State Archives of Florida.

Ringling's elephants receiving a pedicure. Glasier Collection, courtesy, The John and Mable Ringling Museum of Art.

Ringling Bros. Barnum, Bailey Circus
Last Stand Under Canvas
Pittsburg, Pa.   July 16 1956

The final raising of the big top came in July of 1956 in Pittsburgh, ushering in a sixty-plus-year period of arena and coliseum productions.

Perhaps the most familiar descendant of the classical American Circus is the highly stylized Cirque du Soliel, which emphasizes intricate aerial acrobatics, elaborate costumes, lighting, and visual effects.

TWENTY-SIX

THE PRICE OF LOVE

A LITTLE MORE THAN TWO YEARS AFTER AL'S DEATH, YOUNGEST BROTHER Henry passed away in 1918 at age forty-nine, and in 1919 middle son Alfred also died, leaving only Charles and John in a partnership whose holdings had only grown even as its principals dwindled. When the United States had entered the war in 1917, the Ringling show employed about a thousand people and traveled about the country on ninety-two railroad cars, with the Barnum & Bailey show about the same size.

With so many workers and performers gone off to fight, the shows were for the first time in history lacking the personnel to stage full programs and move efficiently about. The Ringling show's 250 canvasmen were reduced to 80, while the property men dropped from 80 to 20, most of them aging 4-F's instead of the burly personnel who had swelled the ranks before the war. As for the cadre of grooms into whose care the show's 335 horses were entrusted, it too had been decimated, for during World War I, a horse cavalry was still a vital component of the forces.

Were all this not enough, in 1918 the Spanish flu epidemic, which would claim more than twenty-two million lives worldwide, swept through the United States, taking tens of thousands of lives and dragging down attendance at all public venues to levels that would not be experienced for more than a hundred years, with the onset of COVID-19. All these factors led the Ringlings to make a momentous decision following the 1918 season: instead of returning the two big shows to their respective winter headquarters—the Ringling to Baraboo and Barnum & Bailey to Bridgeport—all the properties were sent to the Connecticut facility, a decision that would have had Baraboo-boosting Al rolling in his grave.

To John Ringling, however, the move was unavoidable. Not only would the administration and maintenance of a single operation be vastly more practical, but the tax burden in Connecticut was significantly lower than that in Wisconsin. And the truth was that in just a few short years, the circus had lost its virtual monopoly over America's choice for popular entertainment. Movies had matured from minutes-long diversions experienced in storefront nickelodeons to complex, full-length productions exhibited in comfortable theaters, including the first full-length features produced in Hollywood: *The Squaw Man* (1914) by Cecil B. DeMille and D. W. Griffith's *Birth of a Nation* (1915) and *Intolerance* (1916).

In addition, reaching the theaters where films and other more transitory entertainments could be enjoyed had become a vastly simplified endeavor for even the most remote farm family, owing to the ubiquity of the automobile. The first Model T Ford rolled off the assembly line in Detroit on September 27, 1908. Less than twenty years later, the fifteen-millionth would follow. Americans would buy nearly thirty million cars and trucks in the years leading immediately up to the Great Depression, and it is estimated that by 1929 four out of five families owned a motor vehicle. Thus, John Ringling saw that combining the two big shows and confining their appearances to larger population centers only made sense for postwar America. And though many in Baraboo would never get over the loss of the circus, moving central operations to Connecticut, closer to major populations centers and transport lines, was the logical choice.

On March 29, 1919, the Ringling Bros. and Barnum & Bailey Combined Shows opened for the season with a four-week run at Madison Square Garden, with the *New York Times* describing it as "the biggest thing of the kind" the city had ever seen, and lauding the performances of those such as aerialist Tiny Kline, who would remain a show business fixture long enough to perform as the flying Tinker Bell at Disneyland in the 1960s. Reviews also touted May Wirth, who had taken over as the show's featured equestrienne, and the lovely wire walker Bird Millman, whose presence as a songstress and ballerina held the audience spellbound as she performed in solitaire, in center ring, delivering such numbers as "How Would You Like to Spoon with Me." Such diversions, along with bicycling and wire-walking bears, boxing ponies, and dogs somersaulting into the net from the aerialists' lofty perch, proved as popular as ever.

Asked by an American magazine interviewer during that year's tour if the circus would ever be altered by progress, John Ringling exuded confidence: "It never will be changed to any great extent, because men and women will always long to be young again. There is as much chance as Mother Goose or Andersen's Fairy Tales going out of style."

In a way, Ringling's brave assertions would prove true. In fact, the circus would remain relatively unchanged—save those demanded of it—from its golden era quintessence right up to the end of its days. It was the world outside the circus that changed, even if sometimes for the better.

Certainly, the Roaring Twenties provided a fertile environment for the circus. As the economy boomed, a world-weary populace found money in their pockets that they could use to divert themselves from the memories of a relentless, four-waved pandemic and a war so vast in its carnage that it was surely thought to be the one to end all wars. All the shows that had survived the lean years prospered, and new stars arose to capture the imagination of a star-struck nation.

Alfredo Codona, born in Hermosillo, Mexico, had joined the Barnum & Bailey Circus in 1911 at eighteen and moved over to the Ringling show in 1917, where his graceful acrobatics, chiseled physique, and striking good looks eventually earned him the nod as "King of the Flying Trapeze." In 1920, Codona threw his first triple back-somersault, a feat that the Spanish call the *salto mortale,* or "somersault of death," and one that had been accomplished only a few times previously in circus history.

Soon, his ease with the maneuver was effortless and endlessly repeatable. As he told a writer for the *Saturday Evening Post,* "My speed, when I leave my trapeze for the triple, has been accurately measured; I am traveling at the rate of sixty-two miles an hour. At that speed I must turn completely over three times, in a space not more than seven feet square, and break out of my revolutions at precisely the instant that will land me in the hands of Lalo [his catcher and his brother], who, hanging to his trapeze by his hocks, has swung forward to meet me."

Only one time did Codona seriously miscalculate, leaving his bar at what he later determined was about one one-hundredth of a second late. By the time he reached Lalo, that fraction of a section had manifested itself into a four-inch gap between where his body was and where it should have been. As a result, Alfredo's head drove into Lalo's chin, knocking him unconscious. Alfredo continued on, landing face down in the net, the unconscious Lalo tumbling after him. Before Alfredo could roll away, Lalo's dead weight landed on the small of

his back. Alfredo would spend two weeks in the hospital while his five broken
ribs healed.

In that same *Post* interview, Codona provided some insight into the training
necessary to perfect such maneuvers as well as the reasons for the occasional
failure experienced by even the most practiced performers. In essence, master-
ing the sense of timing necessary to perform highly intricate aerial acrobatic
maneuvers is a science to be learned without the aid of a textbook, Codona
explained. A student learning to play the piano might have the help of a metro-
nome or the guiding hand of a master to assist, but Codona said that the circus
acrobat must rely solely on a kind of innate sixth sense.

"You simply learn when to let go," he said, and until you do, you are a failure.
"Even in swinging on a trapeze, there is a split second when the coordinated
propulsion of the body will accomplish more for even a weakling, if applied at
the proper instant, than for the strongest man in the world." For Codona—who
spent five years preparing for the maneuver—it required only two full swings of
his trapeze to gain the speed and height necessary to begin the triple somersault.

As for those terrible moments when all goes wrong during a dangerous routine, Codona described it as a condition known as "casting" among circus performers. "It has to do with that part of an instant when the mind seems to let
go, to refuse any longer to hold to the terrific burden of concentration which
has been placed upon it. . . . Why it happens, or how it happens, a performer
rarely knows. He only realizes that one instant he is apparently as able to do a
trick as ever; the next instant he is a gangling amateur, unable to pull himself
out of psychological transgression that threatens his life."

He went on to describe one season with the troupe, when a series of falls
beset a group of younger female performers engaged in some not-so-demanding
tricks on the fringes of the rings. When the first such accident took place, one
of her colleagues approached the injured girl as she was being carried away on
a stretcher. How did it happen? the anxious friend wanted to know. "I don't
know," the fallen girl moaned. "I just let go."

Codona said a series of falls ensued among the same troupe that season: a
second, a third, a fourth, fifth, and sixth. And each time the explanation was
the same. "I just let go. I just couldn't hold on any longer."

Mistakes of that nature were very rare for Alfredo in the ring, but he would
survive to make more than his share in life. In 1919, a beautiful and talented
aerialist and high-ring artist named Lillian Leitzel, already dubbed "The Queen
of Aerial Gymnasts" for her legendary work in vaudeville, joined the Ringling
show at the considerable sum of $250 per week. In short order, she was making

twice as much and traveling in her own private rail car and enjoying her own private dressing tent, both unheard of privileges for a performer at the time. As her star grew and her beauty blossomed, Leitzel was pursued by any number of luminaries, including senators, assorted millionaire bons vivants, and titans of industry such as Henry Ford, whom she kept waiting outside her dressing tent for unconscionable lengths of time, the bouquet of roses brought for her already wilting by the time she ushered her visitor inside.

Leitzel stood a diminutive four-foot-ten and wore a child's size 1½ shoe. Clad in silk tights and a sheer skirt, her long blonde curls tumbling over a skimpy sequined top, she topped off each of her performances by ascending to the top of the aerialists' web, where, with no net beneath her, she would pass her right hand through a loop attached by a swivel to a dangling rope and begin to swing back and forth until she had launched her body into a spin like that of an airplane propeller while the audience called out the count of the revolutions from below.

The technical term for the movement is the "full-arm plange," or sometimes simply the "dislocate," for each time the body makes such a revolution, the shoulder is dislocated, then snapped back into place. Often, the count of Leitzel's revolutions by the audience reached one hundred before she stopped. Her record was 249.

For years, she and Codona existed wholly within twin universes of Ringling celebrity, but in the end, as if it had all along been a preordained matter, the King and Queen of the company's aerialists would find their way to each other, and in 1928 the torrid affair of two highly temperamental and supremely talented artists was consummated in marriage, at a ceremony in Chicago. Henry Ringling North describes a snapshot of the pair taken as they drove away from the circus grounds with "Just Married" signs plastered to their vehicle. Though Leitzel was in her thirties and had been twice married by that time (she claimed not even to remember the name of the first husband), North describes her as looking as radiant as a high school girl, while the beaming thirty-five-year-old Codona resembled the guileless boy next door.

Of course, appearances are only drawn in order to be deceiving, and the marriage would soon meet rocky shores. Lillian Leitzel had spent twenty years as a principal in the fever dreams of uncountable powerful and attractive men and simply could not turn away from the blandishments of the supremely rich and persistent; Codona, himself one of the most desirable celebrities of his era, derived from a Latin tradition that brooked little tolerance for a wayward or even flirtatious wife. Inside two years, sick with jealousy, he developed the dubious plan to regain Leitzel's exclusive attentions by beginning a barely disguised affair with an Australian bareback rider named Vera Bruce, she herself motivated by the prospect of one-upping the unquestioned queen of the Ringling performance world.

Things deteriorated rapidly, and for the 1930 winter season, Leitzel and Codona embarked upon a series of European appearances separately. It was a Friday the thirteenth in February 1931 when Leitzel, who had dreamed of a fall the previous night, began the climax of her act at the Valencia Music Hall in Copenhagen, with her rigging man standing some twenty-five feet below her. As the audience's rapt count of her speeding propeller revolutions neared the previously agreed-upon limit, the prop man was distracted for a moment, reaching to guide over the rope that she would use to descend to the floor.

It was only a moment, one the prop man would relive for the rest of his life, but at that instant, the brass swivel ring, which was heated to a near-blacksmith's glow by the friction of Leitzel's relentless spinning, abruptly crystallized and snapped. Leitzel plunged twenty feet to the arena floor below. She landed on her shoulders and head, but to the amazement of the crowd bounded almost instantly to her feet. "I'm all right," she told her rigger, intending to resume her act.

"You're going nowhere but the hospital," was the reply, and Leitzel was rushed away.

When Codona heard of the accident, he broke off his engagement at the Winter Garden in Berlin and hurried to Leitzel's side the following day. He found Leitzel the same bright presence who had popped up from the floor of the music hall. She was fine, she insisted. She would soon be back at work, and he should return to Berlin and fulfill his own obligations. Reluctantly, Codona agreed.

On Sunday, February 15, Leitzel lapsed unaccountably into a postconcussion coma and died.

Codona was done in by the loss. He went into solitude for months, and when he returned, his performances changed from graceful aerial acrobatics to extremely dangerous maneuvers that appeared as direct challenges to Death. He married Vera Bruce, the Australian equestrienne, but the intensity of his performances did not subside. Soon he suffered a fall that irreparably damaged his shoulder and grounded him for good. For a time, he and Vera toured with an equestrian show they drummed up where he appeared as director, but the enterprise failed, and Codona soon found himself managing a gas station.

It should come as no surprise that Vera Bruce eventually filed for divorce from this man who had descended from Olympian glory to self-loathing triviality. On July 30, 1937, she asked Codona to join her at her attorney's office so that a division of property could be spelled out, and, surprisingly enough, Codona agreed.

When Codona appeared at the office, he seemed calm and prepared for the inevitable. He asked the attorney if he might have a private word with Vera before they began, and Vera indicated her assent. When the attorney was gone, Codona reached to turn the lock on the door, pulled a .45-caliber pistol from beneath his coat, and fired five shots into Vera's body. The sixth he sent into his own brain, ending his life immediately, though the unfortunate Vera would linger for another day. Ultimately, with one news story declaring that "double tragedy" had written the epitaph to a ruined career, Codona would be buried in an Inglewood cemetery beside the ashes of Lillian Leitzel. "Reunion" is the legend chiseled on the seventeen-foot obelisk that marks the spot.

In his own interpretation of this tragic tale, Henry Ringling North sounds a counterpoint to the underlying analysis of the circus offered by his illustrious Uncle John as "a drop of the waters from Ponce de Leon's spring." North argues that the legacy of the institution that derives from imperial Rome carries with it that era's same dark undercurrent, that of the ever-present specter of death. Whereas it was an absolute certainty, something to look forward to in Roman pageantry, North says, death in the modern circus—though no longer inevitable—is an undeniable presence stalking the high-wire walker or the acrobat performing without a net or the animal tamer who strolls into a ring with little but a bon mot to fend off the charge of a beast capable of human decapitation at the swipe of a paw. Any modern reader who has watched the recordings of Las Vegas megastar Roy Horn being dragged off the stage with his head in the jaws of a white Bengal tiger must surely understand North's point.

As to the Goody Two-shoes of his family's operations, North says that the back lot of the circus, where the menagerie tents abutted those of the one thousand or so razorbacks and roustabouts constituting the main labor force, did in fact resemble a tented jungle. Most of those employees lacked either the desire for or the capacity to acquire permanent jobs, and in the final analysis, North says, they were a tough and unaccountable lot, "a sort of Foreign Legion of the Labor Army." With such a crew in tow, North says, "you have the makings of trouble every day. It is wonderful that we had so little of it."

It was also impossible to shed the company entirely of the host of parasites who followed in its wake, including shell-game operators, confidence men, pickpockets, gamblers, and bootleggers. Every now and again, North writes, "we would have the engineer stop in the middle of nowhere, preferably a desert, and delouse the train. We would go through it from end to end, digging the human rats out of baggage wagons and from under cages on the flats and heaving them ungently to the ground." The malfeasants always managed to catch up eventually, but for a time, operations might proceed without the equivalent of roaches regularly running up the kitchen walls.

TWENTY-SEVEN

LAST MAN STANDING

The death of Alf T. left the brothers John and Charles as the two surviving managers of the combined Ringling and Barnum & Bailey shows, and relations between the two were not always the smoothest. For one thing, Charles's wife, Edith, had become irritated at John's presumption that he was the most important to the show's future and his constant pressing of her husband to "keep up" with him, whether in business or social affairs. If John bought a yacht, then Charles had to buy a bigger one. When John took an interest in the then-hamlet of Sarasota, Florida, and established a bank there, Charles had to start a bank as well, even if the need for even a single such institution was suspect.

Given John's penchant for late evenings and breakfasts that might begin sometime well past noon, Charles insisted that their business meetings start promptly at 9:00 a.m. so that "things could get done." Though claiming that John never failed to show up on time, North suspects his uncle made it only by staying up all night and until the morning meeting.

This rivalry perhaps finds its most striking form in the dueling mansions the two built side by side on the bay in Sarasota, but first a word is in order to explain how Sarasota came into the picture. In 1905, at the age of thirty-nine and after a long stint as a carefree bachelor, John Ringling married the lovely

Amilda (Mable) Burton, thirty, in a ceremony in Hoboken, New Jersey. By that time, the show was prospering and most of the brothers used the winter season as an opportunity to escape the harsh weather they had grown up with to enjoy extended stays in Florida, popular as a winter getaway since railroad and hotel tycoons Henry Flagler and Henry Plant had opened up the state in the 1890s.

John and Mable spent a couple of seasons in Tarpon Springs, then a sports fishing center, on the Gulf of Mexico about thirty miles northwest of Tampa, but the Ringlings found a cool reception from the old money interests in that area. During a boating excursion to Sarasota, about seventy miles down the coast, the Ringlings were entertained by fellow circus manager Charles Thompson, who urged them to start spending their winters there, where no social barriers to "circus people" existed. Thus, in the fall of 1911, Ringling purchased a house formerly owned by Thompson in the Shell Beach neighborhood north of the town center, and soon both John and Mable, who had never owned a house before, were calling Sarasota home, and Ringling was buying up other bits of property in Shell Beach. Soon after, brother Charles built his home in Sarasota, one house over from John's.

The brothers kept yachts docked at the nearby city pier and for the years up through the war enjoyed Sarasota as their winter getaway, though Mable began to spend more and more time there during the rest of the year. During the war, both Charles's yacht *Zumbrota* and John's *Vidoffner II* were commissioned for use by the Navy, but neither encountered action, and the Ringlings, if not excluded by what "society" existed in Sarasota, largely remained outsiders in the community.

All the while, and in contrast to most of his brothers, John Ringling had been expanding his business interests beyond the bounds of the circus. He was a part owner and member of the board of Madison Square Garden, along with J. P. Morgan and William Vanderbilt, and Ringling also became a board member of the city's Chatham and Phoenix National Bank. His familiarity with the rail system led him to the purchase of several short-line railroads, primarily in the West, and when oil was discovered on lands abutting his rights-of-way, he began to speculate in oil leases as well. Ultimately, Ringling laid out plans for a community in the Oklahoma oil lands—Ringling, Oklahoma, remains today a hamlet of some thousand souls in the lonesome flatlands west of Ardmore.

Ringling also owned railroads in Missouri, Ohio, Texas, and Montana, including the rather grandly named White Sulphur Springs and Yellowstone Park Railroad. That twenty-one-mile line began in White Sulphur Springs, Montana, and ran south to connect with the transcontinental Chicago, Milwaukee,

St. Paul, and Pacific line, though it never came anywhere close to Yellowstone Park, which hugs the Wyoming border more than a hundred miles away. The southern terminus was at the unincorporated hamlet of Ringling, Montana (originally known as Leader and renamed in honor of the community's new benefactor), and was meant to be the jumping off point for a resort John Ringling planned to build in White Sulphur Springs. An economic downturn scuttled both development plans and any hope of expansion in the far-flung area. Both of the rail lines were abandoned in the 1980s, though Ringling, Montana, lingers on as an unincorporated community where the phrase "the high, wide, and lonesome" might well have been coined.

Ringling's success in rail was spotty and it was essentially nonexistent when it came to western land speculation, though he did make some profits in livestock trading, which little interested him. His oil investments fared better, though one legal complication and another meant that he saw little of the money during his lifetime. Sarasota, however, was another story, where Ringling found himself already ensconced in a state where unbridled land development would flourish as it had nowhere else.

Teaming up with a local developer named Owen Burns in the early 1920s, Ringling purchased the bankrupt Yacht and Automobile Club, whose holdings included a number of lots in the area then known as Cedar Point (now Golden Gate Point), near downtown, and began dredging operations to expand the property's footprint where John Ringling Estates would be centered. Instead of identifying him as "the noted circus man," local papers instead called him "the New York and Sarasota capitalist," and Ringling's days as an outsider were over.

In fact, Ringling was earning about $300,000 per year from the circus, another $300,000 from oil, and an equal amount from various stocks and bonds. Although being a virtual millionaire did not put him into the economic stratosphere (Andrew Carnegie had recently gone to his grave with the nation's largest fortune of about $450 million, and even relative unknowns as Henry Flagler and Henry Clay Frick had rung up holdings of $100 million or more), Ringling was more than comfortable, with 1922 seeing him take delivery of an opulent new yacht, the *Zalophus*, with six staterooms, five baths, and a crew of ten, and for which he paid $200,000.

In January 1923, both John and Charles were elected to the board of the Bank of Sarasota, at a time when the so-called Florida land boom was about to explode. There was not a great deal of acreage on the mainland near Sarasota available for vast subdivisions such as were proposed near Fort Myers, or for transforming scrublands into something nearly beyond comprehension such as

Addison Mizner's Boca Raton. But John Ringling's imagination had fastened onto the islands protecting Sarasota Bay just offshore from the town. Siesta Key, to the south, was the only one of the low-lying, scrub-covered islands connected to the mainland by bridge, and speculators had already bought up most of the desirable property there. But Ringling knew that bridges were things that could be built and thus he began buying up all he could on Bird, St. Armands, Coon, and Otter Keys and several miles northward on Longboat Key.

St. Armands was to be the keystone to Ringling's plan, with a beautiful shopping plaza as the terminus of a causeway that began on the mainland near Cedar Point and spanned the waters of the bay to connect with a string of paradisiacal "near-tropical" islands with their available homesites. On January 1, 1925, Ringling announced he would build the bridge to St. Armands, and on that date one year and $700,000 later, he sat in a dark green Rolls-Royce limousine as it became the first vehicle to cross the just-completed span. He could not have been faulted for feeling confident about the future as he took that drive, for in the past year more property had changed hands in Sarasota than in any other in its history and the town of just fifty-five hundred seemed poised for takeoff.

An important piece in Ringling's plan remained missing, however, that being the construction of a Ritz-Carlton hotel on Longboat Key, to be constructed adjacent to the new golf course for which Ringling had donated twenty acres, the idea being to demonstrate that Sarasota was an equally attractive destination for the nation's monied set as were Miami Beach and Palm Beach, already thriving on Florida's east coast. A permit had been issued to allow construction to begin on the structure, with its cost pegged at $3 million and Ringling said to have committed $400,000 of his own, but a subscription drive to raise the remainder of the construction capital had stalled, enthusiasm dampened by an epochal stock market dive in March 1926.

John Ringling came up with a somewhat irregular tactic to reenergize the prospects for his adopted city, inviting the director of the Chamber of Commerce to travel with the combined circus show for the 1926 season. The object was to promote Sarasota as a tourist destination and a heavenly domicile in every city through which the circus passed. Every circus wagon was emblazoned with an advertisement extolling the virtues of Sarasota and every program carried fulsome stories of the benefits of living there, where, indisputably, life was "joy."

All was to little avail, however. Negative press coverage in northern cities, with tales of "underwater lots" in Florida being sold multiple times in a single day until prices had climbed to untenable levels, had put a damper on land sales everywhere in the state, and the hurricane of September 1926, which virtually flattened Coral Gables, perhaps the crown jewel of planned cities in the nation, put an end to baseless speculation. Worse yet, that same spring Charles had suffered a stroke, and he and John had met in Baraboo that summer and actually talked about the possibility of selling the circus, even if neither of them could face giving up the vast enterprise they had worked so hard to create.

But that December, with the brothers back in Sarasota, Charles, then sixty-two, suffered another stroke. John ran across the broad lawns separating their houses to find Charles lying unconscious in his bed, attended to by the family doctor. Abruptly, the harsh rattle of Charles's breath ceased and the doctor rose to check his pulse.

Finally, the doctor shook his head, and John heaved a great breath of his own, wiping at his tears. "I'm the last one left on the lot," he said.

The fabled partnership of the Ringling brothers was finally at an end.

TWENTY-EIGHT

PATRIARCH OF PARADISE

UNLIKE SO MANY OTHERS WHO FOUND THEMSELVES DEVASTATED BY THE COLlapse of the Florida boom, John Ringling's interests—the circus not least among them—were too vast and diversified for a real estate collapse to ruin him. The oil wells were still pumping and the circus was still drawing them in, and he had partnered with the legendary boxing promoter Tex Rickard to build a new $4.75 million iteration of Madison Square Garden on Eighth Avenue between Forty-Ninth and Fiftieth Streets that would seat more than eighteen thousand.

Though Ringling was wise enough to understand that the vast boom he envisioned for Sarasota was simply not going to happen and that good sense dictated he would have to stop and cut his losses on the barely begun Ritz-Carlton hotel project, he did not give up entirely on his adopted home. As the 1927 season approached, Ringling managed to convince the city to accept the gift of the $700,000 causeway he'd built to St. Armands, thereby relieving himself of the burden of its maintenance. Then, he called ringmaster Fred Bradna to Ca' d'Zan, his new Sarasota home, and began to outline a brainstorm.

Ringling's enthusiasm was twofold: he had hit upon a way not only to reduce a significant portion of circus overhead but also to deliver a tourist attraction beyond measure to his beloved new hometown. All this was to be achieved, he told Bradna, simply by moving the winter headquarters of the combined shows from Bridgeport, Connecticut, to Sarasota, Florida. No longer would there be heating of blocks and blocks of brick barns during the frigid Connecticut nights; and furthermore, the necessary circus staff could also live far more cheaply and pleasantly in Florida.

Besides, Ringling said, he had found the perfect site in the old Sarasota fairgrounds, which was available for twenty-nine cents on the dollar and was already prepared to house its fair share of horses and domestic livestock—what few alterations were necessary for camels, elephants, emus, and the like could be easily made. But the biggest benefit, in Ringling's mind, traced right back to the cunning Flatfoot circus men of one hundred years before: audiences—especially *tourist* audiences—would flock to tour the winter quarters of the Greatest Show on Earth in Sarasota and pay good money to inspect idle circus wagons and gaze at menagerie animals who were simply loafing through their winter days.

Bradna's reaction ran primarily along the lines of "Well, Mr. Ringling, you're the boss, but where do I come in?" Ringling waved a hand airily. He just wanted Bradna to know, that's all. Though of course he would like Bradna to deliver the news to everyone in Bridgeport.

It was a charge that Bradna undertook less than enthusiastically, for after all, the Barnum & Bailey side of the company had been headquartered there from its earliest days, a half century before, and the upset over the transfer of the Ringling headquarters there had scarcely died down. But as it turned out few argued strongly against the idea of spending the winter in Florida, save for Bridgeport native "Good Luck" Lombard, who ran the speakeasy that catered to the circus crowd. "Say, it isn't true," was his nightly refrain.

In short order, work began on converting the abandoned Sarasota fairgrounds, with barns, menagerie quarters, workshops, rail sidings, and an outdoor arena the size of the floor of Madison Square Garden, where performers could train . . . and—just as importantly—spectators could pay to sit in the bleachers and watch.

By the fall of 1927, the new winter headquarters were complete, and a new seasonal tradition began. The final show of the season was presented sixty miles up the road in Tampa and everyone who could find a way to get there from Sarasota was in attendance, schoolchildren forgiven their absences, workers as well. After the show closed, throngs attended the celebratory return of the circus to its freshly landscaped, palm-studded winter headquarters, all of it made possible by the newly minted hero of Sarasota, John Ringling.

A number of jobs had been created in building the headquarters, some three hundred full-time Ringling employees came to swell the economic base, the population rose by about two thousand altogether, and Ringling's prediction of a wave of tourists proved not entirely fanciful. Daily attendance at the headquarters sometimes topped three thousand and averaged about one hundred thousand each season over the ensuing decade. There were minor grumbles from Sarasota old-timers: many of the circus employees were immigrants from southern Europe who would suffer the same sort of disdain that old money dished out to new at the more rarified levels of a burgeoning nation. And, of course, a fair number of grifters trailed into Sarasota after the show, for cons and dodgers are just as fond of a pleasant climate as the next person. But Sarasota rose above these issues, the populace gradually warming to its new identity as home to the circus. It might have been clear that Sarasota was not going to become the next Palm Beach as a result of what John Ringling had brought, but plenty of struggling communities in Florida would have gladly accepted his beneficence.

If Ringling had finally established himself as Sarasota's number one citizen, he had not neglected his circus altogether. One of his principal additions for the 1928 season was a European troupe of wire walkers who had become famous for composing a four-man pyramid that traveled across the high wire balanced on a bicycle. The troupe was performing in Havana when Ringling tracked them down and signed them, and their first performance for the show was so astounding that the audience was stomping and whistling for an encore fifteen minutes after the conclusion of the act. Ringmaster Bradna went after the troupe, only to find them sulking in their robes in the dressing tent, for in Europe, whistling and stomping are signs of derision. After Bradna's explanation, the Wallendas climbed happily back into their costumes, returned to the ring, and began their rise to circus immortality.

The Flying Wallendas were led by German-born Karl, who would go on to dazzle audiences worldwide for some fifty years, including when he crossed a quarter-mile gap above Georgia's Tallulah Gorge in 1970. The Wallendas also played parts in some of the most catastrophic moments in circus history, having taken to the wire just as the Hartford circus fire broke out in 1944 and suffering a tragic accident in 1962 that killed two of their number.

One of their first near-misses came in 1934 when they were still performing for the Greatest Show after John Ringling had left day-to-day operations. The show had been set up during a spate of bad weather on a muddy lot in Akron, Ohio. The Wallendas were on the wire, engaged in the four-person pyramid climax, rolling high above the area with no net beneath them. Suddenly, a gust from an approaching thunderstorm hit the big top and the wire beneath the bicycle, fastened only to a heavy wooden slab, or "dead-man," on the ground, went momentarily slack when its stakes gave way in the mud.

The bicycle, with Karl Wallenda riding and carrying the other three members balanced on a pole across his shoulders, toppled sideways. Wallenda caught the wire with one hand, then saw his wife rushing past him. He snatched her out of the air with a scissors grip of his legs at the last instant. Karl's brother Herman had also managed to grab hold of the wire as he fell. Miraculously, he caught Joseph Geiger, the fourth member of the troupe, in the same fashion as Karl saved Helen. Herman took himself and Joseph hand over hand to safety at the platform, while Karl and Helen dangled from the wire until a net was rushed beneath them.

For Bradna, the near tragedy was a reminder of John Ringling's overriding concern for the safety of his performers. Ringling had long ago devised a system whereby two telephone poles were driven deep into the ground as supports for the high-wire rig, to prevent just such a slip that had nearly killed the Wallendas. In fact, it was something of an unusual circumstance that Ringling had agreed to sign the Wallendas in the first place, given the extraordinary daring of their act. In 1925, in fact, he had dropped the dangerous wild animal acts from the show, reasoning that it was scarcely worth combating the criticism of animal rights activists when the lives of his people were at risk.

Despite such concerns, and though Ringling was still traveling with his circus in 1928, much of his attention remained centered in Sarasota, where the completion of the new winter headquarters coincided with the completion of the dream house that he and Mable had been planning from as early as 1923. The first house they had occupied after moving to Sarasota in 1911, Palms Elysian, was a comfortable but somewhat pedestrian two-story wood-framed clapboard, with a broad porch and the look of a home one might find on a tree-lined street in a comfortable Connecticut neighborhood.

By the time the twenties had begun to roar, however, well-to-do northerners were flocking to Florida in droves and, particularly in Palm Beach, were striving to outdo each other in the design of their winter homes. With the support of his patron Paris Singer, heir to the sewing machine fortune, Addison Mizner from 1918 on had become the darling of the monied set in Palm Beach and elsewhere on the east coast of Florida, where he combined various features of Italian and Spanish architectures into elaborate designs that his American clients found exotic and perfectly suited to the Florida waterfront landscape and climate.

The design for perhaps the most fanciful of the grand homes on Palm Beach Island, the 126-room Mar-a-Lago (built from 1924 to 1927), was that of Joseph

Urban, sometime architect and famously known as the stage designer for the Ziegfeld Follies. Urban was hired by cereal fortune heiress Marjorie Merriweather Post, who was looking to build "something different," and Urban was more than happy to comply, freely adapting Mizner's neo-Mediterranean concepts and adding in Moorish elements, with the result being a sprawling, multifaceted creation that architectural purists found difficult to characterize but that nonetheless pleased its owners and their guests and that has continued to intrigue the public to this day. (There is no evidence that Ringling ever visited Mar-a-Lago, though Post once brought the circus to the seventeen-acre grounds for a performance in the 1930s).

It was in this expansive spirit that Ca' d'Zan, or House of John, was built between 1924 and 1926, its fifty-six rooms of 36,000 square feet nowhere near the size of the 62,500-square-foot Mar-a-Lago. However, it gives way very little to a Mizner or an Urban design in terms of ingenuity and uniqueness, standing as an intoxicating example of a style that might as easily be described as "Ali Baba comes to Florida."

To enter the Dwight James Baum design is like stepping onto the set of a period film. For Mable Ringling, who adored the Tuscan villas she had toured and who also desired something of the palatial in the aspect of her new home, Baum combined the elaborate detail of a Venetian Gothic palace for the building's western façade on the water with a less decorative, multiplaned façade on the east, all of it gathered around a central tower that commands the approach to the home. Prominent among the exterior features of the home is the use of brightly glazed terra-cotta tile, stained glass, and variegated marble; to approach the home from the right angle in the right light suggests that the whole is constructed of spun sugar instead of the poured concrete that it is.

The rooms are of relatively modest size, much of the furniture placed not by decorators but by the Ringlings themselves, much of it acquired at auction as older estates in the Northeast were liquidated, including a massive set of Empire-styled bedroom furniture that Ringling purchased thinking it had once belonged to Napoleon III (Ringling also had a barber's chair installed in his bedroom, where he sat to be shaved every day). On the ceiling of the grand ballroom, the most expansive room in the home, are found twenty or so canvas panels entitled *Dancers of the Nations*, painted by Hungarian artist Willy Pogany, himself a book illustrator and set designer who had completed stints with Ziegfeld.

In line with the Ringlings' intention that the home be designed for entertaining, Ringling purchased and had installed an intricate brass, burl, and stained glass bar that had once stood in the Cicardi Winter Palace Restaurant in St. Louis, though given that Prohibition reigned, he stored most of his wine and liquors, along with other valuables, in a massive vault hidden behind a false wall on the third floor. An expansive patio spans the western façade of the house, accommodating as many as five hundred and offering a splendid view of the bay. In all, Ca' d'Zan is estimated to have cost about $1.25 million, with the cost of its furnishings adding about another $400,000.

Critics' opinions of Ca' d'Zan have varied widely over the years. Even the first director of the Ringling Museum was known to obfuscate, given the oft-voiced opinions that the building was over-ornate and too diverse in its characteristics to be taken seriously, but such cavils were not unlike those initially aimed at Mar-a-Lago and various specimens of Addison Mizner's work. Perhaps a more useful summation is found in the words of a panel asked to appraise the value of the home in the 1950s: "The total effect inspires interest, fascination, admiration, and awe."

There is less divergence of opinion concerning the other principal building erected on the Ringling estate—the museum housing Ringling's formidable private art collection. In 1925, during a trip to Italy when John was buying up various objets d'art with which to decorate the proposed Ritz-Carlton hotel, he told his adviser, art dealer Julius Bohler, that he and Mable had been talking about the undertaking of some project of special value that they could leave behind for the city of Sarasota after their deaths. In the end, he told Bohler, they had decided to create an art museum. The fact that Ringling had previously expressed little interest in the acquisition of art did not trouble him. He had already had an architect produce sketches of this museum, he told Bohler, and over the next five or six years, he would undertake the assembly of one of the finest private collections of Italian Renaissance paintings in the country.

Fortunately, Ringling had in Bohler an art dealer of acumen and principle, and he also began to devote considerable of his own time to the study of art and art history. In the ensuing months, he purchased a number of portraits, including a pair attributed to Tintoretto and Titian, and in early 1926, made the acquisition that would prove to be the cornerstone of his collection and cement his place as a serious collector. These were four huge, wall-sized cartoons (studies for tapestries) by Rubens that Ringling saw as populating one gallery all by themselves, thus to give his museum an unquestioned sense of grandeur and authority. It was a notion that his background in circus spectacle and poster art may have influenced, and it also turned out to be an inspired decision, serving to this day the function that Ringling intended.

Over the ensuing years, through 1931, Ringling would collect avidly, acquiring more than four hundred works, including those by Rembrandt, Franz Hals, Andrea del Sarto, Velazquez, Breughel, El Greco, Goya, and a host of other major and minor artists, as well as a collection of more than a thousand Cypriot antiquities that the Metropolitan Museum had declared a surplus. The latter made him the largest owner of primitive Greek art in the country outside the Metropolitan. As his efforts continued, Ringling's purchases began to broaden to the pre-Renaissance Baroque as well as to nineteenth-century American works.

And while many of his selections were based on the pedigree of the artist and the provenance of the painting, Ringling often bought works simply because they appealed to him, a practice that sometimes paid significant dividends. In 1929, he purchased a work that spanned two irregularly shaped panels taken from a church in northern Italy that experts at an auction house dismissed as an insignificant copy. The work was later identified as Il Guercino's *Annunciation*, its value vaulting instantly into the stratosphere. Ringling had paid $56 for the two panels, because he admired the quality of the work.

The museum itself was to be located on a marshy corner of Ringling's Sarasota estate, and the architect chosen was John H. Phillips, who had designed the entrance for Grand Central Station and sections of the Metropolitan Museum of Art. He was a regular guest of Ralph and Ellen Caples, whose lot adjoined that of the Ringlings.

Phillips's initial drawings for the museum depicted a U-shaped building far less ornate than Ca' d'Zan but very much in keeping with the Italian villa look that Mable Ringling so adored. The Ringlings were delighted with Phillips's concept and commissioned him without hesitation, but there came one complication when Phillips realized that the size of Ringling's fortune was not quite the Croesus trove that was rumored. Ringling's wealth was estimated at more than $100 million in the mid-twenties, when his development prospects were at their peak, but that would have been primarily paper wealth—so certain aspects of the plan, including an attached College of Art, with dormitories, would have to be scaled back, though most of the proposed museum hall stayed intact.

The interior of the building comprises twenty-one galleries, including two major rooms for the work of Rubens, one containing two tapestries designed by the master and the second the four cartoons. In addition to the artworks on display, Ringling also included entire rooms and architectural accouterments that he had purchased from the Astor and Huntington Mansions in New York. When opened in 1930, *Art Digest* called the Ringling Museum "a museum of architecture," and the *New York World* gushed, "John Ringling, who used to drive a circus wagon, has built one of the finest museums of art in all the world."

For all this, preparations for immortality never overshadowed the fact that the Ringlings had organized their lives at Ca' d'Zan for pleasure and the entertainment of friends. Guests in those halcyon days included the likes of Will Rogers, Flo Ziegfeld, Tex Rickard, New York governor Al Smith, William J. Burns of the Burns Detective Agency, New York mayor Jimmy Walker, New York Giants manager John McGraw, and a host of other notables. A stay at Ca' d'Zan included supercharged conversation, sumptuous meals, no small amount of drinking, and the usual highlight, a jaunt into the bay aboard the yacht *Zalophus*, where members of the Czech orchestra Ringling had imported played dance tunes on the deck into the wee hours.

Ringling understood the boat's uncommon appeal to his visitors and often lent it out to friends. On one such occasion, Mayor Walker had absented himself from the city for a Florida getaway with his showgirl mistress, and Ringling, held in New York on business, gave Walker free run of Ca' d'Zan and its amenities. Ringling thought little of the matter until he got a frantic call early one morning from Al Roan, the captain of the *Zalophus*.

"I don't know how to tell you this, Mr. John, sir," said Roan. "But the fact is we hit an uncharted sand bar right in Sarasota Bay, and *Zalophus* sank."

"Jesus," Ringling replied. "Anybody drowned?"

No one had, Roan assured Ringling, He had gotten Walker and his mistress, along with a noted NYC banker and *his* paramour, to safety in the boat's launch. But the four passengers were acting as if they wished they had drowned, Roan said. "They're scared wild of the publicity."

Ringling paused, then demanded of Roan, "Who knows about this?"

No one knew, Roan assured him. It was the middle of the night when the accident took place.

"Listen carefully, Al," came Ringling's response. "You take those people to Tampa and put them aboard a train for New York or anywhere there's a train going. That boat won't sink until *tomorrow* morning." And according to the subsequent newspaper accounts, that is exactly when the *Zalophus*—with not a single passenger aboard—expired.

TWENTY-NINE

THE LAST RACE

If life at Ca' d'Zan sometimes epitomized the riotous Roaring Twenties, and if dapper, urbane John and lovely Mable might have echoed the celebrity of such contemporary couples as Marjorie Merriweather Post and E. F. Hutton or Scott and Zelda Fitzgerald, it might as easily be understood that the party could not go on forever. "My candle burns at both ends; it will not last the night" begins the well-known poem published by Edna St. Vincent Millay in 1920. The verse ends with a brave assertion—"But ah, my foes, and oh, my friends—It gives a lovely light!"—that only lends poignancy to the end of the decade and especially to its end at Ca' d'Zan.

Early in 1929, as work proceeded on the art museum, Mable Ringling, fifty-four, was to make a startling admission to her husband. Her increasing bouts of exhaustion and abdominal difficulties were the result of an onset of Addison's disease, a failure of the adrenal glands; coupled with the diabetes that she had kept secret for years, the prognosis given by her doctor was grim. Scarcely had she confided in John than she found herself bedridden, and on June 8, 1929, she died.

By all accounts, John Ringling was thunderstruck by the rapidity of Mable's decline and passing. Ringling, who'd never owned a piece of black clothing in his adult life, was forced to borrow a pair of trousers from his butler for the funeral. Ringling told his nephew North that he felt he would never be happy again, and, in fact, made him a gift of his entire wardrobe of carefully crafted suits. North found himself swimming in his uncle's clothing and carried everything off to a secondhand shop in New Haven, where the proprietor took one look at the sewn-in label, "Made expressly for John Ringling," and snapped up the whole on the spot.

At the same time that Mable had begun her swift decline, Ringling was called to a meeting with the officers of Madison Square Garden to discuss the details of the circus's 1930 engagement. Whether it was owing to his preoccupation with Mable's condition or simply to his characteristic indifference to detail, Ringling did not appear for the scheduled meeting. When the meeting was finally reconvened, the directors, long annoyed by Ringling's flippant attitude, explained that the agreement making the garden available to the circus for the following year would exclude any Friday night performances. Those would be reserved by the venue for the presentation of a highly profitable series of prizefights.

When Ringling finally realized that the directors were both serious and absolutely inflexible on the matter, he made a suggestion as to what they might do with their contract and stormed out the door—his circus would play at the 22nd Regiment Armory, he vowed, but rather than proceeding there to watch, he added, the Madison Square Garden directors should instead go straight to hell.

Rather than make that booking, the directors immediately reached agreement with the American Circus Corporation, a consortium of five competitors and the only surviving company that approached Ringling size and standards, to play the Garden's April 1930 circus dates. When Ringling learned of this, and after his anger had subsided, he began to consider his options. For the past fifty years, either the Barnum & Bailey show or the Ringling show or the combined shows had opened at the Garden. In fact, the Garden had been built expressly to house the circus. The very idea of another show taking that place was simply anathema.

In time, he calmed to the point of seriously considering buying the Garden. But that wouldn't accomplish much, he realized, because the American Circus Corporation would still have its contract. It left him only one way out. And so John Ringling bought the American Circus Corporation.

The price reportedly was $2 million and a portion of it was paid in cash. Ringling financed the remainder, $1.7 million, with the Prudence Bond and Mortgage Company. Given that the American Circus Company encompassed five profitably operating companies with 150 rail cars, a two-thousand-animal menagerie, and forty-five hundred employees, Ringling believed in the advice given him by Wall Street investment analysts: though Ringling operations had never gone public, he would simply reorganize the new company and sell its shares to the public. Given the imprimatur of the greatest circus man of all time, it would be a snap. And, of course, it just might have been had Ringling undertaken the project in some year other than 1929.

The stock market, which began its tremblings in September, crashed into veritable oblivion on Black Tuesday, October 29, 1929, when more that sixteen million shares were traded at steadily declining prices until the gains and the freewheeling confidence of an entire decade were obliterated. Any hope of floating a new stock offering would have elicited gales of laughter had anyone on Wall Street been in a laughing mood. Suddenly, Ringling, and by extension his personally held company (Charles's wife Edith and Alf T.'s son Richard had inherited those shares), were saddled with mountainous debt at a time when even his show was having difficulty drawing crowds.

Though he managed to close out the dismal year of 1929 with net profits of $1 million, by 1931, gate receipts had fallen so dramatically that the combined shows were closed on September 14, the earliest date ever. What unfolded in the ensuing months constituted one of the more stunning reversals in the annals of American business.

John Ringling had always possessed an uncanny ability to compartmentalize various setbacks and disappointments. Nephew Henry North says that even as the circus was gasping in 1931, Ringling went off to Europe in July, attending a sale at Christie's where he bought several paintings intended for the museum in Sarasota. In that same year, Alf T.'s son Richard died, having run through an estate of $5 million or $6 million and leaving his widow Aubrey little more than a one-third interest in a show that was on the verge of insolvency. Without batting an eye, Ringling found a way to divert a bit of cash from circus operations to shore up Aubrey.

The beginning of the end for Ringling did not come until the spring of 1932, when he was diagnosed with an arterial clot in his leg that for a time doctors feared would result in amputation. Ringling, sixty-five, pulled through, but his doctors ruled that he would have to absent himself for a time from the stress of circus management and the incessant demands from creditors.

For his retreat, Ringling ensconced himself at the Half Moon Hotel in Coney Island, an establishment owned by an old friend and sometime fellow investor Samuel W. Gumpertz. Ringling was to lean back and rest easy, Gumpertz assured him. He would keep an eye on things and report back to Ringling as needed.

Alas, Gumpertz turned out to be the sort of friend who makes enemies seem superfluous. An interest payment that had come due on Ringling's note with

Prudence Bond—at the time reduced to just over $1 million—went into default, giving impetus to Gumpertz, who organized two groups of investors to purchase the defaulted note from Prudence, which was only too happy to divest itself of what was looking more and more like a millstone.

Gumpertz then approached Edith Ringling, the always envious wife of Charles, and Aubrey, the financially struggling widow of Richard, to argue that John Ringling was terminally incapacitated and unfit to continue to run the show. Left to his own devices, Gumpertz argued, a stubborn, out-of-touch John Ringling would soon have the show collapsed into insolvency and its stock would have lost all value.

In July 1932, John Ringling was summoned to a meeting by Gumpertz, who explained that it was a summit to once and for all resolve every creditor's claim and set the show onto renewed footing. What Ringling heard at the meeting, however, would shake him to his core.

There, Gumpertz revealed to John Ringling that he and his associates, Allied Owners, had secretly purchased the note originally signed over by Ringling to Prudence Bond. Furthermore, Gumpertz said, because that note was in default, Allied could move for immediate settlement of that debt and thereby force Ringling Brothers and Barnum & Bailey into bankruptcy.

While Ringling was surely seething, Gumpertz quickly played his trump card. Allied would forgo their demand if certain conditions were met: the operations of the combined shows and all their holdings would be changed immediately from a partnership to a corporation to be headquartered in Delaware; Allied would receive 10 percent of the stock issue for its work in arranging the matter, and the remainder would be divided into equal portions: 30 percent each for Edith, Aubrey, and John.

As for the note that was responsible for causing the mire into which the circus had fallen, it would be assumed by the new corporation, but John Ringling would be required to pledge all of his personal assets to secure it, all to be held as collateral until such time as the debt was paid off. Gumpertz punctuated the delimitation of the terms by producing a complete list of Ringling's far-flung holdings down to the last oil can beside the tracks of the White Sulphur Springs and Yellowstone Park Railway, a research project Gumpertz had applied himself to while John recovered and Edith and Aubrey contemplated their options.

John Ringling found himself staring at a list of every item of value that he had acquired over a lifetime's struggle, one that had begun with him playing second banana to a flea-ridden goat sixty years ago. Included, of course, were the details of a vast collection of art, which itself contained the solution to the present problem. The sale of a mere handful of Old Masters could have cleared up the entire mess. But that was an unthinkable course for John. He and Mable had dedicated themselves to that collection and it was going to posterity intact and in all its magnificence. To hock those paintings to the two-faced, finger-pointing scoundrel before him was a prospect beyond imagining.

He stared about the table, finding Aubrey occupied with a handkerchief, or a fingernail, or some important detail making it impossible for her to meet his gaze, though Edith glared back at him with a look that conveyed just how long she'd been waiting to see him skewered. A different John Ringling might have risen from his seat at that point and walked out of the meeting with a wave and a dare to Gumpertz to do his damnedest. Even Ringling must have known how long it would take for a claim of default to wend its way through the courts. By the time the matter made its way to the dockets, the economic difficulties of the country would have gone away, audiences would be once again flocking to the Greatest Show on Earth, and all this unpleasantness would have vanished.

But this John Ringling was sixty-six years old, alone and sick, and likely sick at heart at the magnitude of the betrayal he found arrayed before him. There had never been a moment for him like it, certainly not when his brothers were alive. But now, as he never had been before, he found himself—truly—the last one standing.

In the end, John gave in and acceded to Gumpertz's terms—with one exception. He demanded the formation of a separate entity, the Rembrandt Corporation, to which was deeded every item of his art collection. (The museum and the land it sat upon had already been divested from his holdings.) The remainder of his assets and his stock interests were listed as collateral for the delinquent note. Thus did Gumpertz engineer the transformation of the Ringling Brothers partnership into a publicly held corporation.

Perhaps the most disheartening footnote to a more than dispiriting affair came soon after, at the first stockholders' meeting of Ringling Brothers–Barnum & Bailey Combined Show, Inc., when the first order of business was moved and seconded. The resolution stipulated that John Ringling would be named president of the corporation and that he be retained as such at the rate of $5,000 per year (his annual draw had always been ten times as much). But named as general manager of operations with complete authority over circus operations was Sam Gumpertz.

In short order the question was called. John Ringling voted his 30 percent against, and Edith was quick to put her 30 percent for, with Gumpertz adding his 10 to hers. John turned to hapless Aubrey, who clearly would have been anywhere but where she sat at the moment.

In a quiet voice, she did her best to escape, saying, "Now there have been enough votes cast. It's all settled, so I don't have to vote at all."

John Ringling leaned forward. "You *will* vote, Aubrey," he said. "I must know where you stand."

In the end, Aubrey relented. By a margin of 70–30, John Ringling, the last brother on the lot, was reduced to a figurehead and the corporate era of the Greatest Show on Earth began.

THIRTY

AFTER THE BALL

EVEN GIVEN SUCH A HUMILIATING TURN OF FORTUNE, RINGLING DID NOT SET-
tle easily into the role of functionary intended for him. The fall of 1932 found
him still going to his office, still negotiating to bring the best new acts into the
Ringling fold. One such was the Christiani family of equestrians, considered to
be the most accomplished of the day.

One afternoon, as he sat in his office, a telegram arrived, one he supposed
might have to do with his delicate negotiations with the equestrians. He had an
eager glance at the message, then paused and read it again. Suddenly, Ringling
was feeling dizzy. Sensing that something was seriously wrong, he rose from his
desk and stepped toward the door, intending to make his way home. Instead, he
collapsed, the victim of a cerebral stroke.

It was sometime later that the telegram Ringling had been reading was
found in a pocket of the suit he was wearing that day. The message had not
come from the Christianis, nor their agents, but instead from Sam Gumpertz.
The telegram declared that the head of Allied had learned Ringling had been
negotiating with the Christianis, in direct violation of orders that he stay away
from circus operations. Such meddling was to cease immediately, the telegram
read. And if it did not, Gumpertz warned, "we will hold a stockholder's meeting
and turn you out."

While Ringling eventually recovered some use of his paralyzed right side
and found his speech restored after a few weeks, the event marked the true end

of his circus life. He spent the remainder of his days at Ca' d'Zan, where Henry Ringling North came following his graduation from Yale to serve his beloved uncle as, in his words, "business agent, chauffeur, handyman, and sometimes cook." And while the image of an ambitious young man shut up in "a great empty, fading mansion with an elderly invalid who was facing ruin" might conjure grim scenarios straight from *Sunset Boulevard*, North insists that such was not the case.

Through all, Ringling retained the uncanny ability to shut away thoughts of monetary peril and deteriorating health and comported himself, as North puts it, "as though the sap of youth were boiling through his veins and the money were rolling in." Even a heart attack he suffered in 1934 did not daunt him long. Though getting together the cash for groceries was sometimes a chore, the two dined from Spode china and drank well-aged wine from Venetian crystal in the elegant loggia, looking out tall windows at the moonlit bay and the distant shadow of Longboat Key, while Ringling spun story after story of the glory days, including one regarding the painting he'd spotted on a hunch in a New York art shop that—purchased for $200 and its over-painting scraped off—turned out to be a Tintoretto worth $50,000.

One evening during dinner, North went to answer a pounding at the mansion's front door, where he found a US marshal demanding to see Mr. Ringling. North was experienced enough by this point to realize that here was another court summons about to be served.

"I'm afraid he's not in," North told the marshal. At about the same time came Ringling's voice echoing down the hallway, demanding that the nurse bring more wine to the table.

"Well, I'm afraid he is," said the marshal. "You tell him I'm not going anywhere."

When North returned to the table to advise Ringling of the situation, Ringling waved a hand. "Very well. Tell him to wait."

With North back in his seat, Ringling continued a story he'd begun before the interruption, following it up with several more, all the way through dessert, coffee, and leisurely digestifs. When the ceremony of dinner had finally come to an end, Ringling gave a nod toward the great entry hall. "If you'll give me a hand, we'll go see about this fellow."

They found the marshal in the vast hall with hat in hand, looking a bit daunted by the splendor surrounding him, any lingering trace of his bluster flittering away when Ringling greeted him as expansively as a duke welcoming his local magistrate, full of apology for having kept the man waiting. Following another story or two and a pointing out of this artifact and that in the grand room, Ringling ultimately accepted the papers from the marshal, who by that time seemed almost apologetic for his errand. Ringling ushered the man out into the night with a hearty farewell, closed the door behind him, and turned to tuck the papers away in his coat with a wink at his nephew. Whatever was written on those papers, North understood, the eyes of John Ringling were unlikely to ever fall upon it.

Chief among their pleasures together were long car rides undertaken in one of the fine cars Ringling had managed to keep from his creditors, a 1924 Rolls-Royce convertible and a Pierce-Arrow among them. In spring, Ringling might recall a magnificent red-blossoming royal poinciana that he had once seen in Fort Meyers, and off they would go on a 160-mile round trip to see a tree. Another time, Ringling was reading the local paper when he abruptly glanced up at North. The Cole Bros. Circus (perhaps it was actually the Hagenbeck-Wallace) would be appearing in Pensacola—in the Florida Panhandle, more than five hundred miles away—he said, and there was to be a parade, more and more a rarity in the circus world.

It had been fifteen years since even Ringling had seen a circus parade, and he would like to see this, he told his nephew, so off they went. They took the open Rolls to a small Pensacola hotel with a second-story balcony overlooking the main street, and North set Ringling up in a comfortable chair there. Shortly, there came a burst of music echoing around a corner and soon enough there appeared the bandwagon itself, drawn by an eight-horse team, followed by the necessary squadron of elephants. North could spot the effects of the Depression in the flaking paint on the wagons and a missing spangle on a costume here and there, and he made a sidelong check for any disappointment on his uncle's face. He needn't have worried, though. Tears were already rolling from his uncle's eyes. In that moment, North realized, it was not *a* circus parade passing below them but the parade of every circus John Ringling had ever known.

As though our brains were meshed together in telepathic television, I saw with him the Ringling band led by white-whiskered Yankee Robinson come down Broadway in Baraboo—Al and Alf T., Charles blowing mightily on his trombone, and Otto lambasting the big bass drum. . . . Time accelerated and vision overlapped. Now came a multi-team hitch of horses that filled the whole thoroughfare from curb to curb, pulling a crimson-and-gold band wagon as long as a railroad car with thirty musicians playing for dear life. A herd of forty elephants in gorgeous trappings with gorgeous girls on their backs went past; a white horse curvetting all alone carried young Ella Bradna, while further back rode a schoolgirl named May Wirth. Smiling from a splendid carriage was little Leitzel. . . . More and ever more magnificent tableau wagons, iron wheels rumbling on cobblestones . . . Then, blasting us with its cacophony until the buildings seemed to rock, came the biggest steam calliope of them all. Time stopped. The real calliope was passing out of sight, followed by a swarming mass of children.

[Finally] Uncle John pushed himself out of his chair with enormous difficulty, and clung to my shoulder. "Time to go home, Buddy," he said.

★★★

Though his last months were marked by a steadily advancing distrust of most everyone, including nephews Henry and John, those two agreed that whatever conflation of illness and aging had prompted John Ringling's decline would never be allowed to affect their affection for the man they had come to revere. John Ringling died, in New York, of bronchial pneumonia, on December 2, 1936, just shy of his seventy-first birthday. His estate was appraised at $23,500,000. He died with $311 in the bank.

John Ringling's initial will gave half his estate to his sister Ida, mother of Henry and John, with the other half going to the state of Florida to create an endowment for the upkeep and expansion of the holdings of the Ringling Museum. However, most of the assets were still frozen as collateral for the note due Allied Owners, now reduced to about $850,000. In addition, the US government filed a claim in the amount of $13.5 million for estate taxes and unpaid income taxes (John Ringling had found the latter an inconvenience not worth attending to). Then, it was discovered that Ringling had, in a fit of spite shortly before his death, added a codicil to his will, essentially cutting his sister and the two nephews out.

The situation was compounded by the fact that the combined shows, under the management of Sam Gumpertz, had been seeing net profits fall to about $60,000 per year through the lean years of the Depression, compared to the $1,000,000 that Ringling had cleared in 1929. The circus business in general was teetering on collapse: only three railroad shows were operating in 1933 and 1934, and there were but four in 1936 and 1937. By 1939, the number would drop to two.

None of this was daunting to John Ringling North, who had, while his younger brother served as majordomo to their uncle in Florida, spent much of his time as a Wall Street broker struggling to keep the circus from going under. Though Ida and her sons had been cut out of the will, John Ringling—neglectful of detail to the end—had overlooked the need to rescind the position of nephew John and Ida as executors. Armed with his authority to liquidate and dispose of John Ringling's assets, John North approached a friend at Manufacturers Trust Company with a startling request: he was asking for a loan of $1 million, to be used to pay off the Allied note and some minor obligations. It was John North's intention to persuade his Aunt Edith and his cousin Aubrey to close ranks with him and return the combined shows to family management, with himself at the helm.

In the end, both his aunt and his cousin agreed, the loan was issued, the note finally retired, the 10 percent of stock virtually extorted by Allied repurchased, and the company restored to the family, with John Ringling North president of the circus for a guaranteed term of five years and Henry Ringling North his assistant and vice president. Although the Ringling family might have finally rid itself of the opportunistic Sam Gumpertz and his associates, and John North was able to beat the government down to an $850,000 settlement on the tax score, they found that they faced new enemies of a very different sort.

The Depression still gripped the nation and, in 1938, for the first time, union organizing impeded the show when animal handlers and roustabouts went out on strike during the Madison Square Garden opening. The dispute lingered into the summer, forcing John North to fold the tents for the season in June. North salvaged something of the year by sending out nonunion performers from the combined shows under the banner of the nonunionized Al G. Barnes and Sells-Floto Circus, one of the holdings that John Ringling had acquired in 1929 when he bought the American Circus Corporation.

Among the star attractions at the time was Frank Buck, a long-time collector of wild animals for menageries and circuses who had penned a best-selling book, *Bring 'Em Back Alive* (1930), and starred in several feature films based upon his exploits in the wild. After John Ringling's departure, the show had resumed its use of caged-animal acts, including that of Clyde Beatty, who became famous for his "fighting act," entering a cage containing as many as forty lions and tigers, cracking a whip and holding out a chair, a pistol strapped to his belt.

Often criticized for using such apparent cruelty in his training methods, Beatty, who opened for the Gumpertz-led shows at Madison Square Garden for several years, scoffed at such complaints. Only a person interested in a quick and painful death would try to control big cats in that way, he said, for a whip and even a pistol would be precious little protection against the sudden charge of an infuriated cat. The fearsome-looking "fighting act," with its macho trappings, was nothing but deception meant to lend color to the proceedings, he insisted.

"Personally, I believe you can teach an animal nothing," he said. "They show you what they can do and then you develop it." It didn't mean there was no danger involved in the act. In 1932, as he was rehearsing with his cats at winter headquarters in Indiana, a cat named Nero knocked a momentarily distracted Beatty to the ground, then sank its teeth into his thigh. Though the cat was quickly subdued, an infection developed in Beatty's leg that kept him hospitalized for weeks.

Traveling as the chief animal act for John Ringling North's iteration of the combined shows (along with a fearsome-looking gorilla named Gargantua) was the first woman to train tigers, Mabel Stark, billed as "The Queen of the Jungle presenting a Notable Congress of the Earth's Most Ferocious Performing Lions and Tigers." Stark used no whip or chair, running her animals through their routines with voice commands and an assertive attitude alone. The high point of her act was a wrestling match between her and a Bengal tiger several times her size.

One of the most affecting performers for the North show was Emmett Kelly, whose creation of the hobo clown "Weary Willie" struck a profound and unforgettable chord with Depression-era audiences. His sad-sack, shuffling demeanor was quite the contrast to the Bozo-like cavorting of the traditional circus mime, and his image and his humor—including a routine where he patiently leaned on his shovel while the "boss" whirled about trying to get things accomplished—intwined with the very concept of the circus and became an enduring aspect of American culture.

"Weary Willie is a melancholy little hobo who always gets the short end of the stick and never has any luck, but he never loses hope and keeps on trying," Kelly once said about the iconic character he inhabited. A former cartoonist born in Kansas, Kelly also delighted audiences by stationing himself beneath the high wire when acts such as the Wallendas were performing, a handkerchief spread between his hands as a safety net in case they should fall. Winston Churchill once came to the circus to meet Kelly, and Loren MacIver's portrait of the clown has become an image familiar to countless millions worldwide.

In addition to clowns and lion tamers and other traditional components, John North also sought to incorporate more Broadway musical pageantry into the proceedings, including interspersing showgirl-laden dance routines, and—if

it can be believed—"a ballet for the elephant," choreographed by George Bal-
anchine with music by Igor Stravinsky. Though circus purists scoffed, the poet
Marianne Moore witnessed one of the 425 performances of this unlikely number and averred in the publication *Dance Index* that the elephants had more
than held up their end. "Their deliberate way of kneeling, on slowsliding
forelegs—like a . . . ship's slide into water—is fine ballet."

John and Henry North also brought practical improvements to the circus
meant to counter the inroads made by the movie business, with theaters touting their "air-conditioned comfort" since the mid-1920s. It took three flatcars
to transport eight "portable" blowing units purchased from the Buffalo Forge
Corporation, and fifty men to maintain and operate them, but, along with
diesel generators, mechanized booms, mechanical stake drivers, and motorized
tent rope pullers, such constituted the price of progress.

While it might have been assumed that the advent of World War II would
put the same damper on the circus as had the so-called Great War, the position
of the US government was that the circus was in fact an essential industry,
necessary for sustaining the nation's morale. And in fact, gate receipts reflected
the validity of such thinking. Despite all the factors arrayed against it, and even
with a tragic fire in August that consumed the menagerie tent, killing sixty-five
animals, the combined show returned net profits of over $900,000 for 1942,
the first season that followed the attack on Pearl Harbor.

Though nephews John and Henry had decided that they would not take
the show out for the remainder of the war, citing labor shortages and safety
concerns—it was no longer possible to obtain fireproof canvas owing to the
needs of the armed forces, for instance—Aunt Edith and Cousin Aubrey resisted. The five-year agreement ensuring John's supervision over operations had
expired, and in January 1943, there was yet another stockholders' summit at
which John and Henry were cast aside and Edith's son Robert, a former opera
singer, was installed as the new president of operations.

In spite of Robert's dearth of firsthand circus experience, the show did well
in 1943, and the year of 1944 began auspiciously, too. Because of the war, the
circus experienced regular personnel shortages, which often meant problems
with maintaining schedules and ensuring that equipment was properly maintained and deployed. Worse yet, Robert Ringling, who had been traveling with
the circus and had acquired a measure of competence as an operations chief, fell
ill and was forced home to Illinois, leaving operations in the hands of new vice
president Jim Haley, John Ringling's former accountant, and now the husband
of Cousin Aubrey. On the morning of July 6, 1944, Haley, inexperienced as

an operations chief, accompanied the arrival of the show into Hartford, Connecticut, where its forty-one tents were pitched on an expansive lot not far from town.

The show had previously been using a fire-resistant canvas big top, but it had proved to leak terribly in the rain. Thus, the new managers had decided to revert to an old canvas that had been waterproofed with a solution of paraffin and benzene. This canvas shed water extremely well. And, unfortunately, if a match were touched to it, it also burned like tinder.

THIRTY-ONE

OUT OF THE ASHES

ALONGSIDE HEADLINES DESCRIBING THE LIVES LOST IN GERMAN BOMBINGS OF London, the *New York Times* carried the grim news of the 139 lives lost and the 174 badly burned in the circus fire at Hartford. One photographer caught a memorable view of clown Emmett Kelly—the ultimate victim incarnate—running anguished toward the flames with a bucket of water. That powerful image would lead the tragedy to be dubbed "the day the clown cried."

Donald Anderson, a thirteen-year-old, would receive a medal for his actions that awful day: when the fire broke out, he jumped from the top row of the bleachers and sawed a hole in the canvas sidewall with the fishing knife he carried. Hundreds followed outdoors after him, but Anderson barely hesitated, sawing his way back inside through another gap to rescue the elderly man who'd brought him as well as a four-year-old girl who'd been trampled unconscious.

The early reports said that two-thirds of the dead were children, but that proved to be an exaggeration born of the horror of the moment. In time, the verifiable death toll would rise to 167, with 67 of them children under the age of fifteen, hardly a cheerful statistic. The injured numbered 682, and 6 of the dead lay unidentified and unclaimed, including one blonde-haired, blue-eyed little girl who had been trampled to death and whose heart-rending gravestone read "Little Miss 1565." These and other circumstances would be debated ever after, and indeed the incident has become an indelible part of Connecticut history, with every decade's anniversary bringing a fresh wave of books, editorials, library memorials, remembrance services, and the like. "The people of Hartford and the state grieved for years," said one editorial writer on the seventy-fifth anniversary of the tragedy. "The shocking loss of life reverberated through the post-war years much as the Sandy Hook deaths have affected us today."

That same night of the fire, circus vice president Haley was arrested and charged with involuntary manslaughter, along with four other circus officials. When chief canvasman Leonard Aylesworth returned the next day from Chicago where he had been conferring with Robert Ringling, he too was arrested and charged. The courts also ordered all circus property impounded.

In addition to the criminal charges, it was obvious to everyone that liability claims would far outstrip the $500,000 policy that the circus carried, but it was also clear that unless the circus were to continue to operate, only a fraction of those claims would ever be paid. Henry Ringling recalls that some within the organization argued for letting the circus simply enter bankruptcy, but the family vowed to carry on and to pay every cent of its debts. The circus posted a bond of $1,000,000 and thus was permitted to return to Sarasota to reorganize.

In the end, under the terms of what was called the Hartford Arbitration Agreement, the circus was allowed to continue operations, with all net profits going to a special receiver in charge of paying out liability claims. The circus was back out on the road by August, playing arenas and stadiums without a big top for the rest of that season, and actually closing with a profit. Ultimately, about $4 million was paid in claims ranging from $1,000 to $100,000 over the ensuing six years, with no petitioner resorting to trial.

Late in 1944, at the criminal trial, the vice president James Haley was convicted and received a jail sentence of a year and a day, while the others, with the exception of David Blanchfield, received lesser terms. Blanchfield was the only one of the six who had not petitioned to receive a suspended sentence on the grounds that his work was "indispensable" to the continued operations of the circus, his stance one that found favor with the judge. Having been "the only one who told the truth," the judge said, he was free to go.

Though Robert Segee, a Native American man arrested on charges of arson in Ohio in 1950, told authorities he had also set the Hartford fire, he later recanted that confession. And while some fire officials in Hartford remained convinced that the fire was deliberately set—perhaps in the restroom tent—a 1991 reinvestigation ended with the verdict "cause undetermined."

One poignant footnote from the fire lingers even to this day: at the same time that the 1991 reexamination of the fire's cause was going on, retired Hartford fire detective Lieutenant Rick Davey, never able to get the question out of his head, began his own investigation into the identity of Little Miss 1565. Through a painstaking process of interviews with survivors and a gradual process of elimination, Davey arrived at the conclusion that the unidentified girl was actually Eleanor Cook, eight years old at the time of her death. She had gone to the circus on that day with her mother, Mildred, and her two brothers, Donald, nine, and Edward, six. When the fire was over, Edward was found dead, and Mildred, critically injured, was rushed to the hospital where she would stay for many months. Her son Donald miraculously escaped unscathed, but young Eleanor was missing. With Mildred incapacitated, an aunt of Eleanor, Emily Gill, was asked to view the remains of Little Miss 1565. But the teeth were wrong, the hair was wrong, and the clothes were wrong, Gill said. Discounted as a victim of the fire, Eleanor Cook was classified as a missing person.

Though the issue of Little Miss 1565's identity continued to surface in the Hartford media from time to time over the decades, nothing substantial came of it until Lieutenant Davey became obsessed in the early nineties. "Over a period of time I just kind of fell in love with a little girl, the photograph of a little girl, someone I never knew," he said. Ultimately, Davey reassembled all the circumstantial evidence suggesting that Little Miss 1565 was Eleanor Cook, presented his case to Mildred Cook, in the presence of her son Donald, who was ready to assert that the morgue photo was that of his sister. In the end, state medical examiner Dr. H. Wayne Carver issued a revised death certificate: Little Miss 1565 was in fact Eleanor Cook.

It all makes for a wonderful story, providing closure for a long-grieving family, but as Stewart O'Nan, perhaps the most careful historian of the fire, points out, there remains one troubling issue: the dental records of Little Miss 1565 and Eleanor Cook do not match. And at three-foot-ten and weighing just forty pounds, Little Miss 1565 is typical of a girl of six. Eleanor Cook was said to be "tall for her age," her height well over four feet—she would have likely weighed at least fifty-five pounds. Though contemporary DNA testing could likely resolve the matter, no one is left with reason to press for an answer.

In the immediate aftermath of the fire, and through considerable familial cajoling and maneuvering, John Ringling North was able to regain control of circus operations, and the year of 1946 saw $1 million paid over to the receiver in charge of the Hartford fire claims. Though John Ringling North had always maintained the right to vote his 30 percent holdings in the corporation as if he owned it, in truth he was only the executor of the estate of John Ringling, the holdings of which included that stock, and all of which were pledged against any number of claims still outstanding. This was a matter that in fact threatened North's ability to maintain control of an ever-shifting corporate landscape.

The state of Florida had in 1946 accepted a transfer of Ringling's thirty-two acres on Sarasota Bay, Ca' d'Zan, the museum, and a $1.2 million endowment—a gift valued at $20 million in total. The holdings of the Ringling Museum including five hundred or so paintings, themselves valued at about $4 million. But until the still-embattled estate of John Ringling, also deeded to Florida, was settled, there would exist no unfettered trust fund to fund the operations of the museum, including maintenance of the fragile paintings. Florida governor Millard Caldwell was loath to undertake the disposition of the disparate remaining Ringling interests, including the 30 percent share of the circus stock, the still-producing oil wells in Oklahoma, the theater Alf T. had built in Baraboo, and the property holdings in and around Sarasota.

By 1947, an impatient Governor Caldwell suggested to John Ringling North, who was by this time owed nearly $1 million in executor's fees, that he buy out the state's interest in the estate and sort things out himself. The state would take the proceeds of the sale to use for the museum operation and the maintenance of Ca' d'Zan and the grounds. Thus, under the terms of a contract signed on October 8, 1947, for the sum of $1.25 million paid to Florida, John North Ringling was able to take control of his uncle's share of the combined shows, free of encumbrance. When added to his own 7 percent share, along with other agreements he had forged with Aunt Edith and Robert Ringling, he now held 51 percent of the Ringling stock.

The ensuing season of 1948 was the best postwar year yet, with a number of equipment improvements made, including a portable grandstand seating ten thousand that could be erected in less than an hour by a few men. Among the new acts was Unus, the "Upside-down gravity-defying, equilibristic Wonder of the World." Unus, whom John had found working in a Barcelona night club in 1946, had perfected a hand-balancing routine that seemed impossible even to circus old-timers.

For his finale, he would show audiences nothing funny was going on by taking off the white gloves he wore. Then he would don the gloves and climb onto a table beside a lamp with no shade and only a softball-sized glowing bulb. Unus would then maneuver himself into an upside-down position with only his index finger on the light bulb, the rest of his body pointed arrow-straight into the air.

As part of an article titled "The Circus" that he wrote for his friend John North's circus program of 1953, Ernest Hemingway said, "You watch Unus standing on one finger and you think, 'Look at such a fine, intelligent and excellent man making his living standing on one finger when most of us can't even stand on our feet.'"

According to his brother Henry, it was the culmination of a lifelong dream for John to have unfettered control of the family circus, though he quickly began to limn the difficulties that would attend to the achievement. As Henry put it, "The end was written plain in our ledgers for years before it came. But we were deliberately blind."

The principal problem was the complexity and size of the big top–styled production, which in truth required the seamless integration of five business endeavors running side by side. There were railroad operations, moving sixty-seven thousand tons of equipment and personnel some twenty thousand miles each year; restaurant operations, serving about nine hundred thousand meals each year; hotel operations, housing thirteen hundred people in hundreds of locations over a period of eight months; construction operations, requiring the erection and dismantling of a small tented city on a daily basis; and then there was the entertainment business itself, the only one of which produced any income. As costs rose along every other vector, it became more and more difficult to squeeze a profit out of the last.

In the last great year of 1929, John Ringling netted $1 million on receipts of $2.5 million. By 1955, receipts had risen to $5 million, but the tally of costs came to $6 million. There were some one-off windfalls that helped the bottom line: Cecil B. DeMille's 1952 production of *The Greatest Show on Earth*, much of it shot on location at winter headquarters in Sarasota, grossed more than $20 million as the Oscar winner for Best Picture, and it paid the circus more than $1.3 million in royalties. And for several years, John North took a tidily profitable one-ring version of the show to Havana during the winter when most of the troupe was in mothballs in Sarasota.

But costs continued to escalate, especially the freight charges from the railroads, themselves beginning to crumble under the competition from trucking and air freight. A once-efficient rail system was often stranding loaded circus cars for hours in the yards, meaning delays for the starting times of matinees in the next city, and a resulting loss of revenue and cachet among audiences. The brothers discussed the possibility of downsizing the show to save costs but dismissed the notion on the grounds that the show itself was the most important thing of all—how could you promote the Greatest Show on Earth if you knew it was only the greatest show you could afford?

Thus, the season of 1955 began with an all-out bang in Madison Square Garden, when Marilyn Monroe rode a pink elephant around the concourse for the opening spectacle. The receipts from the New York run, along with the windfall from the movies, was enough to eke through the year. But in 1956, even with two hundred tons of "Ponderous, Performing Pachyderms," and such acts as acrobat Pinito del Oro reading a newspaper while balanced on the top of her head on a whizzing trapeze bar with no net below, the show was under water by a million dollars on July 15, halfway through the season.

It was the end, John North cabled brother Henry from Pittsburgh, Pennsylvania. On the night of July 16, 1956, the company gave a performance like no other before ten thousand enchanted fans, and at 11:15, with the performers in their dressing quarters and the two hundred elephants returned to their tents, the canvas big top of the Greatest Show on Earth was struck for the final time.

THIRTY-TWO

ROCK AND ROLL TO THE RESCUE

JOHN NORTH ACCOMPANIED THE RETURN OF THE TROUPE TO WINTER HEAD-quarters in Sarasota where it was gloomily disbanded. For a time, he licked his wounds, pondering a future in which the circus somehow did not figure. But then he began to think about a letter he had received the previous winter from a rock-and-roll promoter who thought the era of the big top circus was at an end. This promoter, however, had some ideas for revitalizing the circus industry that he wanted to discuss. John North's reply at the time had been a polite brushoff. But now, with his life's passion wrapped in a shroud and about to be kicked into the grave, North was developing whole new emotions. Finally, he picked up the phone and made a call to Irvin Feld.

Feld's background was in many ways about as disparate from that of John Ringling North and his forbears as it is possible to get, save for one brush with the entertainment business in his early years, as a snake oil salesman travel-ing the carnival circuit in rural Pennsylvania and Maryland with his brother Izzy. In 1939, tired of the itinerant life, he and his brother, Hagerstown natives, scrounged a loan of $1,000 from the company that supplied them with their snake oil ("Exactly what was in it? I never really wanted to know") and bought a variety store in a Black neighborhood in Washington, DC.

Shortly thereafter, a representative from the NAACP visited Feld, urging him to expand his operation into a drugstore luncheonette, which would be something of value for the neighborhood. Feld was agreeable, leasing the drugstore operations to a team of Black pharmacists, and then opening a lunch counter in what he dubbed Super Cut-Rate Drugs that was the first such integrated operation in the city. The always forward-looking Feld thought he could make out even further by adding a record department, which flourished, becoming a chain of record stores, which in turn led Feld into the formation of his own record company.

Before long, Feld was packaging rock-and-roll tours featuring the likes of Chubby Checker, Bill Haley & the Comets, Fats Domino, Buddy Holly, Fabian, the Everly Brothers, and Frankie Avalon. Later he met a fifteen-year-old Canadian kid who wanted him to listen to a song he'd composed called "Diana." Feld became young Paul Anka's personal manager, put him on tour, and would share in the fortune that came the singer-songwriter's way. And as he booked and routed his team of rock stars, Feld picked up information that would prove as invaluable to an emerging new era in entertainment as John Ringling's encyclopedic knowledge of the American rail system had been: an intimate knowledge of every city in the United States and Canada where there were big, beautiful new air-conditioned and heated indoor auditoriums in which to perform.

As he explained to John North, the circus could live on, playing only in arenas such as Madison Square Garden and San Francisco's Cow Palace and the like, with no need to move tents and the labor required to erect them, with no more menageries, no side shows, no cooking operations, no hotel and travel headaches—the performers would receive travel and per diem allowances and make it to the next venue on their own. In this way, daily expenses would be reduced from $25,000 a day to $10,000, the number of employees cut from fourteen hundred to three hundred, and yet the show itself would remain gloriously untouched.

It was, after all, the way many of the early circuses had been presented. The tent show grew up in the 1830s, the by-product of a rugged frontier country that had few arenas suitable for the mounting of a circus show. Over the past few years, finding a fifteen-acre vacant lot near a city's center to set up forty or so tents had become a near impossibility. But there were 150 or more cities with usable arenas, all of them easily accessible and with plenty of parking. Nor would there any longer be—given that every engagement would be playing indoors—a profitless winter season and headquarters.

The deal that the Felds presented John Ringling was simple: the Felds would book and advertise the circus and pay the venue rents. In return, Ringling would pay them a fixed percentage of the gross receipts. Though he was doubtful Feld could pull off all he claimed, Ringling saw no other reasonable option and signed on the dotted line.

Accordingly, in 1957, the circus season began without a single railroad show in operation. The elephant corps for the Ringling Bros. and Barnum & Bailey show, reduced in number from fifty-five to twenty, traveled along with other trained animals, in baggage cars leased from the railroads. The rigging, costumes, and other necessary properties were moved about in trucks, and most of the personnel, including the performers, were in charge of their own travel.

In terms of the quality of the show itself, what remained may no longer have constituted the Greatest Show on Earth, but it remained the Greatest Show Still Going. Though Emmett Kelly left the circus that year to become a mascot for the Brooklyn Dodgers, such popular acts as the Flying Alexanders and highwire master Harold Alzana stayed on, and a number of new spectacles were added, including an aerial ballet where performer Galla Dawn balanced on her head on a trapeze bar while spinning hoops on both her arms and legs. Thrills came from the sight of "Miss Elabeth" taking a "Desperate Dive from the Top of the Arena," and comic relief was provided not only by the troupe of clowns but also by Sciplini's Chimps, an animal act American audiences had not seen before.

Despite the fact that Feld was jockeying at the last minute for choice arena dates and the show had to crisscross the country a number of times as a result, the 1957 season, forty-six weeks long, actually returned a profit, not bad for an undertaking that had racked up losses of $2.5 million in the two previous years.

But the Ringling show and the circus industry in general had finally found itself up against a force that seemed impossible to contest: that of television. Ed Sullivan and the masters of ceremonies for other variety shows were presenting circus acts every week, for free, and former circus clown Red Skelton had his own show, where he was freed to add a voice to his routines. Most of the Ringlings' best circus clowns would have been perfectly capable of the stand-up comedy that had once characterized clown acts, in fact, but the growing complexity of circus programs and the speed with which most acts proceeded had resulted in the diminishment of clown acts to those solely of mime.

As for other facets of the traditional program, you could get closer up to sea animals and lions and tigers than at any circus show by watching such programs as *Sea Hunt*, *Flipper*, and *Disneyland*, and it became ever more difficult to get audiences up from their couches and easy chairs and down to the circus yards. It was during this period that sponsored shows became popular, where such charitable and civic groups as the Shriners took over financial responsibility for the shows in exchange for a share of the profits, thereby using social obligation as a motivator to turn out jaded audiences.

The 1960s constituted a down period for the entire industry, which not only withered financially but also lost a number of its most accomplished performers to accident. In 1961, the Wallendas first perfected their seven-person pyramid, where four men stood on the high wire holding balancing bars, connected to one another by shoulder poles. One level up, two men balanced themselves on the shoulder bars of the men below. Those two were also connected by a shoulder bar, on which was perched a woman one more level up, seated in a chair, two of its legs wobbling for purchase. The act was short-lived, however. On January 30, 1962, as the group carried out the maneuver at a Shriner's-sponsored circus in Detroit, Dieter Schepp, a young nephew of Karl Wallenda, making his first appearance in the act, began to lose his balance.

"I can't hold on anymore," he cried. And the pyramid crumbled. Karl caught the wire with his legs and was able to snatch his niece Jana, holding her tightly in his arms. But three other members of the act fell to the concrete floor forty feet below. Two died, including Dieter Schepp, and Wallenda's son Mario was paralyzed from the waist down. The tragedy plunged all circusdom into gloom.

Though the seven-person pyramid was forever retired, Karl Wallenda would persevere into his seventies, when he made his way across a 720-foot wire strung between the Eden Roc and Fontainebleau hotels on Miami Beach for a television special. On March 22, 1978, as he was walking a wire strung twelve stories up above a plaza in San Juan, Puerto Rico, he lost his footing and plunged a hundred feet to his death in a parking lot. He was seventy-three.

Along with the general decline in talent, and even though the new network of arenas promised a lucrative, problem-free, and year-round venue set for the circus, competition for dates from smaller and often far less competent producers made it difficult for the bigger shows to plot out a long, efficient, and thus profitable route. Previously, in the middle of the 1958 season, Henry Ringling North, weary of battling the forces of progress, had retired from the circus. Brother John remained in charge of production, but, his fortunes suddenly made flush with the appreciation of his uncle's oil and Sarasota property assets, he left the United States for Switzerland in 1962. His absence from everyday operations of the show was manifested in its steady decline. By 1966, fewer than a dozen acts were left on the program, and the sobriquet of the Greatest Show on Earth had taken on ironic overtones for those who knew the industry.

To Irvin Feld, who had become steadily enamored of the circus, it was an impossible situation. "I couldn't stand to let it go on in the state it was in," he said. "I felt I must do everything possible to purchase the circus. It became an obsession." Feld claims to have put that obsession in the form of a New Year's resolution for 1967, and on that first day of the year he called John North, then in Rome, to begin negotiations. Feld flew to Rome to confer with North, using the argument that the grand old institution had begun to slip to the point where it had become an embarrassment to itself, an assertion that may have stung North but one that produced the desired effect. North finally agreed to sell the circus operations to Feld, for $7.5 million in cash, "not one cent in a note."

Feld found the necessary backing for the purchase from Judge Roy Hofheinz, builder of the Houston Astrodome, and the deal—for $8 million, ultimately—was consummated with elaborate ceremony in the Roman Colosseum, where Feld's daughter presented Feld with a lion cub to mark the occasion. Though some circus old-timers were aghast that a group of "towners" (circus slang for anyone outside the business) was now in control of the Greatest Show on Earth, Feld threw himself completely into the resurrection of the production to its former glory. He traveled Europe to scout acts with the same intensity as a James Bailey or John Ringling, telling a *Time* reporter, "After a couple of weeks on dusty lots in the midst of a blazing Italian summer, you get the feeling you've seen everything. Then, out of the blue comes an act so spectacular that you get shivers up your spine."

Perhaps Feld's greatest early success was the wooing of legendary German animal trainer Gunther Gebel-Williams. John North had tried for years to attract Gebel-Williams, whose talents as a tiger and elephant trainer, an equestrian trainer and rider, and an acrobat led to his unquestioned status as the circus star of the day. To swing the deal, Feld had to agree to the purchase of the whole of the trainer's enterprise, Circus Williams, for $2 million. But in return, Feld could present American audiences with such sights as Gebel-Williams standing on one end of a teeter-totter, an elephant stomping on the other end, and the performer flying through the air in a somersault, to land on the back of a second elephant.

Another Gebel-Williams showstopper was the presentation of this tableau: two horses, each with a tiger sitting on its back, flanking an elephant, also with a tiger on its back, and straddled atop *that* tiger a triumphant, grinning Gebel-Williams. Gebel-Williams's cozy work with the big cats was a far cry from that of Clyde Beatty. "For me, the pistol, and the chair and the noise just aren't right," he said, even though he never lost his respect for the power and the innate wildness of the beasts. "A wild animal trainer who puts total trust in his animals is very foolish. Very foolish." It is advice that Roy Horn might well have recalled before the 2003 Las Vegas show during which he was so severely mauled (the producer of "Siegfried & Roy" was Feld Entertainment, it might be noted).

Another Feld accomplishment was the 1968 formation of Clown College, a training center established in Venice, Florida, about twenty-five miles south of Sarasota, where Ringling winter quarters had been moved in a cost-cutting measure of 1959 (quarters would move to Baraboo in 1993 and back to Sarasota three years later). The college was conceived to provide a steady stream of performers in that genre, prompted by Feld's observation of the aging nature of his company's corps: "I know they can fall down," he said of a group with an average age approaching fifty, "but I don't know if these guys can get up."

Tuition for Clown College was free for the ten- to thirteen-week program so long as applicants agreed to accept a one-year contract with the traveling circus following graduation if they were selected. About fifty students were chosen each year, and for eight hours a day, six days a week, they studied makeup application, costume design, stilt walking, juggling, pantomime, and other clown skills, were encouraged to develop new routines that would "play" to circus audiences, and emerged with a complete, distinctive costume, including a personally molded clown nose and a pair of custom clown shoes. Over the course of its nearly thirty-year history, some fourteen hundred clowns were trained by the college. In 1997, with clowns and mime training back in vogue elsewhere and the needs of the circus more than satisfied, Clown College closed.

One of the most controversial decisions Feld made following his takeover was to form two completely independent shows of equal merit, one which he called "The Red Unit" and the other "The Blue Unit." Feld believed that having two companies to book would actually make it easier to compete for arena dates, though John North—disregarding the fact that the Barnum & Bailey show traveled separately from the Ringling show for more than ten years following their merger at the turn of the century—was irate at the notion. "How can there be *two* Greatest Shows on Earth?" he demanded of Feld, threating to have the Ringling name removed from the marquee. "Which one will be the greatest?"

Feld's reply was Solomonic, perhaps even Barnum-esque. "Both!"

In practice, Feld's assertion proved true. Performers and the public alike found no fault with either version of the production, and Feld's marketing savvy, coupled with an increased focus on food and souvenir sales (movie theater operators had for some time counted on concession sales as much as tickets) led the Gebel-Williams-centered shows to a new level of profitability, doubling the annual gross and leading to the sale of the "new" circus to toymaker giant Mattel in 1971 for an astounding $47 million, quite an appreciation for a four-years-held acquisition, even if most of the purchase was paid for in stock.

Mattel's vision was to create a marketing synergy between the circus and its toy line, but as things developed, it seemed a practical impossibility for a manufacturing company to understand and assimilate such a complicated entertainment entity as the circus. Or, as Irvin Feld put it, "The good Lord never meant for the circus to be owned by a big company." In 1982, the toymaker sold the circus back to the Felds for about half of what it had paid in 1971.

Within two years, Irvin Feld died of a stroke in 1984, at sixty-six (Izzy had passed in 1972), leaving his son Kenneth Feld in charge of operations. Though Kenneth was no newcomer to the business, having been scouting for talent since shortly after his father had purchased the company in 1967, and having conceived of "Disney on Ice" in 1981, the loss of Irvin Feld seemed calamitous, given his Runyon-esque place as a legendary cigar-smoking, storytelling show business character beloved by all. "He was charismatic," Kenneth says, "the kind of individual you met for five minutes and remembered for the rest of your life."

Kenneth Feld carried on, however, introducing such measures as the production of the companies' own sets and costumes and the retrofitting of obsolete train cars for use as circus and show cars (the show had been back on the rails since the early 1960s). In 1995, the company formed the Center for Elephant Conservation on two hundred acres of farmland in Polk City, Florida, about a hundred miles northeast of Sarasota, not far from Orlando. That center, still in operation and home to some forty creatures, is described as a gathering place for elephant behavior research and conservation, and it regularly loans out elephants and provides elephant semen to zoos and breeding programs worldwide.

Well-intentioned as the conservation center may have been, a suit was brought against it by the ASPCA in 2000, alleging maltreatment of the animals after an inspection cited undue use of restraints and deficiencies in health care (one case of tuberculosis was discovered). The case dragged on through the courts until 2009, when the suit was dismissed on the grounds that the ASPCA lacked standing to bring the action. The court directed the ASPCA to repay Feld Entertainment $9.3 million in compensatory damages, and in 2012, the ASPCA complied. Feld Entertainment continued its pursuit of legal fees from other organizations that had joined the suit, and in 2014, the company was awarded another $15.75 million from the Humane Society of the United States, the Animal Welfare Institute, the Fund for Animals, Born Free USA, and other nonprofit animal rights groups.

The disposition of the suits did not put an end to the complaints of animal advocates, who continued their efforts to free wild and endangered species from use across a wide range of amusement attractions. Regardless of whether elephants and lions and tigers are actively mistreated or abused by trainers and handlers, activists say, they nonetheless suffer from the rigors of the circus life, a life that confines them for much of their lives, prevents them from socializing and from moving freely about, and generally forces them to live counter to their instincts and nature. And as for PETA (People for the Ethical Treatment of Animals), its characterization of the circus is "The Saddest Show on Earth."

It was in response to the continuing criticism of the show's ongoing use of elephants that, in early March 2015, Kenneth Feld (by that time joined in the business by daughters Nicole and Alana) decided to drop the elephants from the show. The thirteen Asian elephants still traveling with the show were remanded to the Center for Elephant Conservation, where the herd had grown to become one of the largest remaining of the endangered species. The decision was not an easy one, Feld said, but it was made "in the best interest of our company, our elephants and our customers."

Reaction from animal rights activists was positive, though some lamented the fact that it would take three years to phase out the use of the animals. Feld responded by saying that time was needed to expand the Polk City facility for the new arrivals, where costs to care for each of the animals came to about $65,000 per year. As it turned out, the last day for the elephants came on May 1, 2016, in Providence, Rhode Island, where six elephants danced, sat on their hind legs, and stood with their forelegs on one another's backs in the maneuver known as the Long Mount. Ringmaster Johnathan Lee Iverson thanked the elephants for more than one hundred years of service to the show, adding, "We love our girls. Thank you so much for so many years of joy."

What may be said to have turned out well for the elephants certainly did not turn out well for Ringling Brothers, of course, for the retirement of the elephants effectively signaled the end of the big-time circus on these shores. Nearly a decade earlier, noted circus historian Fred Dahlinger Jr. had laid out a daunting list of challenges the Felds faced, including "GenX and aging audience segments, digital era, restrictive animal laws and governmental regulations, rising expenses, terrorism, railroad limitations, nuclear family division, lessened circus activity and interest."

These, said Dahlinger, were as diverse and threatening as all those that had afflicted owners of Ringling operations from the beginning, with the original brothers combating "peer competition, vaudeville, film, World War I"; Sam Gumpertz; "the talkies" and the Great Depression; and the Norths battling "union activity, dramatic expense escalation, cultural and technological advances, World War II, suburban development, television."

With all that arrayed against it, it might be wondered why anyone with a right mind would undertake a battle for the big top to begin with. But in an earlier interview, Kenneth Feld—who in the 1990s had actually contemplated sending the circus out once again under a newly designed big top—conveyed an adroit answer. "Young people today have a difficult time deciphering what's real and what's not. If you go to a movie and see the digital effects, you don't know what's really real. With that has to come a loss of appreciation for the skill that these performers have. But there's nothing like live entertainment. It gives you an adrenaline rush. No matter what in the world happens, there's never going to be a substitute for what we do."

THIRTY-THREE

WHAT REMAINS

THE GREATEST SHOW ON EARTH MAY HAVE TAKEN ITS FINAL BOW ON DECEMber 21, 2017, but that was by no means the end of the circus itself. Largely nonanimal operations such as New York's Big Apple Circus and such regional undertakings as San Francisco's Pickle Family Circus continue to come and go. Numerous smaller traditional circus shows such as Circus Sarasota, with high-wire walkers and acrobats, riders, dog acts, and more, and the Mendocino-based, have-tent-will-travel Flynn Creek Circus, with its own cadre of experienced acrobats, aerialists, jugglers, hoop divers, and clowns, continue to operate in the United States and elsewhere in the world.

If the scope of operations is somewhat scaled down from the grand forebears, a glance at the reviews posted by various independent clearinghouses bear out the fact that many Americans still find themselves delighted with the entertainment they find even under the not-so-big top. "Expected this to be like a community theater outing," wrote one recent visitor to the Sarasota venue. "Big surprise! Since the end of Ringling Brothers circus tour, there are many fine performers without a suitable venue. Several of them were in Sarasota last night. No second-class acts—just 2 hours of enjoyment."

Perhaps the principal production running in the lee of the Ringling departure is Cirque du Soleil, or "Circus of the Sun," founded in Canada in 1984 by a pair of street buskers. The group limped along in a form not unlike the original Ringling Brothers shows until a grant from the Canada Council on the

Arts gave it the wherewithal to become what Guy Laliberté, one of its founders, described as "a proper circus."

Cirque du Soleil includes no animals in its act, which focuses principally on intricately choreographed high-wire and trapeze acrobatics influenced by ballet and dance, the elaborate shows accompanied by live music, with performers alone in charge of props and equipment. With five permanent installations in Las Vegas (*O, Michael Jackson, ONE*, etc.) and more than forty shows traveling the world, the company, which has subsumed such competitors as Blue Man Group, had a net profit of just under $1 billion in 2018 and employed more than four thousand by the beginning of 2020. However, the COVID-19 spread forced the shuttering of operations and, at the time of this writing, the once-flourishing company, with no income and carrying about $1.5 billion in debt, petitioned to enter bankruptcy.

Though the circus seems destined to be a mercurial and ever-evolving enterprise, the public's fascination with individuals able to transcend the ordinary—to "do crazy things" with their bodies—will likely never abate. A recent episode of the popular television show *America's Got Talent* had ubiquitous winnower of aspirants Simon Cowell marveling at an acrobat performing a handstand a dozen or more feet in the air atop several stacked chairs. "I've never seen anything like that," an astonished Cowell told his cohorts on the judging panel. There apparently was no one there to respond, "I guess you've never been to the circus, then." If the judges were to witness Unus balanced one-fingered on his light bulb, one surmises, they might retire the show's trophies on the spot.

Beyond the smaller circus-styled productions and the television shows and the street mimes (and the occasional popular novel or film such as *Water for Elephants*) are myriad reminders of the power of the big top, from the Barnum & Bailey–styled containers that contain our animal crackers to the line of sophisticated wines produced by the Lodi-based Michael David Winery, with labels for its Petite Petit and Freakshow bearing striking, intricately detailed images drawn from the traditional circus.

There is unlikely to be anything like the Greatest Show, as it was in its prime, ever again, with many ineluctable reasons for that. John Ringling may have won a long-fought battle, but even he could not best Time. Still, in the rise and fall of the American circus, we see much that illustrates the nature of the American character. The Roman circus was essentially formed as an exhibition of might and power and, ultimately, dominance. When the culture from which it grew was dissolved, the notion of such spectacle as entertainment went with it. The

European circus was founded largely upon equestrian skill, with its very best performances reflecting military discipline, order, and mathematical precision, and exhibiting an uncanny communication between masters and their mounts.

The American circus drew from both these traditions, but it quickly broadened in its scope to reflect the rough-edged, sky's-the-limit character of a developing nation. The repertory of equestrian, acrobatic, and juggling acts was soon augmented by Barnum-esque elements of spectacle, oddity, and danger—though shorn of violence—with every newly successful producer consumed with zeal to outdo the one previous and create an ever more stupendous show, all this precisely in keeping with the supremely optimistic frontier spirit.

John Ringling was not incorrect in his assertion that the circus appealed to children as well as the child in every person. Nor was Henry Ringling off the mark when he claimed that the shadow of death that stalks the wire walker and the high-flying acrobat and the lion tamer and even Zacchini the Human Cannonball provided an essential tension for many circusgoers. But the collective, surpassing aim of it all was wonder, wonder that the ordinary limits of human capability could be transcended, even to the extent of cheating death. The clowns were there as a reminder not to take any of it *too* seriously.

In our ahistorical age, there is probably little to say about the value of the traditional circus to those who find distressing the employment of animals in circus acts—whether presently or in memory—and no matter the pedigree or the protestations of the individual production. But at the very least, it would have been hard for most audiences to leave a performance of the Greatest Show on Earth not having had their suspicions confirmed: that animals are in many ways as capable, intelligent, and emotionally endowed as the humans in the ring and in the stands, sometimes more so. If that is only a consolation, it is surely not one without value.

I hark back to the image of those great trained pigs cavorting on the plastic pool slide in a shadowed portion of the ring at Nassau Coliseum on the final night of the Greatest Show, the more glorious acts whirling and roaring above them, all of it about to end forever. Wire walkers were dancing, trapeze artists were flying, and mini motorcyclists spun within a dangling, far-too-small-for-safety cage. And the pigs—their handler busy corralling the troupe of acrobat dogs—they continued to climb and slide and splash down into a tiny plastic swim pool, apparently happy not to be bacon, apparently having fun.

"In the end, the circus endures because it beckons us to contend with our own fragility and potential," cultural historian Janet M. Davis has written.

Semiologist Paul Bouissac, in *Circus and Culture*, goes further: "A circus performance tends to represent the totality of our popular system of the world," he asserts. In Bouissac's view, audiences are particularly satisfied by a circus performance because it presents a microcosm of the known world that can be experienced inside the space of hours: "It is gratifying because it enables us to grasp [our culture's] totality in a limited time and space."

Of particular delight, Bouissac claims, is the inversion of everyday order in many of the circus acts: "A horse makes a fool of his trainer, a tiger rides an elephant . . . an elephant uses the telephone, plays music, or, like man, eats dinner at a table; a clown produces incongruous sequences of objects and behavior. Even the basic rules of balance are seemingly defied or denied." These "transgressive" actions, as Bouissac terms them, delight children because children are not yet fully integrated into and accepting of the order that a society demands, and he suggests that some adults avoid the circus not because the circus is "lowbrow" but because it, in a most sophisticated manner, threatens traditional notions of order.

On a more profound level, Bouissac says, the circus presents a metacultural discourse, one that "leaves the audience contemplating a demonstration of humanity freed from the constraints of the culture within which the performance takes place." As proof of his contentions, Bouissac observes that if only children had patronized the circus, it could have hardly remained a financial success for such a long time. He counts the circus among the "major achievements of mankind, both societal and individual" and suggests that any dismissal of its importance is the result of "hasty judgement and limited experience."

Whatever one might think of the academics' analysis of the circus, anyone who's ever sat in the stands understands the immediate appeal of proceedings where are displayed the athleticism and physical contest of Olympic sport, the spectacle of a Broadway musical, the drama of a lives-at-risk thriller, and the exoticism and mystery of travel to far-flung and fabled lands. It is a veritable compendium of and the precursor for virtually everything Americans have found entertaining.

Furthermore, as Kenneth Feld points out, in contrast to the impossibilities portrayed on film and television and in video games, all of it is real, a distinction cultural critic and historian Ernest Albrecht agrees is crucial. Albrecht speaks of the dissolution of the circus and the diminution of our forms of commonly held entertainment in dire terms: "The trend in technology in recent years has been to push individuals into greater and greater electronic isolation. It seems safe to assume that in the future a sizable portion of our entertainment will come directly into our homes where we will view them as solitary pleasures. As a result, there will be fewer and fewer opportunities to come together with others to create that special group known as an audience." And without the fellow members of an audience to turn to, Albrecht might have added, who is there to celebrate with, who will check the math of our existence?

ACKNOWLEDGMENTS

First and foremost, my thanks go to my wife, Kimberly, who took me aside as I was leaving a talk I had given in 2015 in a ballroom at the Sarasota Ritz-Carlton hotel. "There is something you must see," she told me, and took me out onto the lovely grounds to show me a column where a plaque was affixed, advising that in 1926, circus man John Ringling, as part of a vast vision of development, had begun construction of a Ritz-Carlton in the area, a project that innumerable obstacles kept from realization until the beginning of the twenty-first century. There is not space here to describe all the tuggings on the sleeve-thread of history's sweater that ensued from this simple plaque viewing, but suffice it to say that I, who had no knowledge of any Ringling activity not bounded by the three rings beneath a circus tent, fell quickly under the spell of a story that simply seemed would have to be told. As usual, the exact nature and shape of that story were vague at the outset, but the certainty that there was something in it both important and relatively untrammeled came to me immediately and irresistibly. And here you have the result.

I wish also to thank my good friends Kelly Kirschner, former mayor of Sarasota and dean of Executive and Continuing Education at St. Petersburg's Eckerd College, as well as Dr. Donald R. Eastman III, recently retired after eighteen years as president of Eckerd, for their endorsement of this project, which I began while in residence as Peter Meinke Visiting Distinguished Writer at the college. Special thanks are also due Marshall Rousseau, former director of the John and Mable Ringling Museum of Art, who was of great help in introducing me to the expansive grounds and magnificent holdings of that institution. I am similarly indebted to Stephen High, current director of the Ringling, as well as to Heidi Connor, chief archivist there; Heidi Taylor, associate registrar of holdings; Jennifer Lemmer-Posey, Tribbals curator of circus; and Ron McCarty, who for thirty-eight years served as curator of Ca' d'Zan.

Thanks are also due Neal Adam Watson and Darrell Horton at the State Archives of Florida for their assistance in gathering materials for this volume.

I would also like to give special thanks to John Blades, former director of the Henry Morrison Flagler Museum in Palm Beach, for his encouragement and guidance, as I also happily send them to friend and fellow scribe James W. Hall for being willing to look over my shoulder at every important phase of this undertaking.

It is also a pleasure to send a special thank you to my agent Kim Witherspoon at Inkwell Management, for her unwavering support, along with a shout-out to Kim's assistant Maria Whelan for helping me navigate the dark waters of large-file transmission and the like. Finally, unbounded gratitude goes to my most patient editor Colleen Lawrie for her enthusiasm for this project and her trust that I would see it through (with the valuable, eleventh-hour help of deft copy-editor Christina Palaia and adroit production editor Kaitlin Carruthers-Busser).

Not every writer who becomes convinced of the worth of a project is fortunate enough to see a stirring through a concept into a reality, but this one has, and he is mightily grateful for all the help along the way. Nothing is as important in this life as possibility and wonder—may this undertaking make some small contribution in that regard.

NOTES

Because this is not intended as a work of traditional scholarship, and in the interest of avoiding distraction for the reader, I have dispensed with the use of footnotes in the text itself. Much of the story is drawn from materials that have often been previously reported piecemeal and in varying contexts according to the overriding thesis of an individual volume. The attempt here is not one of historical archaeology, though certain heretofore unexamined materials play their part. The goal is to trace the development of an unprecedented and singularly American institution and its rise to the pinnacle of our popular culture. It is a factual narrative of remarkable, largely other-era accomplishment, with a series of colorful, somewhat larger-than-life individuals as protagonists. Still, to aid those interested in further reading or investigation, I have endeavored to give appropriate credit to sources, either in the text or, where singular contributions seem to merit it, in the notes that follow. Any oversight in this regard is unintentional.

Introduction

The final performance of the Greatest Show on Earth was covered in news outlets worldwide. See Maslin and Schweber for the account in the newspaper of record.

1, World on Fire

The Hartford circus fire was page-one news in most papers, including exhaustive coverage by Berger in the *New York Times*. The authoritative historic volume on the tragedy is by prolific novelist O'Nan.

2. Before the Big Top

Klepper and Gunther's work provides a particularly dramatic perspective of the fortunes of the mighty at times when wealth was far more unequally divided than it is today. Goberdhan is quoted in Maslin and Schweber, *New York Times* (*NYT*). Even the briefest revisit of Gibbon reinvigorates a day, and the whole of the *Decline* is now available at a finger-click—the quote is from Chapter 21, Part 2, paragraph 4, sentence 2. Excesses of the Roman circus are discussed in Murray, 47–48. Early circus historian Greenwood describes the essence of the circus, 8–9. Ghiselin's influential volume is *The Creative Process* (1954). The succinct observation is drawn from the class notes of this writer, fortunate enough to have been a member of the good professor's seminar on creativity in the late 1960s.

3. The Periodic Table of Circus Elements

Murray lays out the elements of the modern circus, 25–26. The events in Constantinople are from Greenwood, 9. Shakespeare, *Love's Labour's Lost*, Act I, scene ii, 48–52. Stokes and other details of the circus in the Middle Ages and Renaissance come from Murray, 60–62, 64–65. Coxe, 213–218, sheds light on the role of the clown. Greenwood, 12–17, details early equestrian activity in England. Astley remains a greatly honored hero in British circus lore: see "Who Is Philip Astley?" at the Philip Astley Project website; Barltrop's contribution "Philip Astley of Hercules Hall" at the *London Revealed* blog; Greenwood, 19–25; Coxe, 28–31; Murray, 80–84, "Circus Life in the Old World." The complete Astley account comes from Ward's *Billy Buttons*. Grimaldi's visit to a therapist: Stott, 200; singing with the oyster: Stott, 225, Murray, 109; buying into Sadler's Wells: Stott, 214; Grimaldi's acting capabilities: Stott, 227–228. Grimaldi as "Joey": Murray, 109–111.

4. On American Shores

Importance of the horse in America, Greenwood, 46. Parliament on the moral turpitude of the theater, see "February 1648" of *Acts and Ordinances of the Interregnum*, British History Online. The Articles of Association (Continental Congress Association et al.) are accessed online at the Library of Congress. Pool as first American equestrian, Greenwood, 53–63. Curtis is quoted in Greenwood, 64. May (18) describes the playbill of the performance observed by Washington. Murray (119) details Washington's activities on the day of his visit to the circus. May (20) describes Ricketts's triumphs. Greenwood (75) details the fire that sent Ricketts into bankruptcy. Culhane (10) recounts the circumstances of Ricketts's demise.

5. Pachyderm on the Half Shell

Greenwood (86–91) discusses the roots of the indigenous American circus. Barnum's quote on clowns is generally listed among his "Top 25." His observation on the importance of elephants is reprinted in Fleming, 15. The "Crowninshield Elephant" is detailed by Culhane, 13–14. Travails of the traveling circus, Coup, 142–143. Barnum passes along the tale of H. Bailey reclaiming his elephant in *Autobiography*, 42–43. Details of the early elephants' contribution can be found in Goodwin's piece for *Natural History*. Brown's as first tent show: Culhane, 22. The "big top" is introduced: Coup, 139. Integration of circus acts and menageries, Coup, 140–141. Flatfoots raise the menagerie to new levels, Murray, 134. Coup on the "million-dollar circus," 13–38 *passim*. The "Flatfoot Era," Murray, 139–141. Coup on the value of the hippo: 141. The "lion's-mouth" song is quoted in Murray, 135–136. The passing of the first famed lion tamer Amburgh is described by Culhane, 24.

6. Readying for Takeoff

Murray (165) provides the poetic description of the circus parade. The calliope's emergence is detailed in Culhane, 56. Contemporary calliope detail abounds on the internet, in Wikipedia, and elsewhere. Lighting and other ancillary accouterments of the big top: Chindahl, 53–54. Showboat circuses, Chindahl, 55–61. Spalding's structural improvements: Murray, 169. Huck's appreciation of the circus is in chapter 22 of the famed classic. Culhane (51) details Nast's use of Dan Rice's outfit. May (66–67) details the sad end for Rice. Blondin's traverse of Niagara Falls Canyon is described in a number of news accounts, including that of the *New-York Daily Tribune*. Blondin's career is documented by Murray, 180. The accomplishments and the couture of Léotard are discussed in Culhane (305) and Murray (184–185).

7. How They Roll

Prices and wages are available from a welter of online sources, including the US Census Bureau and sites such as www.choosingvoluntarysimplicity.com. Spalding's showboat converted, May, 78. Canadian duty list, May, 51. First "road signs," Chindahl, 52. Elephants as tow trucks, Coup, 76–78. Dangers from highwaymen, etc., Chindahl, 54–55. Threat at Cave-in-Rock, May, 51. "Hey, Rube!," "clem," etc., May, 52–55.

8. What's in a Name?

Bailey's 1891 interview, "A Caesar Among Showmen," *NYT.* Sister Catherine identified as abuser, Davis, 54. Bailey on adopting the name of his patron, "Caesar," *NYT.* Civil War service, "Jas. A. Bailey," *Billboard.* Guerilla raids, Chindahl, 86. The account of the prairie fire is among Coup's most powerful writing, Coup, 88–96. Bailey's expertise as advance man is detailed by McCaddon as quoted in Saxon, "New Light," *passim.*

9. Growing a Stake

Bailey's career on the rise, Murray, 239. The account of Lake's death was originally published by Matre in the *Circus Banner Line.* The rise of the after-show is detailed in Thayer, "History of the Concert or After-Show." Bailey promoted to general agent, becomes co-owner: Murray, 240. Problems of early rail transport, Chindahl, 88–93. Bailey's declaration to go to Australia, in "Jas A. Bailey," *NYT.* Bailey on his hatred of "McGinnis": Murray, 240–242. Bailey's somewhat astonishing reunion with his brother, Saxon, "New Light," 5–6.

10. Clash of the Titans

The triumphant version of that tour of the Antipodes was repeated in Bailey's *NYT* obituary, "James A. Bailey, King of Circus Men." Interviewed by a *Times* writer some sixteen years earlier, Bailey said that he had returned to the United States some $12,000 in debt and that the printer had taken a promissory note for the unpaid bill; "A Caesar Among Showmen," *NYT.* The 1891 version is more in keeping with McCaddon's recollection that a number of the performers had to make their own way home from South America, but the discrepancy is also emblematic of the ever-shifting nature of "truth" when it comes to tales told by or about colorful personalities in the entertainment world. Bailey's innovations in circus lighting: Chindahl, 98. Bailey as micromanager: Saxon, "New Light," 8. The Panic of 1873 formed the basis of a PBS *American Experience* episode: www.pbs.org. Impact of the birth of Little Columbia is detailed in Slout, 200.

11. A Showman Hits His Stride

The story of Barnum making fools of his shipmates is repeated by Kunhardt, Kunhardt, and Kunhardt, 7. Barnum tells the tale of himself as gullible landowner: *Autobiography*, 11–13. Barnum's days in the general store: Kunhardt et al., 11. Barnum as a free agent, *Autobiography*, 4. Most of the detail of Barnum's early career comes from the 1855 version of his *Autobiography*, including the hilariously annotated list of uncollectible debts (52). His recounting of the Joice Heth episode (53–67) provides all one needs for an understanding of Barnum's views on the nature of popular entertainment: in Barnum's eyes, only a fool or an enemy would take him for a cynic or a charlatan. On Barnum's interest in Ms. Heth as an instance of slave-holding, see Wilson, 42–43. Also, Reiss, "P.T. Barnum, Joice Heth, and Antebellum Spectacles of Race," 8, *passim*, and Reiss, *The Showman and the Slave*, 26, *passim*.

12. First Tour of Duty

The various biographies of Barnum often diverge in their emphases: Fleming's brings him alive to a new generation of young people, the Kunhardts' lavish production adds a veritable recreation of the shows themselves, Wilson's careful examination elevates him to a status well beyond that of "showman," but all draw their inspiration and organization from the facts of a rather remarkable life, and those are nowhere more eloquently drawn than by Barnum himself, especially in the 1855 edition of his autobiography, a volume free of self-importance and puffery, and hewing by and large to the simple facts of an up-by-the-bootstraps career. Only where it seems necessary to introduce a singular observation have I strayed from a narrative of incidents common to all the accounts or have I attempted to best Barnum's own account of a notable occasion. His account of winning the Scudder Museum (*Autobiography*, 92–100) is a dealmaker's classic. In future references, I refer to the first edition of the *Autobiography* as just that, and to the final, conflated edition of 1927 as *Barnum's Own Story* (*BOS*).

13. Museum Master

The rise of early America's interest in museums is detailed in Alexander, 65–66. Tocqueville's dim view of Scudder's is from the classic by Pierson, *Tocqueville in America*, 150. Murray (129–130) recounts the decision of the early Flatfoot circus men to derive an income from visitors to winter headquarters. Barnum is the source for the details of the Feejee Mermaid exhibition (*Autobiography*, 85–91; *BOS*, 118). In later versions of his autobiography, Barnum went to some lengths to defend his ideas on the legitimacy of his exhibits and point out the popular appeal of his approach, even at the expense of such institutions as the British Museum (*BOS*, 119).

14. General Tom

Barnum provides the details of Tom Thumb's appearance before the Royal Court in *Autobiography*, 92–97. The Kunhardts describe Barnum's ill-fated attempt to buy Shakespeare's home and ship it to the United States (60–62) and details of *Le Petit Poucet*, the play written for the Little General (64).

15. *Est Arrivé*

Barnum tells the tale of the museum customer seeking only a view of Mr. Barnum, *BOS*, 18–85. Barnum on attempts to elevate his image by becoming Ms. Lind's impresario: *Autobiography*, 113. Details of Jenny Lind's arrival in the United States come from "Reception of Jenny Lind," 2, and from Barnum, *Autobiography*, 120. Details of Ms. Lind's first appearance: "Jenny Lind's First Concert," *New Hampshire Patriot and State Gazette*. Contemporary estimations of Ms. Lind's talent: Rogers, "Jenny Lind," 444. Ms. Lind in Cuba: "Jenny Lind at Havana," 4. Barnum on Ms. Lind giving the Cubans what for: *BOS*, 222–223.

16. Riches to Rags, and Back Again

Barnum on his continuing relationship with Lind: *BOS*, 238–240. Success of Barnum's *Autobiography*, Kunhardt et al., 120. The "Fire Annihilator," *BOS*, 258–259. Barnum's financial collapse, Bennett, "Fall of Barnum," 4. Fall of Iranistan, *BOS*, 297. Barnum's rise from the ashes, *BOS*, 307. Chang & Eng: Kunhardt et al., 147. Barnum as slave owner, "Our Foreign Correspondent," *New York Atlas*.

17. The Circus Comes Calling

Building of Waldemere, Kunhardt et al., 212. Barnum chafes in retirement, *BOS*, 401–402. A succinct summary of Barnum's involvement with the Cardiff Giant and the source of "A sucker born every minute" is found at: archive.archaeology .org/0511/etc/giants.html. Barnum's notion of exhibiting sea lions in the East River: Kunhardt et al., 222. Barnum claims to have decided to enter the circus business on his own: *BOS*, 404. Coup approaches Barnum, Culhane, 100. "The checkers can lay where they are": "An Old Showman," *Atlanta Constitution*. Barnum loads up on "oddities," *BOS*, 404–406. Coup on Barnum's ignorance of the circus business: "White Tents," *New York Clipper*, May 16, 1891, 1. Coup claimed credit for adopting rail travel (65). Barnum on the scope of rail operations, *BOS*, 406. "Roll-through" loading, Culhane, 103. Freak show as "ordinary," see Grande, "Strange and Bizarre"; Bogdan, *Freak Show*; and Adams, *Sideshow USA*. An ahistorical age: Wilson, 7–8. It might be worth pointing out that one reviewer of Wilson's volume had virtually nothing to say about the quality of the book but instead devoted several pages to an excoriation of Barnum, calling him "a liar, a racist, and an entertainer who would do anything for a crowd" (Kolbert, "You Can't Make It Up"). Criticism of the size of Barnum's troupe by circus men: Slout, 20–25. First-year profits, in "An Old Showman," 6. The "two-ring" circus, Slout, 63. Barnum on the death of his wife, *BOS*, 410. Barnum on remarriage to Nancy Fish, *BOS*, 414. Barnum's claim that his first wife had prayed for death, Wilson, 240. Barnum's profits from the circus, Slout, 133–145. Advertising budget for Barnum's circus, Kunhardt et al., 250–252. Barnum on his meeting with U. S. Grant, *BOS*, 440. The sort of self-aggrandizement implicit in this anecdote, although often on display in later versions of Barnum's memoir, are nowhere to be found in the first edition.

18. Mr. B, Meet Mr. B

Barnum on his competitors and his telegraphed offer for "The Baby Elephant," *BOS*, 423–424. Terms of the merger of Barnum and Bailey, Slout, 205–206. Announcement of the "three-ring-circus," Slout, 210. "Barnum Day," *BOS*, 426. Bailey abolishes the "privilege" system, Hamilton, "Recollections," 8. Barnum refuses to cancel the purchase of Jumbo, *BOS*, 430. Details of Jumbo's transport to America, *BOS*, 429–432.

19. On Massive Shoulders

Barnum's additions to the Barnum & Bailey repertoire, including the "Grand Ethnological Congress of Nations," Kunhardt et al., 296. Jumbo as the star of the show, Scott, *Autobiography of Matthew Scott*, 78–79. Sleeping with Jumbo, Scott, 75–76. Jumbo saves Scott from the elephant stampede, Scott, 85–86. Jumbo's demise was detailed in newspapers around the globe: "Jumbo's Death: The Official Report," *Chicago Daily Tribune*, September 19, 1885, 2; "The Great Jumbo Killed," *New York Times*, September 17, 1885, 5. And the tale continues to occupy a prominent place in circus lore: Haley, "Colossus of His Kind: Jumbo." Barnum to Harper Bros. and Croffut: Saxon, *Selected Letters*, 266, 273.

20. The Greatest Show

Bailey dismissing the value of Barnum's "name": Hamilton, "Recollections," 8. Bailey's work habits, "A Caesar Among Showmen," 20. "Mister" Bailey: Saxon, "New Light," 8. Barnum to Mrs. Bailey, Saxon, *Selected Letters*, 264–265. "Greatest Show on Earth": Culhane, 140. Nimrod the lion survives the fire, *BOS*, 449–450. Barnum's last words, *BOS*, 452. Barnum's impact on American culture: Kronenberger, 25. Bailey as creator of the modern circus: "A Caesar Among Showmen," 20.

21. Upstarts

Garland's observations on the circus come from *Boy Life on the Prairie*, 232. Ringling historian Apps wonders whether Alf's recollection might have conflated the visit of Dan Rice's circus with that of John Stowe's Great Western Circus, a wagon show that came to McGregor in September of 1869, Apps, 5. Alf's re-creation of the arrival of the circus is found in his *Life Story of the Ringling Brothers*, 25. While Alf Ringling's volume is apparently geared for the younger reader, the chronology and detail therein (1–52) provide—along with the early Ringling route books—the primary source material for Henry Ringling North's treatment of the same era in *The Circus Kings* (1–64). Alf details the return of Albert and promotions for the 1882 season, Ringling, *Life Story*, 83.

22. The Coming Men

Charles's recollections of the first true show for the brothers is from North, 65. The summary of the Ringlings' growing enterprise comes from North, based in large part upon the detailed company route books, as well as upon family lore, including the observation of a cousin that there were simply "so God-damned many of them" (77).

23. Punch and Counterpunch

Various accomplishments of America's so-called Gilded Age have been the previous focus of the present writer, including *Last Train to Paradise*; *Meet You in Hell*; and *Water to the Angels*—most of the ancillary details regarding the general historical and social context in which the circus developed come from those volumes. Bailey's business activities following the death of Barnum are detailed in May (123) and Murray (248). "Rat sheets" and other competitive chicanery are detailed in North, 109–111. The tale of John Ringling's encounter with Cody is in North, 107. North details the rise to prominence of the Ringling operation (112–117).

24. Building a Leviathan

Ringling activities while Bailey was in Europe: North, 118–122. Fred Bradna tells the story of his meeting with wife Ella in his autobiography *The Big Top*, 7–8. Other details are recounted in his *New York Times* obituary of February 22, 1955, 21. The decline of the Barnum & Bailey operations: May, 230–232. Bailey approaches the Ringlings: Saxon, "New Light," 9. Merger of Ringling and Forepaugh-Sells, North, 123–124. Bailey's decision to discontinue the circus parade, May, 232–233. Bizarre circumstances of Bailey's death, in Saxon, "New Light," 9.

25. Terms of Success

McCaddon approaches the Ringlings, Saxon, 9. Merger of Barnum & Bailey with Ringling Brothers, North, 124–126. Introduction of automobile acts, Culhane, 174. Bradna's outrage with Leers, North, 144–145. The "summit of the circuses," Chindahl, 148–149; John Ringling, "We Divided the Job," 57. John Ringling flummoxed by a performer's resignation, Gordon, *Born to Be*, 133. John Ringling's philandering, North, 163. John Ringling outmaneuvers the house detective, North, 133–134. John Ringling as first among equals, North, 151. Ringling on toning down the "death-defying" circus, John Ringling, "We Divided the Job," 182. Number of cars in the respective train shows, Chindahl, 150. White's observations on the circus as microcosm: "The Ring of Time," in *Essays of E. B. White*, 143. Wilson throws his hat into the ring, Culhane, 177. Technological advances in the circus, Chindahl, 151–152. Alf's passing and the withholding of the theater gift to Baraboo, North, 169–170.

26. The Price of Love

Deaths of Henry and Alfred Ringling, effects of Spanish flu and World War I on Ringling operations, North, 171–175. First performance of the combined shows: "Supercircus," *New York Times*; John Ringling, "We Divided the Job," 58. Codona on his trapeze technique: "Split Seconds," 12. Codona on psychic fatigue, "Split Seconds," 6. The Codona-Leitzel-Bruce tragedy rivals the story of Jumbo as oft-told circus legend. The rendition here is drawn from Bradna, 179–197; North, 182–190; and Culhane, 188–189, as well as from newspaper accounts of the time, including "Bullets of Codona Fatal to His Ex-Wife," *New York Times*, 4. North (190–192), on the sometimes disreputable image of the circus.

27. Last Man Standing

John Ringling's daily schedule, North, 195–196. John and Mable Ringling receive the cold shoulder in Tarpon Springs, Weeks, 46. The detail of Ringling's financial speculation in and around Sarasota is drawn from Weeks, 80–154, *passim*. Insight into Ringling's investment in short-line railroads is found in Inbody, "Ringling Circus Family Made Mark on Montana"; "I'm the last one left on the lot": North, 204–205.

28. Patriarch of Paradise

Moving the winter headquarters to Sarasota, North, 209–210. The addition of the Wallendas and their many near disasters are described in Culhane (354–355) and in Bradna (264–265, 269–270). The Florida building boom and its characteristic architecture is the focus of this author's *Palm Beach, Mar-a-Lago, and the Rise of America's Xanadu, passim.* The building of Ca' d'Zan is detailed by Weeks (116–130) and North (196–201). The evaluation panel's summation is quoted by Weeks (130). Citation of Ringling as owner of largest private collection of primitive Greek art is from Weeks (191–192). Acquisition of Il Guercino's *Annunciation*, Weeks, 192–193. Details of the Ringling Museum's Astor and Huntington rooms are in Berry (20). The reviews of the museum's opening are cited in Weeks (205–206). The tale of Ringling averting a public relations disaster for Mayor Walker is from North (210–211).

29. The Last Race

Millay's poem, often quoted as a kind of epitaph for the Roaring Twenties, was published originally in *Poetry* in 1918. Mable's death and its aftermath, North, 216–217. Ringling at loggerheads with the directors of Madison Square Garden, North, 218–220. Ringling's physical decline and the machinations of Samuel Gumpertz, North, 223–226.

30. After the Ball

Ringling's stroke, North, 226. The anecdote with the court deputy is drawn from North (220–221). Dahlinger "corrects" North on the name of the circus production he and his uncle traveled to see ("Afterword," in *Circus Kings*, 389). John Ringling's death: "John Ringling Dies," *NYT*, 2; North, 238. Details of John Ringling's estate, North, 249–251. State of the circus industry, Chindahl, 162–163. John Ringling North becomes COO of the combined shows, North, 252–263. North's bout with circus unions, North, 285. Clyde Beatty's views on the teachability of animals, Culhane, 203–210. A poignant tribute to the talents of Emmett Kelly is found in Browning, "Tears of a Clown." Mabel Stark as lion tamer, Culhane, 180–181; North, 285. Marianne Moore on elephant ballet, Culhane, 246. Addition of a/c to the big top, North, 291. Show profits for 1942, North, 320–321.

31. Out of the Ashes

Further detail on the Hartford disaster: Berger, "139 Lives Lost"; Associated Press, "Little Victim," *Chicago Tribune*, 2. "The Day the Clown Cried" is noted in Browning, "Tears of a Clown." The heroics of young Donald Anderson are detailed by O'Nan (92). O'Nan (196–199) also corrects certain of the immediate casualty statistics. War-related personnel shortage as factor in the disaster's magnitude, North, 326–327. Lasting impact of the fire on the area: "Hartford Circus Fire Scarred the State," *The Day.* Bond posted by circus, North, 329–330. Results of criminal trial of circus officials, Cavanaugh, "The Hartford Fire," *NYT*, 1; North, 331. Fire detective Davey's investigation, Associated Press, "Little Victim," 2. Reasons for Eleanor Cook's classification as a missing person, O'Nan, 172. O'Nan casts doubt on the identity of Eleanor Emily Cook as Little Miss 1565 (344–354). Repayment of claims against the circus, 1946, North, 336. Transfer of Ringling property to the state of Florida: Weeks, 257–285; Meter, "John Ringling" (thesis), 68. Today the Ringling complex in Sarasota, including the art museum, Ca' d'Zan, the Ringling Circus Museum, the Asolo Repertory Theatre, and the surrounding grounds—all of it valued in excess of $500,000—is administered and maintained by Florida

State University and is said to be one of the forty most visited museums in the nation (Meter, 75–76).

32. Rock and Roll to the Rescue

North returns the overtures of Irvin Feld, Culhane, 274. North (377–379), in discussing his operations of the circus in 1957, omits any mention of Irvin Feld's involvement. Culhane (274–277) cites a number of interviews with Feld regarding the changes brought to booking practices, etc. The emergence of "Shriners" and other sponsored shows: Culhane, 277–279. Wallenda tragedy of 1962: Associated Press, "Two of Flying Wallendas Killed," *NYT*, 1. Karl Wallenda's death: "Karl Wallenda, 73, Patriarch," *NYT*, 23. Henry Ringling North, brother of John Ringling North, retires from circus operations, North, 381–382. Feld, on his desire to keep the circus running, Culhane, 283. Feld's attempts to upgrade operations, acquisition of Gunther Gebel-Williams: Culhane, 285–286. Gebel-Williams on his training methods, Culhane, 289. On the mauling of Roy Horn: "Kenneth Feld Remembers Roy Horn." On the operations of Clown College: Walk, "Sarasota's Circus Legacy Lives On." The closing of Clown College, Shea, "Ringling No More: A Former Clown Reflects." Irvin Feld on the possibility of there being *two* "Greatest" shows, Culhane, 285. Kenneth Feld on the reacquisition of the show from Mattel, Feld, "How I Did It." Disposition of animal rights groups' suits against the Feld circus, Allen, "Ringling Bros. Is Gone; What's Next?" Kenneth Feld on the decision to retire the elephants from the show, Littleton, "Ringling Bros. Circus to Drop Elephant Acts." Costs of maintaining elephants on private preserve, Perez-Pena, "Elephants to Retire." Humane Society's suggestion the elephants be moved to alternate facilities, Smith, "Last Dance." List of forces opposing successful circus operations, past and present, Dahlinger, "Afterword," 396. Kenneth Feld considers mounting a new "big top" show, Culhane, 278. Kenneth Feld on the essence of live entertainment, Feld, "How I Did It."

33. What Remains

The "new" American circus, Albrecht, *The New American Circus*, 7–9. Circus Sarasota, see https://circusarts.org/performances/shows/circus-sarasota-2020/. Flynn Creek Circus: see Stockwell, "Flynn Creek Circus Returns." Size of Cirque du Soleil operations, Van Praet, "Caisse Boosts Cirque du Soleil." The circus beckoning to contend with our own fragility, Davis, *The Circus Age*, 237. A circus performance as a representation of the world's totality, Bouissac, *Circus and Culture*, 7. The inversion of everyday order, Bouissac, 8. The circus as a major achievement of humankind, Bouissac, 9. Entertainment and "electronic isolation," Albrecht, *New American Circus*, 243.

BIBLIOGRAPHY

Books (Annotated)

Adams, Rachel. *Sideshow USA: Freaks and the American Cultural Imagination.* Chicago: University of Chicago Press, 2009.
> Providing insight into a once common practice deemed barbaric by many today.

Albrecht, Ernest. *The New American Circus.* Gainesville: University Press of Florida, 1995.
> Focus on the development of the regional and community-based circuses of the latter twentieth century.

Alexander, Edward P. *Museum Masters: Their Museums and Their Influence.* Walnut Creek, CA: AltaMira, 1995.
> Diverting discourse on the creation of notable American museums.

Apps, Jerry. *Ringlingville USA.* Madison: Wisconsin Historical Society, 2005.
> Detailed, fulsomely illustrated regional history focusing on the Wisconsin roots of the Ringling operation through its departure from Baraboo.

Astley, Philip. *The Modern Riding-Master: Or, a Key to the Knowledge of the Horse, and Horsemanship.* Philadelphia: Robert Aitken, 1776.
> In which the peerless rider and circus man Astley shares his secrets, including his first piece of advice: "Approach the Stable alone very quiet, and by no Means diſturb the Horſe."

Barnum, P. T. *The Autobiography of P.T. Barnum.* London: Ward and Lock, 1855.
> The original edition of Barnum's autobiography, perhaps the most disarming in its candor.

———. *Barnum's Own Story: The Autobiography of P.T. Barnum.* Edited by Waldo R. Browne. Mineola, NY: Dover Publications, 2017.
> An illustrated reprint of a volume originally published by Viking in 1927, itself an editing and condensation of all the previous editions of Barnum's autobiographies published between 1855 and 1888.

Berry, David A. *The Ringling Visitor Guide.* London: Scala Arts & Heritage, 2014.
> Detailing the exhibits of the Ringling Circus Museum, Ca' d'Zan, and elsewhere within the Sarasota complex.

Bogdan, Robert. *Freak Show: Presenting Human Oddities for Amusement and Profit.* Chicago: University of Chicago Press, 1990.
> Analysis of the origin and appeal of the time-honored practice.

Bouissac, Paul. *Circus and Culture: A Semiotic Approach*. Bloomington: Indiana University Press, 1976.

Discourse on the suggestive implications of circus methodologies, including such topics as "Equine Exhibitions as Poetic Discourse."

Bradna, Fred A. (as told to Hartnell Spence). *The Big Top: My Forty Years with the Greatest Show on Earth*. New York: Simon & Schuster, 1952.

Recollections of the long-time Ringling show manager.

Canfield, William H. *Outline Sketches of Sauk County, Wisconsin, Volume Second*. Baraboo, WI: A. N. Kellogg, 1891–1896.

Contains a brief, proud summary of the early accomplishments of the Ringlings, possibly penned by one of the brothers.

Chindahl, George L. *A History of the Circus in America*. Caldwell, ID: Caxton, 1959.

Comprehensive history of the circus in the United States from the early eighteenth century into the 1950s, with notes.

Cole, Harry Ellsworth. *A Standard History of Sauk County, Wisconsin*. Chicago: Lewis, 1918.

Contains a summary of the early days of the Ringling company derived largely from the show's route book, "Routes, 1882–1914."

Coup, W. C. *Sawdust and Spangles: Stories & Secrets of the Circus*. Chicago: Herbert S. Stone, 1901.

Colorful memoir by the legendary early circus man.

Coxe, Antony Hippisley. *A Seat at the Circus*. Hamden, CT: Archon, 1980.

Revised edition of a 1951 treatise focused on the analysis of the circus acts, including aerial acts, clowns, riding, and juggling.

Culhane, John. *The American Circus*. New York: Holt, 1990.

Lavishly illustrated, carefully researched, comprehensive history of the American circus from the beginnings through the 1980s.

Davis, Janet M. *The Circus Age: Culture & Society Under the American Big Top*. Chapel Hill: University of North Carolina Press, 2002.

Thoroughgoing cultural history of the American circus with analysis of its impact on society.

Fleming, Candace. *The Great and Only Barnum*. New York: Schwartz & Wade, 2009.

Young adult biography, accurate and inclusive.

Garland, Hamlin. *Boy Life on the Prairie*. London: Macmillan, 1899.

Autobiographical fiction rendering effectively a young man's tender years in rural America of the late nineteenth century.

Ghiselin, Brewster. *The Creative Process: A Symposium*. Berkeley: University of California Press, 1954.

Gibbon, Edward. *The History of the Decline and Fall of the Roman Empire: Invasion of Italy, Occupation of Territories by Barbarians*. Project Gutenberg.

The timeless classic, available in its whole online.

Gordon, Taylor. *Born to Be*. Lincoln: University of Nebraska Press, 1995.

A memoir by John Ringling's former valet, who went on to fame as a Harlem singer—contains glimpses of Ringling's private life and travels.

Greenwood, Isaac J. *The Circus: Its Origin and Growth Prior to 1835*. New York: Dunlap Society, 1898. (Repr., Washington, DC: Hobby House Press, 1962.)

Early, authoritative account of the European circus and its transition to the United States in the early nineteenth century.

John Ringling—Dreamer, Builder, Collector: Legacy of the Circus King. Sarasota: John & Mable Ringling Museum of Art, 1996.

An account of the creation of the Ringling Museum of Art and appreciation of its varied holdings.

Klepper, Michael, and Robert Gunther. *The Wealthy 100: From Benjamin Franklin to Bill Gates—a Ranking of the Richest Americans, Past and Present.* New York: Citadel, 1996.

Lays out the case for evaluating personal fortunes of the past as a percentage of the gross domestic product of the time.

Kronenberger, Louis. *Company Manners: A Cultural Inquiry into American Life.* New York: Bobbs-Merrill, 1954.

Interesting commentary on the essential features of American popular entertainment.

Kunhardt, Philip B., Jr., Philip B. Kunhardt III, and Peter W. Kunhardt. *P.T. Barnum: America's Greatest Showman.* New York: Knopf, 1995.

Fulsomely illustrated history of the legendary promoter, including a wealth of detail concerning his more popular exhibits and undertakings.

May, Earl Chapin. *The Circus from Rome to Ringling.* Toronto: Dover, 1963.

Despite the title, it is principally a detailed summary of the history of the American circus through the 1920s, including personal observations of the former advance man and circus bandmaster.

Murray, Marian. *Circus! From Rome to Ringling.* Westport, CT: Greenwood, 1956.

General history of the circus from Egyptian times to the 1950s.

North, Henry Ringling, and Alden Hatch. *The Circus Kings: Our Ringling Family Story,* with an afterword by Fred Dahlinger Jr. Gainesville: University Press of Florida, 2008.

Reminiscences of John Ringling's nephew, who lived with Ringling during his final years and eventually took over circus operations.

O'Nan, Stewart. *The Circus Fire: A True Story.* New York: Doubleday, 2000.

Comprehensive treatment of the Hartford circus fire of 1944 and its lasting impact on the area.

Pierson, G. W. *Tocqueville in America.* Baltimore: Johns Hopkins, 1996.

The perceptive appreciation of the tour of early America by the noted Frenchman, originally published in 1938.

Reiss, Benjamin. *The Showman and the Slave: Race, Death, and Memory in Barnum's America.* Cambridge, MA: Harvard University Press, 2001.

Ringling, Alf T. *Life Story of the Ringling Brothers.* Chicago: R. R. Donnelley and Sons, 1900.

Essentially a young adult summary of the early years of the Ringling circus, often cited by Ringling historians.

Saxon, A. H. *Selected Letters of P.T. Barnum.* New York: Columbia University Press, 1983.

As described in the title, and an enjoyable, insightful companion to Barnum's own autobiography.

Scott, Matthew. *Autobiography of Matthew Scott, Jumbo's Keeper.* New York: Trows Printing and Booking, 1885.

Shakespeare, William. *Love's Labour's Lost*. Shakespeare online. http://www
.shakespeare-online.com/plays/LLL_1_2.html.

Slout, William L. *A Royal Coupling: The Historic Marriage of Barnum and Bailey*.
San Bernardino: Emeritus Enterprise, 2000.
The only in-depth consideration of the creation of the fabled partnership.

Standiford, Les. *Last Train to Paradise: Henry Flagler and the Railroad That Crossed
an Ocean*. New York: Crown, 2002.

———. *Meet You in Hell: Andrew Carnegie, Henry Clay Frick and the Bitter Partnership That Transformed America*. New York: Crown, 2005.

———. *Palm Beach, Mar-a-Lago, and the Rise of America's Xanadu*. New York: Atlantic Monthly Press, 2019.

———. *Water to the Angels: William Mulholland, His Monumental Aqueduct, and
the Rise of Los Angeles*. New York: HarperCollins, 2015.

Stott, Andrew McConnell. *The Pantomime Life of Joseph Grimaldi: Laughter, Mad-
ness and the Story of Britain's Greatest Comedian*. Edinburgh: Cannongate Books,
2009.
Compelling account of the life of the singular comic talent of nineteenth-
century Europe, often referred to as the original modern clown.

Twain, Mark. *Huckleberry Finn*. New York: Charles L. Webster, 1885.
The original edition of the classic.

Ward, Steve. *Father of the Modern Circus "Billy Buttons": The Life and Times of
Philip Astley*. Barnsley, UK: Pen & Sword History, 2018.
Engaging biography of the eighteenth-century British rider and entrepreneur
often identified as the original circus producer.

Weeks, David C. *Ringling: The Florida Years, 1911–1936*. Gainesville: University
Press of Florida, 1993.
Thoroughgoing academic study of John Ringling's time in Sarasota and his
legacy there.

White, E. B. *Essays of E.B. White*. New York: Harper Colophon, 1979.
A gracefully drawn collection by the author of *Elements of Style* and the inimitable children's classic *Charlotte's Web*.

Wilson, Robert. *Barnum: An American Life*. New York: Simon & Schuster, 2019.
A carefully researched and thoroughgoing appraisal that makes for an interesting counterpoint to Barnum's own autobiography, which informs much of
the prior canon regarding a fabled career.

Articles

Allen, Charlotte. "Ringling Bros. Is Gone; What's Next?" *Los Angeles Times*, May
22, 2017, A13.

"America." *Times* (London), June 28, 1851, 5.

Associated Press. "Little Victim of Harford Circus Fire 50 Years Ago Has a Name
at Last." *Chicago Tribune*, July 6, 1994, 2.

Barltrop, Chris. "Philip Astley of Hercules Hall." *London Revealed*, June
2017, updated October 20, 2018. https://www.londonrevealed.co.uk/post
/philip-astley-of-hercules-hall.

Bennett, James Gordon. "The Fall of Barnum." *New York Herald*, March 17, 1856,
4.

Berger, Myer. "139 Lives Lost in Circus Fire at Hartford." *New York Times*, July 7, 1944, 1.

"Blondin." *New-York Daily Tribune*, July 1, 1859, 4–5.

Browning, William. "Tears of a Clown." *Paris Review*, July 6, 2016. https://web .archive.org/web/20170416192954/https://www.theparisreview.org/blog /2016/07/06/tears-of-a-clown/.

"Bullets of Codona Fatal to His Ex-Wife." *New York Times*, August 1, 1937, 4.

"A Caesar Among Showmen." *New York Times*, April 19, 1891, 20.

"Calliope." Miner Company. https://minercompany.com.

Cavanaugh, Jack. "The Hartford Fire, 50 Years Later." *New York Times*, July 3, 1994, 1.

Charles, Lucile Hoerr. "The Clown's Function." *Journal of American Folklore* 58, no. 227 (January–March, 1945): 25–34.

"Circus Life in the Old World." *New York Clipper*, June 12, 1875, 1, https://idnc .library.illinois.edu/?a=d&d=NYC18750612.2.4&e=—en-20—1—img-txIN—.

Codona, Alfredo. "Split Seconds." *Saturday Evening Post*, December 6, 1930, 12– 13, 76, 79.

Continental Congress Association and Peyton Randolph, et al. "Agreements by Colonies." October 20, 1774. Articles of Association of the First Continental Congress. The Thomas Jefferson Papers Series 1. General Correspondence. 1651–1827. Library of Congress. http://memory.loc.gov/cgi-bin/ampage ?collId=mtj1&fileName=mtj1page001.db&recNum=325.

Dahlinger, Fred, Jr. "Afterword." In North and Hatch, *Circus Kings*, 384–400.

"February 1648: An Ordinance for the utter suppression and abolishing of all Stage-Plays and Interludes, within the Penalties to be inflicted on the Actors and Spectators therein expressed." *Acts and Ordinances of the Interregnum, 1642– 1660*, 1070–1072. British History Online. https://www.british-history.ac.uk /no-series/acts-ordinances-interregnum.

Feld, Kenneth. "How I Did It." *Inc.*, August 1, 2007. https://www.inc.com/magazine /20070801/how-i-did-it-kenneth-feld.html.

"Fred Bradna of Ringling Circus, Its 'Field Marshal,' Dies at 83." *New York Times*, February 22, 1955, 21.

Goodwin, George G. "The Crowninshield Elephant." *Natural History*, October 1951. http://www.naturalhistorymag.com/editors_pick/1928_05-06_pick .html?page=2.

Grande, Laura. "Strange and Bizarre: The History of Freak Shows." *History Magazine*, September 26, 2010.

"The Great Jumbo Killed." *New York Times*, September 17, 1885, 5.

Haley, James L. "Colossus of His Kind: Jumbo." *American Heritage* 24, no. 5 (August 1973).

Hamilton, B. F. "Recollections of the Great Showman James A. Bailey, Told by Press Agent." *St. Louis Daily Globe-Democrat*, April 14, 1907, 8.

"Hartford Circus Fire Scarred the State." *The Day* (New London, CT), July 8, 2019.

Inbody, Kristen. "Ringling Circus Family Made Mark on Montana." *Great Falls (MT) Tribune*, April 6, 2016.

"James A. Bailey, King of Circus Men, Is Dead." *New York Times*, April 12, 1906, 1.

Jando, Dominique. "Philip Astley, Circus Owner, Equestrian." Circopedia. www .circopedia.org/Philip_Astley.

"Jas. A. Bailey Dies at His Mt. Vernon Home." *Billboard*, April 21, 2006.

"Jenny Lind at Havana." *Rochester (NY) North Star*, March 20, 1851, 4.

"Jenny Lind's First Concert." *New Hampshire Patriot and State Gazette*, September 19, 1850, 2.

"John Ringling Dies of Pneumonia at 70." *New York Times*, December 2, 1936, 2.

"Jumbo's Death: The Official Report." *Chicago Daily Tribune*, September 19, 1885, 2.

"Karl Wallenda, 73, Patriarch of the High-Wire Troupe, Dies in 100-Foot Fall." *New York Times*, March 23, 1984, 23.

"Kenneth Feld Remembers Roy Horn" (press release). Feld Entertainment. https:// www.feldentertainment.com/kenneth-feld-remembers-roy-horn/.

Kolbert, Elizabeth. "You Can't Make It Up: What P.T. Barnum Understood About America." *New Yorker*, August 5 & 12, 2019.

Littleton, Cynthia. "Ringling Bros. Circus to Drop Elephant Acts by 2018." *Variety*, March 5, 2015.

Maslin, Sarah, and Nate Schweber. "A Final Bow for the Greatest Show on Earth." *New York Times*, May 22, 2017, A21.

Matre, Van. "Agnes Lake and Emma Lake." *Circus Banner Line*, October 1, 1978. In Culhane, *The American Circus*, 90–91.

Millay, Edna St. Vincent. "Figs from Thistles—First Fig." *Poetry: A Magazine of Verse* 12, no. 3 (June 1918).

Monga, Vipal. "Cirque du Soleil Files for Bankruptcy Protection in Canada." *Wall Street Journal*, June 29, 2020.

"An Old Showman." *Atlanta Constitution*, February 23, 1891, 6. In William L. Slout, *A Royal Coupling*, 4–5.

"Our Foreign Correspondent." *New York Atlas*, July 21, 1844; February 16, 1845; April 20, 1845. In Wilson, *Barnum*, 101.

"The Panic of 1873." *American Experience*. www.pbs.org/wgbh/americanexperience /features/grant-panic.

Perez-Pena, Richard. "Elephants to Retire from Ringling Brothers Stage." *New York Times*, March 5, 2015.

"Reception of Jenny Lind." *Farmer's Cabinet*, September 12, 1850, 2.

Reiss, Benjamin. "P.T. Barnum, Joice Heth and Antebellum Spectacles of Race." *American Quarterly* 51, no. 1 (March 1999): 78–107.

Ringling, John. "We Divided the Job but Stuck Together." *American Magazine*, September 1919.

Rogers, Francis. "Jenny Lind." *Musical Quarterly* 32, no. 3 (July 1946): 437–448.

Saxon, A. H. "New Light on the Life of James A. Bailey." *Bandwagon* 4 (November–December 1996): 4–9.

Shea, Andrea. "Ringling No More: A Former Clown Reflects on the End of 'The Greatest Show on Earth.'" WBUR. https://www.wbur.org/artery/2017/05/05 /ringling-brothers-final-shows.

Smith, Michelle R. "Last Dance: Final Performance for Ringling Bros. Elephants." Associated Press, May 2, 2016.

Stockwell, Tom. "Flynn Creek Circus Returns to Calistoga with Funny, Athletic, Edgy Performance." *Weekly Calistogan* (California), August 3, 2016.

"Supercircus Draws Crowds to Garden." *New York Times*, March 29, 1919, 25.

Thayer, Stuart. "The History of the Concert or After-Show." *American Circus Anthology: Essays of the Early Years*. https://classic.circushistory.org/Thayer/Thayer1f.htm.

"Two of Flying Wallendas Killed in Fifty-Foot Plunge." *New York Times*, January 31, 1962, 1.

Van Praet, Nicolas. "Caisse Boosts Cirque du Soleil Stake with Deal to Buy Out Founder." *Globe and Mail* (Canada), February 1, 2020.

Walk, Deborah. "Sarasota's Circus Legacy Lives On." The Ringling. May 22, 2017. https://www.ringling.org/sarasotas-circus-legacy-lives.

White, E. B. "The Ring of Time." In *The Essays of E. B. White*. New York: Harper, 1979.

"White Tents—The Greatest on Earth." *New York Clipper*, May 16, 1891, 169.

"Who Is Philip Astley?" Philip Astley Project. www.philipastley.org.uk/philip-astley/.

Unpublished Thesis

Meter, Amanda Ellen. "John Ringling: Story of a Capitalist." Tallahassee: Florida State University, 2009.

Newspapers

Atlanta Constitution
Essex Journal (Newbury-Port, Massachusetts)
Great Falls (MT) Tribune
New Hampshire Patriot and State Gazette
New London (CT) Day
New York Atlas
New York Gazette
New York Herald
New York Times
New-York Tribune/Daily Tribune
Philadelphia Packet
Rochester (NY) North Star
Rocky Mountain News (Denver, Colorado)
St. Louis Daily Globe Democrat
The Times (London)

Websites

Choosing Voluntary Simplicity: http://www.choosingvoluntarysimplicity.com/what-did-things-cost-in-1860/

Circus Arts Conservatory: https://circusarts.org/performances/shows/circus-sarasota-2020/

US Census Bureau: https://www.census.gov

INDEX

Les Standiford is the author of more than two dozen critically acclaimed books, including *Last Train to Paradise*, *Meet You in Hell*, and *Bringing Adam Home*. His book *The Man Who Invented Christmas* was a *New York Times* Editors' Choice and was made into a feature film starring Christopher Plummer and Dan Stevens in 2017. He is Distinguished University Professor of English and founding director of the Creative Writing Program at Florida International University and Peter Meinke Writer in Residence at Eckerd College. He holds an MA and PhD in literature and creative writing from the University of Utah. He attended the US Air Force Academy and Columbia School of Law and is a former screenwriting fellow and graduate of the American Film Institute in Los Angeles. He lives with his wife, Kimberly, in Pinecrest, Florida.